Stephen Holbrook

OUT OF THIS
WORLD

By

James Christie

Mage Publishing

Wizards Eight, Sun Inn Cottages, Colton Tadcaster, LS24 8EP

Published in Great Britain by Mage Publishing 2002
Second Edition, Mage Publishing 2003
Copyright © James Christie & Stephen Holbrook

ISBN 0-9527109-2-7

"Out Of This World" can be ordered through most major bookshops by quoting the above ISBN code or alternatively by mail order direct from the publishers at the recommended retail price of £8.99 (plus £1 p&p). For details of future publications and to find out where Stephen is demonstrating next, please visit our website at

www.steve-holbrook.co.uk

Printed by TJ International Ltd, Padstow, Cornwall

Among the mundane
as I meander,
everyday ways
of being hold me,
yet echoes inside
of the spiritual,
the slowly distant spirals,
call
'hear me, hear me!'
Then falling open,
I let their fair message
widely unfurl;
'familiar spirits,
take me – take me
out of this world'.

Adrian Spendlow

Who's you bin talkin' to, mah fine coloured boy,
An' jus' where the hell have you bin?

Ah bin talkin' to angels down by the river
An' the spirits they welcomed me in.

1920's blues spiritual, anon.

For
Caroline and Joanna

ACKNOWLEDGEMENTS

We would like to acknowledge the valuable contributions made by those people who have received messages from Stephen and have allowed us to incorporate them in this book. Also many thanks to all those who have kindly sent emails to the website, some of which have been included in the penultimate chapter.

Special thanks must go to Caroline, Robbie, Sue and Jo for their literary contributions and Stephen would especially like to thank Margaret 'Hot Lips' Holbrook for her garage and for making sure he has a birthday every year.

We would like to thank Martin Steers and Roger Hunt for their technical support; this was invaluable and very much appreciated. Thanks also to Roger and Jill Prior for manning the website (www.steve-holbrook.co.uk) and to Pat Johnson aka The Rottweiler, for acting as chaperone and for providing conversational services on long drives home along the M62 (watch out, my son, there's another speed camera!).

Stephen would like to thank James for taking most of the photographs. James would like to thank Stephen for posing for most of the photographs – and he would also like to apologise to the readership at large for the photographs he wasn't allowed to publish.

Finally, Mage Publishing would like to thank John Olivey and his team at T J International Ltd of Padstow for their consistent support and highly professional service.

Out Of This World

INTRODUCTION

In Stephen Holbrook's highly complex mind there is one bright and shining thought – which is that you cannot die! As a spiritualist, he is totally committed to the concept of life after death, which is, of course, the most fundamental cornerstone of the spiritualist faith. However, unlike many others who share this belief, Stephen goes one critical step further and provides hard tangible *proof* of a spiritual afterlife.

He does this, night after night, in towns and cities the length and breadth of Britain, by demonstrating his gift of clairaudient mediumship.

For people who know nothing of this concept, Stephen is able to forge a link of communication between people who have died and 'passed over' – and their loved ones left behind. He hears 'spirit' voices and following the instruction and guidance of those voices, he is able to convey messages of love and support to relatives and friends still alive on this Earthplane.

It is through this process that hard evidence of post-mortem survival is provided, for if Stephen Holbrook is able to approach a total stranger and say *"your father died on the 14th of August in Ward 10 of York District Hospital after suffering two strokes and a heart attack – his name was Geoffrey, and he's telling me that before you closed the coffin lid you straightened his hair and put a St. Christopher medallion in the casket – and yesterday you broke a milk jug while you were doing the washing up, and by the way, you once had a pet canary called Charlie..."* and be absolutely 100% correct in these statements corroborated by the recipient of the message, this information must come from *somewhere!*

It is Stephen's belief (and that of The Spiritualist Church) that the information comes directly from the spirit of the deceased. There are, of course, sceptics who deride this proposition, but when those same sceptics are presented with the evidence and are asked to come up with an alternative theory as to how Stephen does what he does, their best shot is to cry "fraud" and to claim that the medium has got plants in the audience.

This accusation is without logic or foundation, especially in Stephen Holbrook's case. He is a particularly busy medium, demonstrating three or four times a week in three or four different towns: on average he will bring over twenty messages in any one night, which means that he'd have to have at least eighty people on his payroll for any one week!

I first met Stephen in the spring of 1999. From that meeting came an informal business partnership, a firm friendship, and a close collaboration on Stephen's first book "The Light In The Darkness". In researching that book, I attended about a hundred of Stephen's demonstrations and very rapidly came to the conclusion that (a) here was a very genuine article who would not and *could* not cheat in the acquisition of his material, and (b) that he was an exceptionally sensitive clairaudient, proven by the incredible amount of highly specific and deeply personal detail that came through in his messages. I was also privileged to speak with many of the people who had received messages through Stephen and to assess not only the accuracy but also the impact of those messages, and I have to say that I am not the only person who believes that Stephen Holbrook is the most consistently accurate medium demonstrating in Britain today!

Anyone who sits through one of his demonstrations cannot fail to be affected in *some* way; there is always lots of laughter and there are frequent floods of tears, but above all there is a tremendous sense of crackling energy and excitement that lifts the spirit – even if you yourself are *not* getting a message from the other side, you'll be sitting near someone who is, and you cannot fail to be aware of the fact that you are taking part in something incredibly special. Stephen does not preach and he does not actively go looking for conscripts to the spiritualist faith, but at his demonstrations I have seen grown men cry and even the most cynical sceptics have come away having to review their position in the light of what they've just witnessed and experienced.

Writing "The Light In The Darkness" was a roller coaster ride of clandestine conversations, tape-recorded interviews, frantically clicking keys of the word processor and the ever present pressure of a self imposed copy deadline. The idea to write the book was mooted late in 1999 (Stephen was not at all enthusiastic) and the first words went down on the PC screen in February of 2000. The book was written in real time – in other words I was writing about things virtually as they happened – determined that the book would be out by the autumn of the year ready for Christmas. In short, the book was written, printed and published in less than seven months, and although it was a marvellously exciting chapter of my life, filled with fun and an increasing degree of camaraderie as Stephen began to warm to the project, it was also an incredibly frustrating experience.

I was aware that I only had so much time and space – that I could not get *everything* into 186 pages of 11 point typescript – and at best I could only provide a thumbnail sketch of Stephen Holbrook, both the man and the medium. Stephen himself was not always helpful… We could be meeting at the Queens Hotel in Leeds to discuss the book and I would say something like "Right Stephen, chapter nine is all about reincarnation, so can you tell me what you think about this concept?" – and he would look at me blankly and say "Sorry James, I haven't many thoughts about reincarnation at all, except that there was this one old lady who was worried that her husband had been reincarnated as a sheep…"

I admired his honesty, but as his biographer there were times when I wanted to strangle him!

"The Light In The Darkness" has been a qualified success, and on the strength of that success I am easy in my mind about embarking upon its sequel "Out Of This World". With *this* book there will be more time and space, none of the pressure to meet a publishing deadline (self imposed or otherwise) and with Stephen's commitment and enthusiasm, we will try to put some leaves on the branches and some flesh on the bones, exploring in greater depth and detail some of the ideas and concepts that make the subject of the book so irresistibly interesting and intriguing. As with "The Light In The Darkness" it is being written in real time.

There is, of course, the ever present problem of writing a sequel insofar as the author must consider how many readers will be coming fresh to the Stephen Holbrook story, and how many will have already been introduced to him through book one. The author must avoid repetition, but he must not leave his new readers dangling through lack of terms of reference. I will try to find a happy balance, but must apologise to both groups of readers if I get it wrong.

CHAPTER ONE
London At The Beginning

We stood there, me, my wife Joanna, and Steve Holbrook, staring up at the floodlit building in front of us. The tea time traffic roared through the height of the London rush hour and rain fell in torrents, bouncing off the pavements, shaking the leaves of the trees that offered us some small measure of protection, and painting the evening city with an opaque wash that blurred the outlines of tall buildings and turned double decker buses into giant red dragons.

People hurried through the wet streaks of neon light, huddling beneath dark umbrellas that threatened to drag their owners skywards with the next gust of the stormwind that cannoned through the concrete canyons of London's West End... Well not *exactly* the West End, but Southampton Row in the heart of Holborn, which as far as we were concerned was close enough to make no difference. Not to us anyway.

I won't say that we were oblivious to the rain and the wind and the traffic, but in that one brief moment caught in time, our attention was grabbed by the elegant modern edifice of The Cochrane Theatre.

Built in the style of 1960's pseudo art deco with sweeping lines of curve and corner, it featured a long window that gave drinkers in the theatre bar a great view of the street below. The main entrance led into a brightly lit foyer and box office, but the thing that held us spellbound was the large electronic notice board that arched across the right hand quadrant of the theatre surrounded by silver stars of fairy lights.

Every ten seconds or so, bright red letters three feet high stabbed out into the night as Stephen's name was flashed across the board...

Tonight! Tonight! Steve Holbrook! Britain's Top Medium
in an evening of Clairvoyance!

This, I thought with a feeling of smug satisfaction, was a bit more like it! A far cry from places like Little Dinthorpe Social Club and the Ilkley Floral Hall that had been Stephen's staple diet of venues for the last few years. Okay, it wasn't a big theatre, (just three hundred seats) but it *was* a theatre and it *was* in the heart of London, and all three of us knew that although it would be a very tough night for Stephen, there was a spiritual reason why he had to do this particular show and that something very significant would come of it, if not straight away, then at some time in the future. We didn't know exactly what that *something* was, but we just knew it was there, hanging in the ether all around us, even as we stood on the street corner getting soaking wet. We'd spoken of it during the journey down from Yorkshire, and indeed, a few times even before that, but talking about it and actually *feeling* it as we were doing right then, ah well, this was very different.

I felt a grin spreading across my face, then caught Jo's eye, and saw that she was wound up in the magick of the moment just as much as I was. My grin broadened to a smile, and I patted Stephen on the shoulder.

'Well, Mr Holbrook, what do you think about *that*?' I said, nodding up at the flashing sign that projected the legend of his name out into the cold autumnal night... and I suppose that it was only then that I realised that Stephen wasn't taking this the way that most people would take it.

'What do I think of it James?' There was a note of disquiet in his voice. 'Oh God, I don't think I like this at all, I'm scared stiff!'

I suppose, when I thought about it, Stephen had good cause to be nervous and apprehensive about this particular demonstration. I don't think he was too worried (or even all that impressed) by the venue – I mean, he will work in a club, a civic hall, an hotel, the local spiritualist church, even a barn in the middle of a field, and it's all the same to him. He'll still deliver the goods – but on this occasion I know that he was very worried about what kind of audience he was going to find once he walked out there onto the stage.

This London audience would not be made up from people who knew him or were familiar with his work. There'd be nobody there who had come on the strength of his formidable

10

reputation in the areas where he was well known and there would be no friendly smiles from the familiar faces of people he had helped in the past. There would be nobody there who had come in hope of getting a message from a loved one and there would be nobody there looking for any kind of spiritual enlightenment.

This audience would consist entirely of members of the national media. Hard-bitten reporters from the press would rub cynical shoulders with representatives from a variety of radio stations and television companies. There would also be a number of editors from some of the UK's top glossy magazines... All there because their bosses had *told* them to be there or turning out in response to the PR pitch made by the team responsible for bringing Stephen to the nation's capital. Perhaps a few of them might be mildly curious, but the vast majority would be looking for a free night out with the opportunity to socialise on someone else's bar bill.

The thought of facing such an audience obviously worried Stephen, and to tell the truth, had been worrying him for many days.

'I'm not too bothered about impressing people,' he'd said on the drive down earlier in the day, 'but on the other hand, I do want to do my best and put on a good evening... but how can I do that when the circumstances are so unnatural? I'm a *natural* medium and for my clairvoyance to work properly I need a natural atmosphere and I know that I'm just not going to get it with a theatre full of press people all waiting for me to fall flat on my face! God knows what's going to happen or what the clairvoyance will be like!'

'Hey, listen Stephen,' I'd soothed placatingly, 'just relax and go with it. If you do fall on your backside, it won't be the end of the world, but things are going to be fine. Whoever is in the audience, they're only people, just like the rest of us, so don't let them intimidate you!'

Which was all very well to say when you were still half way up the motorway with the demonstration still several hours ahead! Now, as we moved into the last forty five minutes before the demonstration, I began to feel very nervous – not for my own sake, but very much indeed for Stephen's.

To help take his mind off things we took him across the road to The Holborn Hotel and bought him a very large and very expensive glass of wine. We chatted for a while and were joined by Henrik Brixen and his colleagues who were responsible for Stephen's London debut. Henrik, ever cheerful and full of Scandinavian charm, was very excited about the evening, but although Stephen joined in the chat and the laughter I could sense that he was only half with us. What he needed at that time was some solitude, some space to gather his thoughts and find that inner psychic consciousness that enabled him to tune into the spirit world around him. I hoped that he might get some time to himself in his dressing room, but when the minutes finally ticked away and we moved back over the road and entered the theatre through the stage door, Stephen's dressing room was already full of people who wanted to talk to him before the evening started.

I wished him luck and then left him in the arms of the London Promoters. I had no role to play in this operation and courtesy and common sense dictated that I should drop out of the circle at that time. Feeling very much like a spare part, I wandered up to the bar and ordered a brandy and coke. Propping myself up by the window, I stared moodily into the wet night, not too happy in the depths of my own thoughts and concerns, and worrying too about what kind of response Stephen might get from the evening.

I watched as the audience began to arrive and congregate in the bar, and a knot of tension twisted in the pit of my stomach. As individuals I'm sure they were very nice people, but as a group they were noisy and abrasive: there were lots of "dahlings" and "luvvies" and a plethora of posturing in the game of one-upmanship. These people came from a different world, a world of their own making in which they were the elite. They knew it, they revelled in it, and they wanted every one else to know it too! As they posed and preened, I watched from my corner, feeling increasingly isolated and out of place. And yet I felt no envy. Once their world had been my world too, but I'd left it behind years ago in search of other things. But this was the world that now reached out to touch Stephen, and although more than any man alive I wanted him to succeed and find the recognition he so richly deserved, I worried for him in fear that the bright star of his spiritual integrity might become contaminated by this lower commercial vibration.

12

Eventually the bell sounded and the media corps moved down to take their seats in the auditorium. Jo and I found places right at the very back and we were both twitchy with tension. I found myself crossing my fingers and sending out a mental prayer of love and support...

And then the house lights dimmed by half a degree and the stage lighting came up a couple of notches and a very different Stephen to the man we knew and loved so well marched out onto the stage.

'Good evening ladies and gentlemen, my name is Stephen Holbrook. I'm a medium and I'm here to prove that you cannot die – not for the life of you...'

CHAPTER TWO
Retford On The Up...

Six weeks before the London debut we'd launched our first little book in York and then we'd hit the road in a mini promotional tour.

Although we were buzzing with the success of the book, it had been an incredibly busy year and we were both very tired and somewhat stressed out. For my part I was beginning to look forward to a double heart by-pass operation with more impatience than fear, and as for Stephen, he was carrying a tremendous amount of weight upon his shoulders as he considered two important choices that would inevitably change his life.

Through his links with Jane McDonald and her manager/husband Henrik Brixen, there were some serious offers of high profile exposure on national television, and at that time he was weighing up the pros and cons and coming to very few hard and fast conclusions. He was well aware of the fact that from a financial point of view he would be in a position to provide a greater degree of security and comfort for his family, but he also shied away from the idea when he considered the lack of privacy that would inevitably follow on the heels of celebrity status.

One day it would seem to be a good idea to be a television personality, but then the next he would have second thoughts and retreat from the concept at full tilt. With or without the TV carrot being dangled in front of his nose there was also the idea of giving up the hairdressing salon which he had run in Leeds city centre for the previous umpteen years, and I have to say that at that time while I was advising him to go forward and test the waters of television, I was also strongly in favour of him giving up the hairdressing salon.

He would frequently leave his home at five thirty in the morning to be at the salon for six fifteen to start work on his first client of the day at half past six... and I wasn't backwards in coming forwards by suggesting that both Stephen *and* some of his clients needed to get a life! Steve would work a twelve hour day in the salon and would *then* hit the road to God knows where in the great North of England to function as a clairvoyant. He was exhausting himself and there were none too subtle signs that his health was beginning to suffer. There were fairly constant headaches, one bad cold seemed to follow another and, more worryingly, his voice had acquired a permanent croak.

There was one occasion half way through a particularly stressful day when he answered the phone to someone who wanted to book tickets for one of his demonstrations and he said "I'm terribly sorry madam but we're actually fully booked up for that venue"... At least, that is what he *meant* to say, but with tiredness tying up his tongue, it didn't quite come out that way. Somehow fully became bully – and with a bit of imagination I dare say you can guess the rest! Talking about it some months later he was able to see the humour, but at the time he was mortified with horror. If nothing else it alerted him to the fact that he was under far too much pressure and he knew that something had to change! And yet, paradoxically in typically Taurean fashion he sought to avoid change by battling on and making the best of the status quo until he felt sure he knew which was the right pathway to follow.

Anyway, as my old mother used to say, the show must go on, and the first stop on our list of promotional dates saw us returning to one of our favourite and most successful venues.

On the evening of Monday 4th September 2000 the atmosphere in Retford Little Theatre was positively crackling. This was Stephen's third visit and tickets for the evening had changed hands more than once at vastly inflated prices on an unofficial black market. This, when we'd been told about it, had made us both feel very uneasy, although there was nothing that either of us could have done to prevent it. Market forces are market forces, and RLT's limited seating capacity combined with Stephen's growing reputation in North Nottinghamshire had provoked this somewhat unnerving situation.

Stephen had spent the first ten minutes of the evening talking to the packed theatre, explaining how his clairvoyance (or to be more accurate, his clair*audience*) worked, and now he was pacing up and down the stage like a caged wildcat, clicking the fingers of his right hand while his left arm began to cramp into the familiar frozen paralysis, which is always a sure sign that his principal

15

spirit guide Archie May is with him, preparing to marshal the spirit people on the other side who are waiting to get a message across to their loved ones in the audience.

Stephen paused mid-stride and peered into the auditorium. 'I want to come to the lady in the cream jacket, over here, on the left, three rows back... Yes, you, my love... I've got a gentlemen with me who passed over within the last year as a result of a heart attack. He's telling me that this didn't come as any great surprise to him because he knew his heart wasn't in good condition, and he's also telling me that you weren't surprised either because you'd been fearing the worst for at least a couple of years before the actual event. Now, my love, just give me a yes or a no... does this mean anything to you?'

'Yes!'

The lady in the cream jacket called out in a nice clear voice – and from where I was standing in the wings of the stage, I let out a sigh of relief. Getting any message through is hard enough (despite what Stephen sometimes says) and getting an unambiguous confirmation with the first link of the evening indicated that we were off to a good start.

'This gentlemen wants me to tell you that he's sorry he didn't listen to you... He says he knew he shouldn't have been smoking, and he knows he shouldn't have been drinking, but he's going on to say that it got to a point where he felt it didn't make too much difference what he did... In other words, even if he'd knocked the fags and the booze on the head, the heart was still too weak to carry on indefinitely... Does any of *this* make sense to you, my love?'

'Yes, it does...'

'Good, now can I just tell you, my love, that he's holding up a packet of cigarettes... A very distinctive box, red and white Marlboro, and he's giving me the number 30... So does the number 30 mean anything to you or is it that he's just trying to tell me that he was on thirty fags a day?'

'Thirty that he'd admit to – and yes, he did smoke Marlboro cigarettes!'

The lady in the cream jacket, about forty years old, sounded incredibly bitter. There may have been some deep emotion there, in fact I'm sure there must have been, but the energy that fuelled

16

her response was anger... Which was something Stephen picked up on straight away.

'I know,' he said, 'that you've been very upset and very angry and that you feel cheated... This gentleman can't have been very old, still only in his mid or late forties, but he's telling me that we've all got to go some time, and that he's all right where he is now... He's showing me the number fourteen... and he's giving me the name of Ellen or Helen... Can you give me a yes or no, please?'

'Yes. He died on the 14th of March and my name's Helen...'

'And who is Andy or Andrew?' Stephen snapped his fingers impatiently. 'Living! Alive, down here on the Earthplane!'

'Andrew is my son,' the lady said quietly.

'And has there been something about an exam or a test that's put Andrew in a bad mood recently?'

'Yes – he took his driving test last week, and failed!'

'Well, this gentleman is telling you to tell Andrew not to worry – he'll get through it next time round... Now, have you just done something with the sum of £54?'

'Er... No, not that I can think of.'

Stephen didn't back down. 'Please think very carefully. The sum of fifty four quid, spent in the last week or ten days.'

'No, sorry.'

'My love, you have definitely spent £54 on something in the last week or ten days.'

There was a trace of hostility in the lady's voice. 'I definitely have not!'

'Yes you *have*...' Stephen looked over his shoulder and said "Yes all right, I'll tell her," as though communicating with some presence clearly seen by him but invisible to the rest of us. 'Do you have your cheque book with you, my love? If you do, just have a quick flick through the stubs, and it'll be there somewhere. I don't mind waiting while you look.'

Bearing in mind the fact that this conversation was being held in public, in front of a hundred and fifty nine people who were hanging on to every word that was said, it is testament to Stephen's powers of persuasion that the lady opened her handbag, pulled out her cheque book, and as instructed, went through the stubs.

'I... Oh, er, yes, I did write a cheque last Tuesday, but it wasn't for £54 pounds.'

'Oh,' Stephen said curiously, 'well how much was it for?'

The lady in cream sounded sheepish. '£53.95!'

There was a ripple of laughter from the audience but Stephen ignored it.

'Well listen, my love, we're not going to argue over five pence, but this gentleman I've got with me, he's telling me that you spent the money on your teeth. So was it a dentist's bill you paid?'

'Yes it was,' the lady confirmed, eliciting a gasp of amazement from the crowd.

'Yes, well the only reason he knows it was your teeth is that he was standing there next to you while you were having a tooth capped, and I hope that you can take this as a little bit of evidence that indicates that although this gentleman passed over in March with a heart attack, he isn't really dead – he's still here, keeping an eye on things for you, looking after you while you have your teeth done and making sure that Andrew passes his driving test next time round and...'

Stephen faltered for a moment. "My love, I've got to ask this. Was there something very significant about that trip to the dentist last week? Was it the first time you'd had your teeth fixed since your husband passed over? And why is this gentlemen making a buzzing sound in my ear, almost like he's mimicking the sound of a dentist's drill?'

'He was a dentist himself,' the lady said. 'He always did my teeth because he knew I hated having them done – and last week was the first time I'd ever been to anyone else in twenty years!'

There is a round of applause from the audience – something that Stephen absolutely hates – but by then he'd begun to move away.

'Thank you, my love, God bless and good night.'

Stephen strode across the stage for a few seconds and then homed in on a large gentleman sitting on the front row.

'I want to come to you, sir. I've got a lady here who is telling me that she's your Mum, that she's been passed over about two years, and she's shouting in my ear "tell him about the maroon car!" Does this make any sense to you, sir? Just yes or no, please?'

'Yes, it very definitely does.'

'...And this lady is telling me that although there were other people who *should* have done it, it was you who took responsibility for all the funeral arrangements, and that you were surprised not only by the *number* of people who came to the service, but at just who *did* come and who didn't. Can you understand this, sir, just yes or no?'

'Yes...' The gentleman responded in a low voice, and from my position in the wings, I could see that he had his head down, and was trying to avoid looking at Stephen up on the stage. This is not uncommon, for many people are shy about speaking in public and although most people come to Stephen's demonstrations hoping they are going to get a message, there are always a few exceptions to this rule. Then, of course, there are the people who do want a message but who are loathe to take it in front of everybody else. I may have been wrong, but from my limited view of the front rows, it seemed that the gentleman Stephen was linking with fell into that latter category.

'Well, sir, this lady is telling me that you weren't the only one who was surprised, because she was there watching it all, and she was surprised as well!' This elicited a chuckle from the audience and I watched the large man nod knowingly, but Stephen ploughed straight on, hardly pausing for breath.

'She's telling me that someone called Sarah should have been there, but there'd been some sort of unexpected problem and Sarah deliberately stayed away... Can you link with this, sir, again please, just yes or no?'

'Yes... sort of.'

I could see that the gentleman was longing to say more, but with the imposition of Stephen's "just yes or no" rule and the inhibitions caused by the environment, all he could do was shift uncomfortably in his seat. Stephen, however, is a man who can respond quickly to most circumstances, and either consciously or through some element of spiritual intervention, he knows when to relax the rules, and frequently asks a question that cannot be answered simply with a yes or a no.

'Who is Joyce?'

'That's my mother's name.'

'And who is Julie? Alive, still living, down here?'

'That's my wife.'

'Umm,' Stephen became very thoughtful and reflective. 'Let's see if I can sort this out. You arranged the funeral, and you were at the funeral, along with your wife Julie and the rest of the family... but Sarah wasn't there, although she *should* have been there, and this is something that your Mum was aware of. Sir, had Sarah had some kind of an accident, and was she in hospital having a leg or an ankle strapped up, even as the funeral was taking place?'

'Yes. She'd fallen down the stairs in her rush to get to the taxi and broke her leg so the taxi took her to the hospital instead of taking her to the church.'

'And who is Frank? Did someone called Frank attend the funeral and was Frank someone who no-one had thought would turn up?'

'Yes. Frank's my brother, and he came over from Canada especially for the service and, no, none of us thought he'd bother to come.'

'And do you drive a maroon car?'

Despite himself the large man on the front row managed a half smile. 'I did, but I've just sold it.'

'Well your Mum's telling you it was a bloody good job you did because it was a load of old rubbish.'

There was more laughter from the audience and only a few people would have heard the gentleman's defiant mutter: 'Maybe, but *I* liked it well enough!'

I heard it, and obviously so did Stephen.

'Sir, this maroon car wasn't just an ordinary car, was it? Was it some kind of classic car, a very old motor that had been around for a long time?'

'Yes, you're right,' the gentleman responded with some warmth.

'And did you get £4000 for that car when you sold it... or if not exactly £4000, something around that figure?'

Now, in talking about this car of all things, not only did Stephen have the gentleman's undivided attention, but also for the first time in the whole conversation there was some energy and animation in the man's responses.

'As a matter of fact I got *exactly* £4000!'

'Your Mum still thinks it was a load of old rubbish, and she isn't the only one, because she's telling me that your wife didn't like the car much either.'

The large gentleman said nothing, but he looked grim in his defeat.

'Sir, I could tell you that the car you sold was one of those big old gas guzzlers, and the car that you've bought to replace it is a modern little Ford or something like that, none of which is really important. What *is* important is the fact that your Mum's been watching all this going on around you. She knows that Frank made the effort to be at the funeral and that it wasn't Sarah's fault that she wasn't, and she knows that it was you who did all the arranging and sorting out when it really shouldn't have all fallen on your shoulders. You were right to expect a little bit of help and you were right to be disappointed when you didn't get it. And she wants to say to you that nothing in this life is perfect or exactly the way we'd like it to be, but just like the rest of us, you've got to get on with things and make the best of them, and in your case it should be a little bit easier now, knowing that she's alive and well, and helping you as much as she can from the other side...'

Stephen brought through another half dozen strong messages in the first half of the evening and then we broke for the interval. In the early days of our association the interval had always provided a pleasant opportunity to chill out and relax for half an hour, but with the advent of "The Light In The Darkness" our mid-evening break was committed to the selling and signing of the books. We sold half a dozen copies and were absolutely delighted. On this particular trip to Retford we had Jo with us and as she was nominally in charge of the box office and book sales this gave me the chance to locate and have a chat with the gentleman who had been the owner of the maroon car.

His name was George Morrison and he willingly confirmed the detail and the content of Stephen's message, even down to the marque of the car that had been mentioned. He'd sold a maroon 1947 Triumph roadster for £4000 and at the insistence of his wife, he *had* bought a Ford Fiesta to replace it – although we both agreed over a hurried gin and tonic that a Ford Fiesta, even a brand new Ford Fiesta, was no replacement for the Bergerac

21

Special which had been the love of his life, even though it had cost him a fortune to run and maintain. George was quite happy to talk to me – he'd been genuinely amazed by the message he had received from his mother and, like many other people, he wanted to know the nuts and bolts of how Stephen did it. I gave him some quick answers and a free copy of "The Light In The Darkness", full well knowing that he deserved a lot more.

In the second half of the demonstration Stephen was able to forge another nine links with members of the audience, and in each case the messages were clear, detailed and unambiguous. At the end of the evening there was a thunderous rumble of applause, and we managed to sell another few books, much to our delight and surprise.

Driving back up the A1 in the elderly Volvo towards Wakefield, our mood was effervescent and convivial. Without arrogance or conceit we were both extremely pleased with the way in which the evening had gone. Although I had never seen Stephen give a poor performance, some nights were better than others, and our third visit to Retford had been one of his best.

'I wish every night could be as good,' he commented as we were coming on to the motorway.

'Yeah, but you don't really have *bad* nights, do you?' I challenged.

'Oh, don't you believe it,' he shot back.

Bearing in mind I was already in the process of making notes for this book, his response got me thinking. 'All right,' I said, 'tell me about one of the bad nights. In fact, think back, and tell me about the *worst* night you've ever had...'

CHAPTER THREE

Knottingley On The Down

As we cruised home along the quiet motorway Stephen took me back in time to the late 1990's.

'There are,' he said, 'some days that start off bad, and you know in your water that whatever you do, they're not going to get any better. On this particular day, and if I remember right it would have been in the middle of November, I overslept... Not by much, but it was enough to put the whole morning out of kilter, and I found myself rushing around like a blue-tailed fly trying to get everything done. I'd been demonstrating the night before and it had been a long drive home and I'd ended up having a much later night than usual, and I just slept through the alarm.

'Anyway, Robbie, that's my eldest son, would have been about three years old, and Bradley was still only a very small toddler, and that morning they were all over me, clamouring for attention while I was trying to eat a slice of toast and have a half serious conversation with Caroline. All the time the phone was going with people wanting to book seats for the next week's demonstrations, so when I finally did get out of the house, I was even later than I'd been to begin with. I was so frazzled that I wasn't concentrating properly on my driving, and I missed the usual turn off for Leeds and I ended up getting into the city centre by an unfamiliar route.

'I knew my first hairdressing appointment was at 8.45 so instead of parking in my usual carpark, I parked somewhere else, and literally ran for half a mile through the freezing rain to get there on time. I made it – just – and that was the start of a very long morning.

'Ten appointments, one after the other, with ten different people who not only wanted their hair done, but who also wanted to tell me their life stories and all the time, the flipping phone is constantly going like the clappers. By half past ten I had the most incredible headache, and by half past twelve, I knew I had to have a break otherwise I'd start being ratty with people – and you just can't do that, can you, no matter how grotty you're feeling.

Generally speaking I've always loved being a hairdresser and I'm quite convinced that the job has helped my communications skills when I'm dealing with messages from the platform. I mean, whatever you're doing, you've got to know how to talk to people in a language they can understand. But on this particular morning I just wanted to be on a Jumbo jet flying a million miles away from the grey skies of Leeds and everybody else's problems.

'Anyway, around about half past twelve I took a phone call from my sister Adele, who is a professional model. She was ringing to say that she'd got her first proper spread in the Sun, and would I get a few copies because she was going to be in the studio all day and was afraid there mightn't be any copies left by the time she finished work. So I used this as a marvellous excuse to get out of the salon for half an hour. I bought thirty copies of the Sun and walked them back through the rain and dumped them in the boot of the car, put some more money in the machine and then slogged it back through the rain for the afternoon session, where I had *another* ten people who wanted their hair dressing and who also wanted to tell me *their* life stories!

'I'd got very wet three times that day already and by three o'clock I was beginning to sneeze and feel very cold and fluey. I knew I had a demonstration that night in Knottingley, but I figured that if I was lucky I could be through by half past nine, and be tucked up in bed with a Lemsip by eleven o'clock.

'The only thing was that when I got back to the car park at five o'clock, the car park was still there, but my car wasn't... Some mean minded sod had pinched it, although why anyone might want to pinch a battered old Montego when there were dozens of better and more modern cars to choose from is anyone's guess.

'So I phoned the police and, not knowing what to do, wandered back towards the salon worrying like mad about getting to Knottingley on time. I knew I'd probably have to get a taxi, and I was worrying about how much it might cost and if I had enough cash with me to pay the bill.

'Anyway, the police came to the rescue and they phoned me within half an hour of me phoning them to say that my car had been found abandoned at a filling station on the M62... So I grabbed a taxi and battled through the rain and the traffic to this particular filling station. Sure enough, my old Montego was

24

there, still more or less in one piece, but with two of the windows smashed and the boot lid wide open. There were a couple of policeman there looking at these thirty copies of the Sun, half a dozen of which were opened either by the wind or policemen's inquisitive fingers at page three, and I felt so embarrassed. They must have thought I was a right perve or some dirty old man with a fixation for this particular model, otherwise why were there thirty copies of the same newspaper featuring the same girl...

'I mean, I could have told them that it was my sister, but I remembered the old saying that when you're in a deep hole you should stop digging, so I simply filled in the paperwork as quickly as I could, reclaimed the Montego, and set off for Knottingley. The car was in a state, and so was I and when I finally did get to Knottingley, I was ten minutes late. The audience was sitting there waiting for me to start and wondering where I was, and for the life of me I didn't know what to do. I was soaking wet, my head was pounding, and I was sneezing, and as for any degree of calm or composure, well forget it!

'What I really wanted to do was just cancel the demonstration and give everyone their money back, but there was this little voice nagging inside my head, saying that some of these people had travelled a long way to be here tonight and that maybe, just maybe, I might get a message through that could help someone. So I had a mouthful of tap water, ran my fingers through my soggy hair, had three drags on a crumpled fag, and walked out onto the stage...

'The audience was grumpy at having been kept waiting for so long, all of my spirit guides were there but I couldn't hear any of the voices, and I simply stammered and stumbled through the first half hour until things slowly began to click into place.

'The first ten or fifteen minutes of any demonstration is always a tense time – I mean, I go out there onto the stage every night taking it as an article of faith that the spirit world will be with me, filtering the messages through, not knowing what I'm going to say or who I'm going to say it to, but trusting that the spirit people will put the right words in my mouth that will mean something to the right pair of ears. But that night in Knottingley there was just a clamour of psychic activity all around me and I had to work incredibly hard to pick out what was being said.

This wasn't spirit's fault, it was mine. I was so stewed up and feeling so ill that I just couldn't make the connections.

'I think that there were maybe two or three half decent messages, but the rest was just a load of old rubbish, and when I finally got home that night I just wanted to climb into bed and die.

'I was flat on my back with flue for three days and in a way I was glad because it gave me an excuse to stay away from the world for a while.

'Anyway, that was probably the worst night I've ever had. I can't think of a worse one, but maybe some of my audiences could give you some more examples.'

Stephen fell silent, and for a few seconds we watched the unwinding ribbon of road unfolding ahead of us. The silence was finally broken by Jo's soft voice coming from the back seat of the car... Joanna – quiet, calm and stoic with the ability to get to the heart of the matter quickly and eruditely.

'I wouldn't worry too much, Stephen,' she said. 'I've seen enough of your demonstrations by now to know that your bad nights are probably ten times better than everyone else's good nights, so you're still well ahead of the game.'

He immediately denied this, but Stephen isn't always right, especially in the realms of self-assessment, and this time around my dear wife had very effectively knocked the nail on the head with the hammer.

CHAPTER FOUR
Concepts of Clairvoyance

George Morrison of Retford is not the only one who'd like to know how Stephen's clairvoyance actually works. To tell you the truth, I'd like to know a bit more myself and, for that matter, so would Stephen!

And if that sounds a bit lame, consider this – we all use electrical appliances, taking electricity for granted, but not knowing exactly how it works, and many of us drive our cars up and down the motorways with little or no knowledge of the workings of the internal combustion engine.

And so it is with Stephen. He is a totally natural medium. He has never had a formal lesson in mediumship, has never attended a school or college of clairvoyance, and although he did sit in a few development circles when he was still in his teens, this is a far cry from experiencing an academic education on the subject of life after death, not that this subject is covered in the curricula of the colleges and universities of the world anyway!

His first brush with spiritualism came at an early age. He woke in the middle of the night to find his grandfather sitting on the edge of the bed – which was more than a little odd, considering the fact that his grandfather was very sick in a hospital ward at the time.

John, Stephen's grandfather, said that he'd just popped in to say goodbye, and that Stephen shouldn't be upset or worried about anything – and then Stephen blinked and John was no longer there. The bedside clock was ticking its last few seconds towards four o'clock in the morning and Stephen, partly bemused and just a little disturbed, drifted back into sleep. The following morning there was a telephone call from the hospital to inform the family that Stephen's grandfather had passed away in his sleep, and the time of death was given as 3.55 AM.

This incident seemed to act as a catalyst and over the following couple of years Stephen became increasingly aware of an incessant babble of voices echoing round in the back of his head. It became extremely difficult for him to cope with his

27

schoolwork, for half the time he couldn't hear clearly what his teachers were saying because of all the other voices shouting inside his skull.

At sixteen years old he went to seek help from his local GP and this very enlightened gentleman directed Stephen to the local spiritualist church. This was an epiphany for the young schoolboy from Wakefield, for here he found acceptance and explanations.

He was told that he was a natural clairaudient and received some basic terms of reference with regard to the broad concepts of spiritualism.

It was not as difficult for Stephen to embrace these concepts as it might have been for someone who had not spent the previous couple of years going through seven kinds of hell trying to figure out what the blazes was going on inside his ear-drums.

Under the care and patronage of people like Janet Ferguson (diva Jane McDonald's grandmother) who was the leading light of the Peterson Road Spiritualist Church and took Stephen onto the public platform for the very first time, and a quite remarkable lady called Una Pearce, he managed to gain control over the voices in his head and began to learn how to channel his rare and very powerful gifts.

In one sense, the concept of spiritualism is really very simple. The central tenet of belief is that you cannot die! Oh certainly, the body flakes out at a certain time along the life journey, but the spirit carries on in perpetuum throughout eternity. Furthermore, the spirit retains *identity* and memory of its time on the Earthplane, and maintains its links with loved ones left behind – helping, guarding, guiding and protecting whenever it can.

However, for there to be any form of communication between these two spheres of existence, there has to be a medium, and although The Oracle at Delphi or the scrying bowls of the ancients might, in an abstract sense, be described in this light, for there to be any level of personal communication and proof provided of post mortem survival, the medium must be something – or someone – who can not only understand language but also have clear comprehension of abstract concepts such as love, duty and emotion. In other words, the medium must be human with a distinct and definite awareness of spirit.

28

Enter the likes of Stephen Holbrook and his kind!

There have been mediums since the beginning of human time, but in relative terms they have been and indeed still are few and far between. We are not talking here of seers such as Cassandra, or Biblical prophets like Isaiah... We are not speaking of those who can survey a spread of Tarot cards or who are adept at reading the lines on the palm of the hands making comment about character and forthcoming events of interest to the enquirer, but of someone who through some quirk of genes or DNA has the ability to sense and communicate with the sentient spiritual energies of people who have died on this plane and have moved on to some other concept of life in another sphere of existence. Far removed from the world of prophecy and fortune telling, these few souls are more in tune with the tradition of shamanism insofar as they forge and provide a link between this world and the next.

All mediums, be they modern or historical, have their strengths and weaknesses. Stephen Holbrook's strength lies in the consistent accuracy of the evidence that he channels through from the world of spirit, naming names, times of events, birthdays and anniversaries etc., and even identifying the health condition that took someone through the veil from this world to the next. His weakness lies in the fact that he has little knowledge as to where his remarkable gifts come from, or indeed the mechanics of how they actually work.

Having said that, I know many mediums who could give you all the theoretical information in the world about clairvoyancy and life after death but, when it comes to proving it, they turn out to be pretty poor mediums and therefore, in my opinion, their 'theories' become highly questionable, to say the least!

I suspect that Stephen has the better part of the bargain, and if he has chosen not to question the origin of his gift, then this is not through blind arrogance but through gentle faith.

We were talking about this recently during a long drive up the A1 to Durham, and I have to say that driving anywhere with Stephen while Stephen is doing the driving is an experience and a half, all by itself! Very sensibly, he has a "hands free" mobile phone system with an earpiece and a mike, and on the dash board of the car (another venerable Austin Montego) there is a small voice

29

activated Dictaphone... Any conversation one tries to have is constantly interrupted by an unremitting barrage of telephone calls (16 between Wetherby and Scotch Corner) from people who want to book seats for any one of the dozen demonstrations Stephen will be advertising at any one time.

As soon as there is an incoming call, Stephen will activate the Dictaphone and go into a well rehearsed response to the incoming call – *Hi this is Stephen Holbrook, three seats for Ossett Town Hall on the 6th of October? Yes, that's fine just come along and pay on the door* – and later, at journey's end, he just transfers the reservation into the tattiest scraggiest excuse for a notebook you've ever seen. Caroline, his long suffering wife, is constantly having a "go" at him about this system of taking bookings, but in his own defence Stephen points out that this is the way that he's done it for the last ten years, and that it works very well indeed, so why bother trying to fix something that isn't broken? As a fellow Taurean I understand totally where he's coming from, but I can also understand how it must drive our more sensible womenfolk to distraction.

But anyway, as I was saying, on the drive up to Durham we were talking about Stephen's clairvoyance, and I did actually ask him why he has never investigated or questioned the source of his gifts.

'I suppose,' he said thoughtfully, 'that I did question it, you know, back in my teens when I had all that babble in my head and I didn't know what it was, but then Una Pearce and the Spiritualist Church provided me with the answers that I needed, and I was able to accept those answers because they did just feel so naturally right to me... They sounded like the truth and somewhere very deep down inside the pit of my stomach, they *felt* like the truth. But I know where you're coming from, and I suppose that I didn't question the source of the gift because I felt just so pleased and privileged to have been given it... and I suppose that's the way I've always felt really.

'Maybe I don't want to look at something too closely that I cannot explain properly, because I don't want my faith in spirit undermined in any way – but it isn't just that, because I really do believe in spiritualism and I am totally convinced that what I experience and pass on to other people is real and true. Maybe I just don't know how to go about questioning it, or maybe I'm a bit frightened that the source of the gift might think I'm being too cocky and presumptuous – you know, looking the gift horse in the mouth, sort of thing...

'But at the end of the day, I'm not sure that it's all that important. What really is important is the fact that my work as a medium proves that there is life after death and that sooner or later we are reunited with our loved ones and relatives who have passed over before us. I know this is true because I am given proof and evidence of it every time I walk out onto the platform and, of course, the people that I talk to at my demonstrations are also given their proof and evidence... and although I also know I've got my fair share of critics, sceptics and non-believers, what they've got to do is come up with a plausible alternative theory that explains how I can do what I do.

'I mean, if I've got a lady with me on the stage who wants to talk to her husband on the fifth row and she tells me that her name is Gladys and that her husband's name is Tom, and that she died of a heart attack back in 1993, and that there are three surviving children called Fred, Dick and Harry, and that the numbers six and nine are very important – and then the gentleman on the fifth row, who I've never met in my life before, confirms that his name *is* Tom, and that his wife *is* called Gladys, and that she *did* die of a heart attack in 1993 – at 6 o'clock on the 9th of April – and that there *are* three sons called Fred, Dick and Harry, then as far as I am concerned, this information is coming through from the spiritual entity of Gladys herself... If Gladys's spirit had not gone on to an afterlife, she wouldn't be able to talk to me, would she?

'So, if there's someone out there saying that the information has not come from Gladys herself, just let them please tell me where they think it has come from! I'll tell you what, I'd be very pleased to hear from them!

'The only trouble is,' Stephen's voice became a little more philosophical, 'there are so many people out there who don't like the truth when it's presented to them that they go miles out of the way to come up with an alternative truth, but that alternative is usually so far off the wall that it lacks any credibility.

'Why is it that so many people have such a great problem in believing that there is life after death and that it *is* possible to communicate between the two worlds?' He sounded genuinely

31

perplexed. 'To me it's the most natural, and also the most logical thing imaginable, so what on earth are they so frightened about?'

The answer to this question is relatively straight forward. People are and always have been frightened by the unknown, and there has always been a resentment within the human condition directed against anyone who knows more than we do. Little wonder that the mystics of old led solitary lives, frequently being forced into the role of the hermit and, in extremis, it is the same energy that pushed our forefathers into burning little old ladies at the stake for practising a little innocent herbalism. Basically, wherever there is ignorance there is also fear, and this fear manifests itself in many different forms. In our modern times the biggest fear factor that Stephen comes up against is the fear that he might be right, in which case the critics, sceptics and disbelievers are put in a position where they must question their own belief structures and the foundation stones of their own perceptions. They don't want to do this for a plethora of different reasons and therefore it is much easier to take the simple stance of declaring themselves right and Stephen wrong. Nothing feeds fear more than fear itself!

The Mother's Tale

From Margaret Holbrook

The middle of a heat wave with melting tarmac, and at last after sixteen hours of purgatory I gave birth to a healthy baby boy, weighing 7 pounds and 9 ounces! This was on 29th April 1966 at The Southmoor maternity hospital in Hemsworth. I had thought 'is this baby ever going to arrive?' – he was already two weeks overdue, but with the help of some inducement, forceps and midwives running around like scalded hens, Stephen finally made his entrance into the world. An hour and a half later when he had been taken from me to be cot-nursed due to the difficult birth, one of the midwives said that I deserved the VC!

Stephen was never an easy baby and right from day one he seemed to like the sound of his own voice. Somehow I knew even though Stephen was my first child, he was certainly going to make some impact on the world, although quite how, I wasn't sure. My peaceful existence was changed forever. Sleep was of no interest to Stephen whatsoever, consequently neither me nor his father had a normal night's sleep until he was almost three years old. His father started suffering from boils and carbuncles due to the stresses and strains of fatherhood, which might be something to smile about now but it wasn't at the time. I, however, battled on as mothers do.

I could have set the clock by Stephen's twenty minute sleep pattern. There's an indelible picture in my mind of Stephen fast asleep in his pram and the twenty minutes almost up. Within a second his eyes would spring wide open, and at the sitting up stage he would sit bolt upright waiting for the next episode of his life to unfold. Really he was only ever happy when he was on the move.

As time went on my favourite name for him was "90 mile an hour Joe" because everything was done at such a speed. The local shopkeeper's name for him was "Captain", because wherever he went he would always have an entourage of pals with him and he was always in charge. He would often bring home hedgehogs and injured birds and, once, even a fish. Our neighbours affectionately called him "Nature Boy".

33

To illustrate this, one Sunday morning he brought back a three and a half pound carp that he'd caught in The Walton Canal and much to my surprise I found it swimming round and round in his paddling pool. 'I've got to keep it, I've got to keep it!' he cried... Stephen was never one to reason with, but after a long verbal battle about cruelty to animals in general and fish in particular, he despondently walked back to the canal with the fish to give it backs its freedom.

By the age of twelve he wasn't quite so easy to sidetrack, and for eighteen months he pestered me for a dog. Considering that we only had a small bungalow, and that by that time Stephen's two sisters had come along, there wasn't a lot of room, and I wondered if there was any room for a dog... But as mothers often do, I relented and Stephen got his first dog, Theo, a beautiful golden Labrador. Stephen took Theo to the Wakefield and District Canine Training Club, and as he showed great potential for his age, the organisers suggested that he aim for Crufts obedience competition when he reached fifteen. The only problem here was that for this, he would need to have a border collie, which was a more suitable breed for obedience training. So, after another year of constant bombardment – 'Oh please, please, please, mum, I'll look after them and you won't have to do a thing!' – I relented again and Chad the border collie became the new member of the Holbrook family, joining his sisters' three rescued cats and an elderly gerbil called Midge. We were literally full to capacity, that's when I put the "no vacancies" sign up in the hall.

A year later lightening struck. Stephen suddenly discovered girls. Dogs were past history and it doesn't take a genius to work out who became responsible for all the pets. Despite the fact that it was Stephen who wanted the dogs, I would not turn the clock back for the dogs brought such a lot of happiness into the family and both lived to ripe old ages.

I wouldn't say that Stephen was accident prone, exactly, but he's certainly had more than his fair share of narrow escapes. Back in 1970, Stephen and his friend had those little pedal cars and they had hours of fun playing racing drivers until his friend's mother brought the squashed car to the back door with many apologies. It seemed that Stephen had "parked" his car in her driveway and she had reversed over it before she'd known it

34

was there. Needless to say it was beyond repair, and we had the usual tears.

A couple of years later he was in the bath with Joanne, who was still only two years old. Stephen had seen his friend squirting water through a bicycle pump, and he thought it was a great idea, so he smuggled his own bicycle pump into the bathroom and as soon as I was out of the room, had a trial squirt. The water shot into the air, burst the heat and light bulb, bringing instant darkness, shards of flying glass, and two terrified children screaming their little heads off. There were no injuries, thank goodness!

In 1975 he was playing conkers in the school playground and got hit in the eye with a conker. He was rushed off to hospital and was diagnosed as having hyphaema – a serious blood clot behind the eye. He had to remain very quiet and still, in case the blood clot moved. Within less than half a day the boy in the next bed had to be moved because he and Stephen had been flicking peas at each other! Neither of them realised the seriousness of Stephen's injury.

In 1980 he went on a holiday with some friends to a chalet in Chapel St. Leonards... It should have been perfectly safe, but one day Stephen swam out a bit too far and got into difficulties, and ended up being rescued by the lifeguard. The other thing was that dogs were not allowed on the site, but they smuggled one of their pets along anyway, and on the second day of the holiday she gave birth to a litter of six puppies. How they kept it all a secret, I really don't want to know!

In 1981 Stephen broke his arm swinging on a tree that he been told time and time again not to climb... But by then I suppose I'd become a bit fatalistic. Even if he wasn't in trouble, he'd go and find it somewhere, and one thing about him that I noticed is that even if things aren't happening directly to him, things always seem to be happening around him.

Having said all that, I must just finish by saying that Stephen is and always has been a wonderful son and if I'd been able to choose his character and temperament, I'd have chosen exactly what God has given him. He's always been a free spirit and an independent soul. He's always responded to an adventure. He's never easily accepted words like "can't" and "no" and he's always been my best friend.

35

CHAPTER FIVE

Old Pete & The Guild Hall

The biggest fear in life is the fear of death. We can proclaim our spirituality in very loud voices but even the most spiritually advanced guru is inclined to become a wee bit circumspect when it comes to looking death in the face. Even the most ardent spiritualist who is totally convinced of post mortem survival is seldom anxious to take that final step across the threshold between the two worlds. If, however, it can be proven (not conjectured but actually proven) that death is not the end and that there is life *after* death, how much richer and more lighthearted our lives down here on this azure planet Earth might be. Indeed, to what extent would the whole world order change in the light of such knowledge?

Certainly the orthodox religions of the world would have to change their act and update some of their policies, as would politicians, the captains of industry and even the common man in the street. Consider the implications! How would we behave towards one another, nation to nation, man to man, if we all knew as an absolute certainty that we were going on to another sphere of existence after death, and once in that other world of spirit we would be held accountable for our actions – and also our lack of action – down here on the earthplane, receiving recognition where it is deserved and making reparation where it was due? Surely this would change Man's attitude towards his fellow men and surely this would be a worthwhile foundation stone upon which to build a better world?

There are, of course, other fears. Everything from the fear of snakes and spiders to the fear of rejection, the fear of illness and old age, the fear of isolation. But perhaps the greatest fear is the fear of the unknown and the most obvious example of this fear is the fear of death itself. Therefore anything that Stephen Holbrook can do to remove this fear has, in my opinion, got to be seen as a step in the right direction.

I am aware that some people might take issue with this statement, for there are those who fear life more than death and see death as a final release from the trials and torments of this world. For these people life is a painful and a bitter experience and in extremis suicide is seen as the only escape from suffering.

Peter Cooper didn't quite fall into this category, but towards the end of the first year of the new millennium, he was getting pretty damn close.

Better known as Old Pete, especially to the residents of the Bishophill area of York, Peter was a familiar sight, shuffling around the narrow terraced streets in his shapeless trousers, always with a thick shaggy jumper in the summer and an old duffel coat in the winter. Initially there would be a degree of aversion from new people moving into the area, but as Old Pete had lived there longer than most, and as it was obvious that he was not a tramp but just an odd and rather scruffy old man, the aversion usually transmuted into begrudging acceptance before very long.

He lived in an end terrace, siding onto the scooped moat of York's famous walls, and although the curtains were invariably drawn shut, denying the passer by any vista of his home, it was noted that both the door and the windows were kept clean, even though no one ever recalled seeing Old Pete doing any cleaning.

What they did see was the unkempt shuffling figure, with the mass of matted grey hair and long beard and moustache; invariably he would be muttering unintelligibly to himself, eyes fixed on the yard of pavement immediately before him. Occasionally he would be seen carrying heavy plastic bags, and every Saturday night he could be found sitting in the corner of The Golden Ball, smoking a gnarled old briar pipe and sipping at a pint of cheap beer, making it last the night, from opening time 'till closing.

He didn't talk to people and, by and large, people didn't talk to him, although frequently they would talk about him. Some wished that he lived elsewhere while others pointed out that he didn't do anyone any harm, and that whatever else he was, he was neither a nuisance nor a homeless beggar. Many guessed at his age – he could, it was generally agreed, be anything between sixty and ninety, and a few pondered the possibility of some secret history that might, were it to be made public, invalidate the old man's right to live his late years within the framework of the community.

Old Pete's problem was that despite the fact that he kept himself to himself, he looked like trouble… the archetypical tramp, the beggar, the mad child molester… and although it was patently obvious that none of these things were true about him, his general dishevelled and down at heel appearance caused people to think the worst and give him a wide berth – which, as Pete told me a few weeks ago, suited him just fine!

I came to "meet" Old Pete in a rather curious way. Curious, in the sense that like many other people, I'd seen him slouching around York and, equally like other people, had heard some of the unsavoury rumours surrounding his history, but I never actually spoke to him until the evening of Stephen's demonstration of clairvoyance at The York Guildhall on 23rd November 2000 and, even then, it was just to thank him for his help in sorting out a problem we had with the seating arrangements.

There are some nights that go like absolute clockwork and there are others that are so incredibly fraught that I sometimes wonder how Stephen actually manages to make the connection with the other side. In a perfect world there needs to be a calm atmosphere – a mood of expectation and excitement is fine, but tension and contention are to be avoided at all costs. Energies of anger and hostility are the kiss of death to spiritual communication and unfortunately the evening of November 23rd was filled with so much tension and contention before Stephen even drew breath to try and make contact with the world of spirit, that the event very nearly didn't happen at all.

During the preceding three weeks York had been hit by some of the worst flooding in living memory and a tremendous amount of damage had been done. The Guildhall, situated literally right on the riverbank, had had its cellars and storage rooms inundated, and half of its chairs had been ruined beyond repair. Unfortunately, nobody had thought to notify Stephen and, thus, when he arrived expecting to find all the seats as promised, they were eighty seats short, without any chance of getting any more at this late stage. This was a scary situation as he'd already sold all the tickets for the event! To make matters worse, he was in the depths of a very bad cold and was nursing a headache that had been with him pretty incessantly over the mainstay of the day – and to add insult to injury, he'd had to walk for twenty minutes through the freezing cold rain because being a Thursday evening in the run up to Christmas, all of the streets leading to and from York's city centre were closed to traffic to give priority to pedestrians in their pursuit of late night Christmas shopping.

If there had been some sympathy and a little more co-operation from the evening staff on duty at The Guildhall things might not have been so bad, but as far as the evening shift were concerned, it wasn't their fault that there were eighty chairs missing and it hadn't been their responsibility to inform Stephen of the situation. This gung ho couldn't care less attitude brought Stephen as close to losing his temper as I have ever seen him come in all the time I've known him, and even as the audience began to arrive the situation had been far from resolved. The only thing we could do, we realised, was let people in on a first come first served basis and when all the chairs were filled, we would then admit anyone else who wanted to pay half price for standing room only.

This, I have to say, did not go down well with every member of the audience and there were mutterings and grumblings, especially from the people who found themselves having to stand at the back of the hall.

Stephen was trying to sort people out down at the front, Jo was manning the door, and I was quietly tearing my hair out, wishing I could find somewhere to hide. We simply had to find more seats, but the only thing available were some rickety old trestle tables tucked away behind a screen, and we'd been told in no uncertain terms by the caretaker that these were not to be used to sit on because they weren't safe. In the end, I thought 'sod it' and started pulling them out anyway. There was a small cheer from the audience and many hands reached out to help – and that's when I noticed Old Pete, quietly working away, putting four trestles beneath each table rather than just two... The four trestles created a much safer situation and I wondered why hadn't I thought of doing it myself!

With the crowd mucking in and the extra support, we got six long tables sorted out at the back of the hall that provided seating for another thirty people. It still left much to be desired but it took some of the pressure off: I went over and said thank you to Pete and he gave me a small nod in return and then disappeared into the shadows by the entrance as Stephen started the demonstration. I briefly wondered whether he was there as a member of the audience or whether he was helping out as a casual hand on the caretaking staff, but there were so many other things going on in my head that I didn't give it any more thought than that.

It took Stephen quite a while – certainly much longer than usual – to tune in and even after he had done so, I have to say it wasn't the best demonstration of clairvoyance I've ever seen him present. The links seemed tenuous and he was unable to develop the depths of detail that were usually such integral parts of his evidence. That he came up with anything at all is quite amazing, given the way he was feeling and all the hassles we'd had. Having said that, the audience seemed more than well pleased with what he was giving them and there was much laughter when he brought through a member of the judiciary who'd basically drunk himself to death and wanted to apologise to his wife for collapsing over the dinner table and ruining her much treasured set of antique Royal Doulton – and inevitable tears when Stephen made contact with two little boys who'd been electrocuted on a railway line...

Oddly, the most specific message of the evening was a message that nobody claimed.

When Stephen said he wanted to talk to someone at the back of the hall, a gentleman he thought, who had links with Spain, my own ears pricked up immediately. I have always had and still maintain very strong links with Spain and two very special friends have both died on Spanish soil during the past few years. Furthermore, although I'd always hoped I might get one, during my association with Stephen, I've never received a message through him, and now I thought this might be it. My hopes were soon to be dashed however.

Stephen must have seen the look on my face because he immediately said 'No, James, I know about your Spanish links, but this isn't for you. I want to talk to someone with a Spanish name, who lost his wife to the spirit world through cancer – but this wouldn't have been recently – and I know for sure that she wouldn't have died in this country but in Spain, and that it would have taken her a very long time to pass over and she would have been poorly for a long time before anyone realised just how poorly she was...'

He waited, hoping that someone might pick up on this information but nobody did, so he tried to make the link through a different tack.

'I've got a lady here and I'm getting the name of... well it sounds like *Marrie* but I suppose it could be Mary or Marie or even Maria, and she's talking about "the flying horses". She's got a young boy with her now, and this young boy, he'd only be a lad really, six or seven years old, went over to the spirit world very quickly *and it would have had something to do with the flying horses!'*

Stephen paused and waited yet again, but again there was no response. Someone near the front coughed and there was the sound of a scraping chair. The audience was getting restless and Stephen was getting frustrated to the point where he kicked tact and diplomacy out of the window.

'Look,' he said 'I know there's someone here tonight, a gentleman somewhere towards the back of the room, who knows exactly what I'm going on about. I'm getting a strong letter P and there's something significant about a Sunday and if you don't want the message, sir, then that's fine, but just give me a wave and tell me so that I can pass on to the next link without spending all this time wasting my energy trying to get a message through to someone who doesn't want it. I've got Mary or Maria, and a little boy. Mary would have died of cancer at least ten years ago and the little boy would have passed over in some kind of accident with a horse... So please, for the last time, anyone here tonight from Spain who can make sense of this for me? No? Okay, well I'm going to pass on, but let me just say that Maria and the little boy are sending out lots of love and support and they're saying you have to be patient, that this is not the time for journeys and reunions.'

I scoured the back of the hall, looking at all the male faces that I could focus on, trying to wring a clue as to the identity of the person Stephen was trying to link with. There were more than a dozen men present and, to a man, they all looked as perplexed as each other.

'Okay, I'm moving on now...' Stephen turned on his heel and moved back into the centre of the room. I could see that he was very tired and wasn't surprised when he brought the evening to a close five minutes early.

The audience duly filed out leaving us to pick up the pieces. Stephen was drained and exhausted, but relieved to have got through the evening.

'Was it as bad as Knottingley?' I asked.

'Close, but *nothing* could be as bad as that night in Knottingley!'

We talked for a while about how annoying it was when a strong message got lost because nobody would claim it and we talked for a while longer about the cock-up over the seats, then with books and posters under our arms, made our exit and walked back through the freezing night to where we'd parked our cars.

I woke up the following morning to realise that I'd caught Steve's cold and he woke up to the realization that he had flu. The next ten days were fairly grim for the pair of us, and I'm sure that we both forgot about the details of Stephen's demonstration in York. If we remembered anything, it was the panic over being eighty chairs light, and unconnected links with a lady called Mary or Maria who had died in Spain of a lingering cancer went completely out of our minds.

But a significant footnote to this story was waiting to be written, although not until almost a fortnight later.

CHAPTER SIX
Death In Spain

For a number of years now I have enjoyed a marvellous friendship and most unusual collaboration with Yorkshire's inimitable action poet, Adrian Spendlow. Ade's poetry is totally contemporary, more suited to performance than life on the printed page, and my admiration for this man knows no bounds. He gave up a "safe" job a few years ago to see if he could make it as a jobbing poet and with the mouths of three children to feed this was an extraordinarily brave move to make. And yet he *did* make it, and made it successfully, writing dramas and poems to order for schools and old peoples' homes, and finding some degree of fame and notoriety compèring folk festivals, writing introduction poems for every act on the bill – sometimes at incredibly short notice and with frequent moments of panic when the acts are changed at the very last minute. The mainstay of his work, however, is as a free lance poet, persuing gigs wherever he can find them.

Adrian and I have worked at putting music to his poetry, usually on a blues/jazz theme wrapped around guitar and vocals, and if you'll forgive my immodesty, this has proved to be an exciting fusion of something exhilaratingly fresh and different. The only problem has been (and still is) finding the right audience for this poetic and musical experience, and it was in search of an audience and a venue that we found ourselves going up to The Golden Ball in Bishophill to have a chat with some people about staging an event in the pub.

The Golden Ball is one of those lovely old-fashioned places with lots of nooks and crannies and three or four small bars rather than one big modern lounge. In some ways it's still a working class establishment with a hard core clientele of old regulars, but increasingly it's started to get very popular with York's yuppies, and it has always been the alternative watering hole for the city's disenfranchised poets and folk musicians.

We had a reasonably successful meeting and hung around afterwards to have a few drinks. Generally speaking I dislike a

but tend to make an exception for places like
which are genuine and unpretentious, and tend
eatening ambience than some of the modern gin
ɟh Street.

; to Adrian about working an arrangement of
Concerto around a Spanish poem he was in the
;, when in one of those rare moments of total
anced up and noticed Old Pete sitting in the
̱̱̱ ̱̱̱ ̱̱̱ ̱ ̱̱̱ feet away from us. It was fairly obvious that not
only was he openly eavesdropping our conversation, but also that
he recognised me from The Guildhall. He nodded and offered me
half a smile and I suppose I grinned back, before getting on with
what I was discussing with Adrian... But ever after, I was aware
that Old Pete was watching me and listening in, and I wasn't too
sorry when Adrian suggested that it was time to go.

As we got up to leave, Old Pete got up and left with us. Out
in the street it was an icy December night and as Adrian climbed
astride his battered old bike I told him to be careful, then patted
him on the back as he peddled off towards home. I watched him
wobble down the road, then fumbling for the keys, turned
towards where I'd parked the car – and nearly jumped out of my
skin, because as silent as a shadow Old Pete was standing right
behind me.

'Do you mind if we have a quiet word?' he said softly, and
his voice was something of a revelation. Rather than the thick
Yorkshire accent that one might have expected to go with the
rough appearance of the man, it was low and well modulated, not
particularly Southern, but devoid of any kind of regional accent.

'You *are* the chap who works with Stephen Holbrook, the
medium, aren't you...?'

'Yes,' I said. 'I suppose that's me.'

'Well look, I'd suggest we went back into the pub for a few
minutes but then either you'd feel beholden to buy me a drink or
something or I'd feel embarrassed because I certainly can't afford
to offer to buy you one – but listen, my house is literally just half
a minute round the corner and I'd be more than happy to make
you a nice cup of tea in return for a few moments of your time.
Tell me, sir, now what do you say?'

I was cold and I was tired and I really wanted to get home to
my wife, but my curiosity was aroused and working more on

psychic instinct than common sense, I agreed to his request and allowed him to lead me around the corner to his home on the end of Fairfax Street.

These little terraced houses don't look very special from the outside, but inside they can be extremely characterful and comfortable. Both descriptions were applicable to Pete's small home, and if there was a heavy layer of dust over some of the furnishing and fittings, it was friendly dust that had found its place in life with absolutely no intimation of dirt or squalor. Two ancient leatherback chairs sat either side of a Little Wenlock stove and Pete's front parlour was a snug corner of warmth and soft colour (rust red carpet, damson drapes and curtains, flickering embers from the fire) on this freezing winter's night.

While Pete clattered round in the kitchen, I sank down into one of the armchairs and studied the several very good photographs that hung on his walls. I'm a very keen photographer myself, and as I've already mentioned, I have an obsessive passion for Spain and all things Spanish, and therefore I was particularly interested to note that the photographs, mostly moody black and whites, were of a part of Spain that I knew very well. There was a vista of the harbour at Algerciras, a snowscape of The Alhambra in winter, and a stunning night time shot of the Giralda in Seville. Whoever had taken these pictures was clearly a master of the photographic art... and I told my host as much as he brought two chipped mugs over to the stove.

'Oh I took those a good few years ago on an old Pentax Spotmatic, but I think the images weather the test of time...' He looked at me shrewdly. 'I used to live in Spain... Is the tea all right, by the way?'

'Yes, thanks, it's fine.' And then in a moment of flashing psychic insight I suddenly knew what this was all about. 'Stephen Holbrook's last message at The Guildhall a couple of weeks ago – it was for you, wasn't it?'

'Yes,' he admitted, 'it was. It threw me a bit at first because the timing was out... but even when I realised that I was the chap he wanted to talk to, I found that I couldn't speak or own up to it.'

'It's a great shame,' I said, remembering how cheesed off Stephen had been at the time. 'Stephen hates it when a message gets lost.'

'Oh but it didn't get lost,' Pete replied immediately. 'I understood every word of what was being said to me, and I just found that I couldn't respond to it because, well...' he gazed into the murky depths of his mug for a moment, then met my eyes directly, '...because for one thing, I was so choked with surprise and emotion, and for another, even if I'd had all the calm in the world, I'm not the kind of chap who likes to draw attention to himself in public... not these days anyway.'

Not these days, no, but twenty years earlier it had been a rather different story.

Pete had started his working life in the merchant navy, and being gregarious and personable by nature, it hadn't taken him too long to make the jump into the burgeoning cruise ship market of the sixties and the seventies. By 1978 he'd attained the heights of being cruise director for one of the major shipping lines, and by 1980 he'd got tired of the whole thing and at just forty years old decided to retire from the sea for a while and opened a cabaret restaurant on the Costa Del Sol.

Here he met and subsequently married Maria Gutiez – who he would frequently call Marrie rather than her given patronymic, while she, along with all their Spanish friends, would invariably call him Pedro. There was a huge age gap between them. At the time of their meeting Pete was forty two years old while Maria was just nineteen, and this was something that didn't go down too well with Maria's very traditional parents. None-the-less, true love conquers all obstacles and in 1982 they married in Gibraltar and two years later she proudly presented him with a son who they called Patrick after Pete's father and Domingo after Maria's father. Domingo, by the way, is also the word in the Spanish language that means Sunday.

Sadly, even the birth of their son failed to heal the deep rift between Maria and her family, and indeed it seemed that Maria became increasingly depressed about the whole situation. The depression, which manifested itself in a number of ways, tended to conceal the fact that Maria was frequently far from well, and therefore when she was diagnosed with cancer of the lymph glands (lymphoma) in 1985, the cancer was relatively advanced.

Pete did his best to run the restaurant, bring up his son, and nurse his terminally ill wife all at the same time. It wasn't easy,

46

and when Maria Gutiez Cooper finally passed into spirit in the autumn of 1986, as well as being wracked with grief, Pete was also wracked with guilt – guilt at feeling such a sense of relief that the long protracted ordeal was over. The feeling of guilt never ever left him and to compensate he threw his whole life into bringing up his son... 'Probably overcompensated and spoiled the kid rotten,' Pete mused rheumily, 'but he had no family, only me. Maria's people didn't want to know us, and her Mother even said that we'd all got what we deserved for going against the tradition of the family. Terrible, isn't it, the way that people will hold grudges and point the finger of blame.'

As is often the way, disaster seldom strikes with a single stroke in a man's life.

To celebrate Patrick Domingo's sixth birthday, Pete took him to the annual fair in the border town of La Linea. Here there were hot dog and candy stalls, ghost trains, big dippers and a ferris wheel... and one particular ride that fascinated the young six year old.

'I suppose you'd kind of call it a flying horse ride. There was a horse, a little like what you'd find on the carousel roundabout, but in this case, the horse was on the end of a long chain, and as the ride got faster and faster, the horses would take off and fly in a wide circle, almost a full forty five degrees to the central pillar. I got Patrick at the front of the horse and was sat behind him, one arm around the grab handle, and my other arm around the boy, and there we were flying round and round having a high old time... and I didn't actually realise that the chain had sheared until we were flying over the fairground and heading for Algerciras bay at a great rate of knots...'

A later accident investigation concluded that a bolt had sheared through metal fatigue, close to the central console of the ride, allowing Pete's horse to be flung free. While the velocity held, the horse maintained height, but once the velocity subsided, horse and riders began plummeting to the ground.

'I knew we were going to die. I could see the fair, the main road, the beach and the water, all rushing up to meet us... I could hear Patrick screaming in my ears and I just closed my eyes, wrapped my arms around him and waited for the end. I remember thinking that we'd be reunited with his mother in a few seconds, and then I don't remember anything else at all...'

Pete "woke up" in an Algerciras hospital after having been in a coma for the better part of five weeks; he'd broken his left leg in three places, had broken both his arms and had dislocated both shoulders and collar bones. Five ribs had been smashed and he had a fractured skull. His son, Patrick Domingo had broken his neck and the poor little boy was dead even before the ambulance and paramedics had arrived in response to the telephone calls to the Spanish emergency services.

'I wanted to die myself and I waited for it to happen, but it didn't happen and each day I got just a little better. I couldn't believe it. I knew I should be dead and I tried to die. There was nothing at all in my life left to live for. Everything I'd ever loved was gone and I wanted to be gone too.'

To cut a long story short, Pete was in the Algerciras hospital for the better part of six months, during which time his cabaret restaurant in Marbella went bust and he had to sell everything to pay the bills and avoid bankruptcy (a significantly more serious situation in Spain than it is in the UK). At the end of the day there was just enough cash left in the kitty to get back to England, where he raised enough capital to put with the insurance money to be able to buy the house in Bishophill.

'It was the logical place to come to. This town and these streets, this is where I was born and grew up. Initially, I tried to get a job, but I was fairly unemployable and quite honestly it was just so easy to sit back and let the state pay for everything.'

The seasons and the years blurred for Pete Cooper, and then 'I woke up one morning, just a few weeks ago, and thought this is it, I've had enough of being on my own and I'm going to join Patrick and Marrie. Wasn't quite sure how I was going to do it, mind you, but there are enough ways, aren't there, especially if you're being serious about it. I mean you can jump into the river or off the top of the Minster, or take a couple of hundred paracetamol... I didn't particularly want to die, but the pain of living had become just too much to bear. Not a day, good God, not an *hour* goes by without me thinking about Marrie and Patrick and what we could have had together if things had worked out differently for us all. I'd thought of committing suicide many many times, and I suppose I'd already tried to kill myself through drowning my sorrows at the bottom of a bottle, but I'd always been pulled back at the last minute. But anyway,

48

like I said, there was this one morning a few weeks ago... I suppose I'd been sinking lower and lower into a never ending mood of depression, which you do when you wake up every morning dreading the day ahead and realising that you've got absolutely nothing at all to live for, and I thought to myself, enough is enough and it really is time to go. I've put in enough wasted years of penance and remorse and it's time to be with my family again... And then I had this quite terrible thought that shook me to the foundations. I thought "Oh my God, what if they're not there, over there on the other side of the grave? What if there *isn't* any life after death, despite all that I've read over the years and all that my senses tell me?"'

'Anyway, I was thinking about all this when I was looking through an old paper and saw your man's advert for the night at The Guildhall. Reckoned I'd go along and see for myself, and you know the rest.'

This conversation with Pete has led to several other conversations over the last eight months and as I write, he's still here on this side of the veil, taking solace from the message he received from Stephen back in November of 2000.

I remember leaving him on that first night and driving home to tell Jo all that had happened, except that she was asleep. So, rather than waking her, I made my notes, feeling a strong affinity with the subject of my scribblings for the places which had played such a vibrant and important role in his life; Marbella, La Linea, Gibraltar and Algerciras. They had played an equally important and vital role in my own life for the better part of half a dozen years. I tried hard to remember exactly what Stephen had said on the night of November 23rd.

...A link with Spain, a Spanish name, Mary or Maria or Marrie. The strong letter P and something about Sunday being very significant. Death from a lingering cancer, and a little boy, about six years old, passing over with some connection to the flying horses. Not a time for journeys or reunions...

As I think about it now, as I thought about it then, all the hairs at the back of my neck rise up with bristling sentience. Just how accurate can you get? Just how relevant do you have to be to prove post mortem survival? Okay, Stephen was a little out with his timing, but this is surely within acceptable limits if you consider that time does not work in the same way in the spiritual time/space continuum.

Another thought that I have is that in any given demonstration there are always a couple of messages that don't get taken, links that do not get forged, and I know just how deeply frustrating this is for Stephen. On the other hand, I now realise through the incident with Pete Cooper that although the links may not be acknowledged by members of the audience, the chances are that there *is* someone out there who knows exactly what Stephen is talking about and that Stephen's message does have meaning and impact, even though he may not be given the satisfaction of knowing this himself.

CHAPTER SEVEN

Suicide in Scarborough

There is still a widely held Christian belief (and indeed a written dogma – although views are softening in the 21st century) that suicide is a damnable sin and that, at worst, suicides go to hell, and at best they serve their time in a state of limbo. Even some members of the spiritualist church become nervous when confronted by this subject and the consensus of thought (as portrayed in the Robin Williams film "What Dreams May Come") is that suicides survive but in a morass of their own negativity - the same negativity which caused them to terminate their earthbound existence in the first place.

And yet this is a parochially western school of thought dismissed by other faiths and cultures all over the world, based on traditions and belief structures that differ very greatly from our own.

Among certain tribes of North American Indians, notably the Suix, Apache and Commanche, a member of that tribe, sensing that it is time to move on from this plane of existence to the next, will separate himself from the rest of his tribe in search of a remote and silent place where he will prepare himself and wait for death. The fact that this death inevitably comes in the form of starvation and exposure does not abrogate the individual from the responsibility of the decision.

The Islamic warrior engaged in jihad believes that suicide in the name of Allah guarantees him a favoured place in paradise and the Japanese Samurai (both the medieval and 21st century versions) ardently believes that suicide is the most honourable of deaths – so much so that until relatively modern times the Samurai was only allowed the privilege of self termination through direct petition to and permission of the emperor himself.

This belief structure is so alien to the western mind that it is little wonder that the American forces serving in the Pacific during world war two were totally phased and terrified by the Japanese kamikaze attacks launched against them at Okinawa in 1945. And yet while the Americans trembled in their gun turrets as wave after wave of Japanese aircraft deliberately crashed into the fleets of aircraft carriers and armoured transports, Japanese airmen wept with shame and grief when they were not selected to fly the next suicide mission.

All this is somewhat by the by, for as far as Stephen is concerned suicides are no different from any other soul which has transcended this life in favour of the next. Stephen has a number of different guides which connect with different types of spirits trying to communicate with their loved ones left behind on the earthplane. There is a young boy called Christopher who helps form the link where children are concerned and there is a black gentleman called Warren who brings through the suicides and occasionally the victims of murder or some other violent demise.

Although Stephen does not have a two way link with his guides and although his gift is clairaudient rather than clairvoyant, he has over the years built up a psychic impression of Warren... 'Warren is black, of course, and I think he must have had a terrible life. He would certainly have spent a lot of time in prison or police cells and I think he must have had to cope with a lot of suffering and brutality. I'm not sure, but I even think that Warren might have ended his own life by hanging himself in a police cell somewhere... it's just an impression I get. But when he comes through as a guide he always does it with a lot of power and dignity.'

In Stephen's mind there is no difference in either the strength or the source of the contacts (in other words they're all coming from the same place) and it's Stephen's perception that links with suicides are particularly strong. As an impartial observer this is something that I am well able to confirm. To be sure there is a high percentage of drama and trauma in the messages, and there isn't always a lot of laughter with these links, but the evidence is always exceptionally detailed. Stephen will handle these links with great tact and sensitivity, but he seldom pulls any punches.

What is of some notable interest is an audience's reaction to a suicide link. In the face of such tragedy, people sit a little more upright in their seats and there seems to be a heightened sense of attention, almost as though there's a group feeling of 'there but for the grace of God go I!' It isn't ghoulish but it does make me feel that for every one person who has actually committed suicide, there are maybe a couple of hundred souls who have at least contemplated the action at some time in their lives.

Of extra special interest is the response to a suicide link from the person in the audience who is the specific recipient of the message. For the better part there is a profound sense of relief and great thankfulness that the loved one has transcended death regardless of the manner in which they passed over, but there are the odd few who give Stephen a hard time by refusing to acknowledge that the passing has been caused by suicide. There is, after all, still a lot of stigma attached to the subject, and incredibly it's not so long ago that suicide was a criminally indictable offence in this country. *Attempted* suicide, however, was not and therefore by the letter of the law you had to be dead before you could be prosecuted. This stupid law was only repealed in the late 1960's and it always reminded me of the old witchcraft law where the suspect was thrown into a river. If they floated they were guilty, fished out by the neck then either hanged or burned at the stake. If they sank and drowned they were pronounced innocent of all charges!

Stephen will, as I have said, be incredibly gentle and sensitive when delivering evidence to people who have been bereaved by a suicide, and I have even known him to back off completely rather than risk controversy or the chance of upsetting somebody... But I remember a particular evening during the summer of 2000 at The Hotel Saint Nicholas in Scarborough, when he wasn't having any of it.

This particular evening got off to a bad start insofar as there had been a cock-up with the booking and we found ourselves relegated to a different function room to the one we had reserved. It was all a bit cramped and murky and there was a lot of noise coming from above our heads where the local Rotarians were holding a fundraising dinner and disco in the ballroom (which *should* have been our room for the night!). Steve was stressed out from the pressures of work – he'd just done a twelve hour shift in the hairdressing salon and had then slogged his way through sixty miles of eastbound holiday traffic. I had an abscess on my tooth which was driving me up the wall and Jo, who was manning the door, was suffering from a really awful cold. None of us was in a great mood and we were all a bit disappointed by the relatively low audience figures. Nonetheless, Stephen went on and did his best in what, to say the least, were fairly trying circumstances.

With all the background distractions it was not always easy to place the links as they came through and the audience seemed either shy or reticent in claiming the information that was on offer. Therefore, when one particularly strong link *was* forged, Stephen responded with alacrity and, understandably, was loathe to let it go.

'The 14th of July,' he said. 'Does anyone understand the significance of this date? I've got a lady who couldn't walk without sticks during the last years of her life and she's telling me to mention the 14th of July!'

A middle-aged woman with frizzy red hair put up her hand. She was sitting towards the back of the room and I could see her quite clearly from where I stood by the box office table. She seemed tired and drawn and wore a stonewall expression on her face which could have been interpreted as fear or disbelief. I doubt that she would have put her hand up at all had it not been for a younger woman sitting next to her in a beige coat who gave her a jab in the ribs with her elbow and hissed 'Moira, put your bloody hand up for God's sake. That has got to be for you!'

So Moira (and I've changed this lady's name, by the way) put up her hand.

'What do you understand, my love?' Stephen called out from the front of the room.

'My mother was on sticks for the last three years of her life and she died on July 14th.'

There was a harsh northern clarity to this lady's voice, and I sensed a tone that seemed to say *'I don't want to hear any of this and I'd be a lot happier if you went on to talk to somebody else.'*

Stephen, undeterred: 'She's telling me about the pains in her legs and she's saying that all the pain has gone now, that she's thrown the sticks away and she's telling me that she's seen Frank. Who's Frank, my love?'

'Frank was her husband.'

'Your Dad then?'

'No, my stepfather.' There was an undisguised coldness in Moira's voice, but it was a coldness that began to thaw a few seconds later.

'Well, who is Fred, because I've got Fred here as well?'

'Fred was my real Dad.'

'Fred's telling me about his feet and he's wiggling his toes, and he's telling me that this should mean something to you – and he's also telling me about December 9th?'

'December 9th was his birthday.'

'What about his toes or feet?'

'He never had any toes on one of his feet,' Moira said, somewhat brutally. 'Got gangrene from a war wound and they chopped 'em off.'

'Well he's got them back now,' Stephen chuckled good naturedly, 'and he's as pleased as punch with them... He's also telling me, so can I just ask you, have you recently changed some curtains in your house?'

'Yes,' Moira sounded surprised, 'as a matter of fact, I have.'

'And was this quite recently? Within the last week or so?'

'I did it the day before yesterday.'

'And did you take red velvet curtain downs or did you put them up?'

Moira actually smiled a thin little smile. 'I took them down.'

'Red velvet curtains?'

'Yes, that's right, red velvet curtains.'

'Yes, well Fred was watching and he's telling me that it was about time they were changed!' Stephen was grinning from ear to ear. He was on a high roll of positive response and he, in turn, responded to it with enthusiasm, little suspecting that this roll was to bury itself in quagmire within a very few minutes.

'Who's John?'

'John's my son.'

'Spirit side?'

'Yes.'

'What does Thursday mean? In connection with John?'

'John died on a Thursday.'

Now Stephen suddenly became cautious, his mood and his delivery changing perceptibly.'

'My love, did John die in a car? Just yes or no... Did John die in a *blue* car?

I watched Moira's lips tighten into a thin straight line. This was a dialogue that she was obviously unhappy with, and if she could, I think she would have fled the room there and then.

'My love,' Stephen persisted. 'I've got to ask you this… What is the connection between your son John and a blue car? Was he in the car when he died, or what?'

'He died in a blue car!' The words were torn from Moira's lips almost against her own volition.

Stephen fell silent, head lowered towards the floorboards of the little stage. His brow was furrowed with contemplation and concentration. When he did start speaking again he chose a gentle tone that did nothing to nullify the enormity of what he was saying.

'John is telling me that it wasn't your fault,' he began. 'He's saying that he'd been very unhappy for a very long time, and that things were all muddled up in his head because of Elizabeth. Do you know who Elizabeth is, by the way?'

'Oh yes,' the words came out almost like a snarl caught up in waves of loathing and contempt. '…I know who Elizabeth is, all right!' …and if words alone could kill, "Elizabeth" whoever she was and wherever she was, would have been laid low to the ground in that single venomous moment in time.

'John's telling me that it wasn't an accident and that he knew exactly what he was doing. He's telling me he's very very sorry for all the trouble he caused, but he was in so much pain himself…' Stephen coughed and for a second he didn't look at all well.

Moira chose this moment to interrupt. 'I know what you're saying, but he never killed himself. He never did it. He *wouldn't* do it!' Her exclamation was a half shouted challenge and you'd have had to be deaf not to hear the note of desperation in her voice.

Stephen looked down at the stage again for a second, then looking up to meet this sad lady's eyes, his tone of voice changed yet again taking on a very matter of fact down to earth quality that indicated he had no intention of getting into a public argument or slanging match.

'My love, I know this is all very sad and distressing, but just take this with you…' He held up one finger. 'Your Mum who died on the 14th of July has thrown away her walking sticks.' He held up a second finger. 'And she's reunited with Frank who was her second husband.' A third finger… 'That your Mum and Frank are with Fred, your Dad, who can wiggle his toes and

whose birthday is the 9th of December.' A fourth finger…
'They've all been helping you change your red velvet curtains
and,' he splayed open his right hand, 'and they've got your son
John with them, who died on a Thursday in a blue car, who
wasn't very happy before he went over because of Elizabeth, but
who is happy now, and who I know *did* kill himself because I can
smell the exhaust fumes in the garage…'

Stephen broke the link at that point and I watched Moira
shrivel back into her shell of bitterness and remorseful self
recrimination. I felt desperately sorry for this lady – desperately
sorry that she had not been able to take something wholesome
and positive from the messages she had received. At the same
time, I felt proud of Stephen for rising to the challenge and not
backing away from the confrontation.

I also felt a tiny qualm of concern, because just for a split
second up there, when he'd been bringing through the link with
John, he'd turned a ghastly grey/green colour and he looked as
though he was taking on the physical symptoms of the carbon
monoxide poisoning that had killed John in the blue car. This
physical manifestation of death symptoms is rare among even the
most powerful and most experienced of mediums – and it can
also be very dangerous.

CHAPTER EIGHT
The Media

Putting an advertisement in a newspaper can be a very risky business and it can also be expensive – especially when the typesetters get it wrong. A pal of mine once placed an advert to announce the opening of his new brasserie restaurant, and on publication of the newspaper he was both amused and annoyed to read that he was opening not a brasserie but a brassiere! For my own part, I was once blazoned across a Nottingham newspaper as being "James Christie – International Physic". Steve Holbrook can go one better, for when he and fellow medium Sue Cunningham were booked into a town hall (interestingly enough, also in the Northern Midlands) they were billed as being Stephen Allcock and Sue Cumminham! The examples of cocked-up adverts would fill a book in their own right, and you'd be amazed at just how difficult it is to get an advert in print just *exactly* the way you have specified. But if getting an advert right is difficult, then believe me, getting any editorial coverage is ten times as hard.

A few weeks ago, I sat reading a copy of The Stratford Herald becoming more and more frustrated with the turn of every page. While our advert was there (4x3 reverse block with star border) quite prominently in the entertainments section of the paper, nowhere was there any editorial coverage of Stephen's impending visit to The Falcon Hotel. From past experience I've learned that ten centimetres of editorial coverage is worth fifty centimetres of advertising, and therefore as well as being annoyed, I was also disappointed.

Just because a newspaper accepts a "paid for" advertisement, there is no guarantee that it will run an editorial story – that is, it won't unless you're prepared to pay for half a page which inevitably costs many hundreds of pounds, and in which case the paper simply "writes off" the editorial coverage as part of the paid for advert.

From a small advertiser's point of view, working on a very limited budget, it seems most unfair that you can spend £800 on your half page and get a few lines of editorial, but spend the same £800 on four smaller ads each costing a couple of hundred quid and spread over a month, and you don't!

In the case of The Stratford Herald we'd spent a small fortune over a two year period advertising Stephen's demonstrations at the fabulous old Falcon Hotel – we'd been diligent in providing press releases with up to date information, and as always we'd been generous in offering complimentary tickets, either to be used by the newspaper staff or as prizes for any competition the paper might want to run. And still not one bloody word!

I threw the paper down in disgust and pondered on the professionalism of provincial newspaper editors. This august body of people is responsible for providing you, the reader who has bought their newspaper, with THE NEWS! While there can be no doubt that two points off the interest rate is news, as might be the Prime Minister's decision to resign, or Israeli tanks blowing up a Palestinian village, these items are mainly dealt with by the national press, and the provincial editor's task is to provide you with the local news – the plans, say, for a new by-pass, or the council's decision to increase local taxes, or possibly the conviction in court of a high profile resident who's been caught with their fingers in the till. If a Hollywood film company decided to use your town in which to film its next epic blockbuster, this would be news, or if the rock band from round the corner had a hit record, or if the local 4th division football team beat Manchester United, if someone found a treasure trove of Roman coins or Nazi gold in Farmer Giles' forgotten acres, then, yes, these items would all be highly newsworthy.

But it doesn't quite work like that, does it? I mean, when was the last time *your* local football team beat Manchester United seven nil?

Time after time I've toiled through the pages of local journals to be assailed by stories of a gold watch being presented to Fred Smith for thirty years loyal service down at the gas works – I've celebrated the fact that Bernard Bloggs has been successful in breeding a champion ferret and thrilled at the news that Mary Brown (47 from 32 Acacia Avenue) has been reunited with the purse she thought she'd lost in Tesco's supermarket, containing £19 and last week's (losing) lottery tickets... Oh how I've frowned with sympathy to learn how a whole family was *totally devastated* when the council refused them permission to paint their front door sky blue pink, and how often have I felt a sense of justification to learn that some idiot has been fined fifty quid (fifty whole pounds!) for dangerous driving, especially when he's been doing it without tax or insurance and has asked for ninety three other offences to be taken into consideration.

The question is, IS THIS NEWS? – And I suppose the answer must be yes it is, if there's nothing else happening. But hey, hang on a minute! There *is* something else happening. Someone is coming to town who can hear the voices of dead people and who can communicate messages from beyond the grave – and my God, if he can do that, hasn't that got to be front page news? And even if he can't do it (although he's got a proven track record that suggests that he can), hasn't the fact that he *claims* that he can got be more newsworthy than ferrets, gold watches and lost purses?

Of course it has!

But there is a hidden agenda here maintained and promoted by the establishment that seeks to avoid rocking any kind of boat, that seeks not to offend what it perceives as being its orthodox readership – that stands upon the rock of Christian fundamentalism and lumps clairvoyance and clairvoyants into the same basket as fakirs, fortune tellers and hypnotists. This does not stop them from taking your money to run the adverts, but be damned if they are going to run any kind of story which might (a) upset the local vicar, (b) challenge the orthodox church, (c) offend the sensibilities of a few bigoted but quietly influential individuals in any given town who don't hold with anything to do with spiritualism, and (d) go against the editor's personal prejudices. If, for example, your local editor is a staunch catholic or Calvinist, then bugger the principles of newsworthiness, equality and free speech, there's *no way* that a story about clairvoyance or spiritualism is going to get past that editor's desk and your press release is going to end up in his bin faster than it takes to open the envelope which contains it.

We came across this attitude very forcibly with a newspaper called The Glaswegian. On three separate occasions we'd spent what for us was some very serious money advertising Stephen's visits to Glasgow. On each occasion we'd sent off press releases

60

along with photographs and complimentary copies of his book – all to no avail. Never a single line of editorial. In the end, my wife Joanna decided to take the bull by the horns, and took it upon herself to telephone the editor in question to find out why The Glaswegian seemed so reticent to run a story on Stephen. The telephone conversation was not a success. It went like this:

"Good afternoon, is that Mr ------"

"Yep!"

"Oh hello, my name is Joanna and I'm with JCP and I'm just calling to ask if there might be any chance at all of a few lines of editorial to back up our advertising campaign for Stephen Holbrook's evening of clairvoyance at The Swallow Hotel?"

"No."

"Oh... Er, that seems to be a little bit final... I mean, can you give me any reason for this?"

"No."

"Er, can I just point out, sir, that we have actually spent an awful lot of money on advertising, and if this next evening doesn't work, then we..."

"The answer's still no."

"You do realise –" there's a note of steel making its presence felt in Joanna's voice in response to the editor's peremptory and somewhat belligerent tone, "– you do realise that this might mean we have to put our advertising budget with another newspaper that *will* give us a few lines of editorial?"

"That's up to you. Put your money wherever you like!" said the editor, then he terminated the call by hanging up on Jo, leaving my poor wife seething at this gentleman's lack of manners and undisguised aggression.

I'd intended writing to the press complaints commission and kicking up all hell, but I'd just come out of hospital and was supposed to be avoiding stress. Also, we were incredibly busy at that time arranging Stephen's 2001 tour, so I let it go for the time being. But this editor's attitude rankled to the extent that when we went back to Glasgow a few months later I did switch the bulk of our advertising budget over to another newspaper, and when The Glaswegian's advertising sales manager wanted to know why, I wasn't backwards in coming forwards in letting her know the reason. My critics might call me petty but as far as I was concerned there was a matter of principle at stake and the

61

editor in question might do well to remember the old adage about the pen being mightier than the sword.

To be fair, there are some newspapers that do carry our press releases and report (frequently with much praise and enthusiasm) on Stephen's activities. Ladies and gentlemen of the press, you know who you are, and we thank you very sincerely for your open mindedness, your professionalism and your integrity.

During the winter of 2000/2001 Stephen came under an increasing degree of pressure to commit himself to working on national television. There were firm offers from a number of different sources and, on one particular occasion, a TV producer who had travelled up from London to see Stephen demonstrate in Hull was so moved by the emotion of the evening that he sat there on the back row reduced to tears. I'm told that the tears became tears of amazement and disbelief when Stephen politely but firmly turned him (and his TV programme) down.

Stephen's reasons for turning down the television offers were reasonably straightforward. "James, I just don't feel that I'm ready for television yet. I certainly couldn't cope with the celebrity status and you know I don't like that aspect of this work at the best of times. I'm not a star or particularly clever – I'm just a medium who can make contact with people from the spirit world, and if that sounds amazing to you or anyone else, then I can understand that, but it isn't amazing to me because I've lived with it for most of my adult life and it's all completely natural.

"You know, Caroline and I were with Jane McDonald and Henrik the other night, and between the car park and the restaurant Jane was stopped a dozen times by people who either just wanted to say hello or who wanted her autograph, and then, when we were in the restaurant, everyone kept looking over at our table, talking about us behind their hands... and God, I'd *hate* that if they were doing it to me.

"Did I tell you about the other day? I was out with Robbie, my eldest boy, going for a bike ride. Two of his mates were playing in the street, and as we peddled by they called out 'Hi Robbie' and Robbie waved at them, and then they called out to me 'Hi Robbie's Dad,' and I waved at them, and then just as we'd got past them I heard one little boy say to his friend, 'Hey, d'you know Robbie's Dad is a wizard?' Look, I know they never meant anything by it, but it brought a few things home to me all the same. My kids are very *very* important to me, and I owe it to them to give them as normal a life as possible. I don't want them going through school with any more problems than they're going to have anyway."

Which, of course, is all perfectly understandable.

From my own point of view I had (and still have) mixed feelings. On the one hand, promoting a TV personality could be highly lucrative, but on the other hand I'm all too well aware that until very recently (the last six months or so) television's portrayal and treatment of clairvoyants and mediumship, as indeed anything at all to do with mysticism and the paranormal, has been absolutely appalling in its presentation.

In a worse case scenario a TV company in the process of producing a programme about the paranormal will go out of its way to find the weirdest and wackiest people, be they seers, psychics, mystics, pagans, prophets, clairvoyants or whatever, not because they are in any way representative of the dedicated groups of practitioners they purport to be a part of, but because they *are* weird and wacky, eccentric and colourful characters who might not know a widdershin from a deosil, but that doesn't matter a damn because they make interesting TV. They make a total mockery of the sincere souls who are working alternative spiritual pathways, but that is hardly something that a television producer is likely to lose much sleep over.

In a best case scenario, TV will present what purports to be a serious and unbiased report, but they do it with their tongues ever so subtly shoved into their cheeks or with a highly patronising attitude that seems to say "we're broadcasting this programme because our market research teams tell us there is an increasing element of interest in this sort of thing, but nobody really believes this load of old rubbish, do they?"

It is a sophistication of the provincial newspaper editors – purporting fairness but refusing to rock the orthodox boat. Little wonder that Stephen was – and still is – extremely reticent about stepping into this world of potential mockery and ridicule.

For Heaven's sake, don't think that Stephen cannot take criticism, for nothing could be further from the truth... But he doesn't suffer fools gladly and he hates being criticised by people who obviously have no terms of reference other than their own half-baked preconceived ideas, and who haven't really got a clue what they're talking about.

A classic example of this occurred in a radio station interview only quite recently. Stephen had been invited into the studio as a certain well known presenter's special guest. He had assumed that it would follow the mold of scores of other very successful interviews he had done with local radio, but this was not to be. Initially he was made to feel very welcome and relaxed but the moment the microphone went live and the show started going out over the airwaves the presenter's attitude palpably changed.

'So Stephen, you're a clairvoyant medium, right? And you do these demonstrations up and down the country? Can you tell us, what does this entail, exactly? I mean what do you do? Go out there and feed off people's vulnerability when they're down...?'

Stephen's response was controlled but his voice was filled with ice as he thoroughly demolished the presenter, live and over the air with a million people listening in.

'Well, it's absolutely obvious that you've never been to one of my demonstrations otherwise you wouldn't have said something quite as stupid and inaccurate as what you've just said! Let me tell you that when I walk out there onto the public platform I don't have a clue as to who's in the audience, but my guides help me make contact with the people I need to talk to... I'm given a name or a date which enables me to go on and bring through the evidence, and if I can say to a lady "your name is Molly and I've got your son here and he's telling me that his name is David and that he was killed in a motor bike crash last December and that you broke a flower vase this morning when you were tidying, and by the way he likes your new hairstyle but he doesn't think much of the carpet you just had put down in your lounge" – and if I can be right about all the things I'm saying, that the lady is called Molly and that she did have a son called David who was killed on a motor bike last December, and that she has just broken a vase and that she has just had a new carpet laid in her lounge, this is not playing on her vulnerability! It's giving her proof of life after death, and if what people have been telling me for the last fifteen years is right, then I actually bring a lot of strength and comfort to the people I'm talking to...

So obviously you haven't done your research properly, and just as a matter of interest, you *haven't* attended one of my demonstrations, have you?'

'Er, no, actually I haven't…'

I wasn't with Stephen in the studio for this travesty of an interview, but I did hear it on the car radio, and I really found myself cheering for Steve that day. He didn't raise his voice or lose his temper, but in this instance he certainly put "the media" in its place and an independent contact that I have at the local radio station told me later that when the interviewer left the studio he was ashen faced and somewhat subdued. Stephen is a very mild mannered man, but when someone really rubs him up the wrong way and he passes the point of just being a little bit hurt and upset, he can be quite withering and his scorn can cut you to the bone.

Someone somewhere higher up in the echelons of the local BBC hierarchy must have been made aware of the incident for when Stephen was invited back on the show a few weeks later the presenter was a changed man and treated Stephen with a modicum of respect and courtesy.

CHAPTER NINE
Please, Mrs Robinson

Of course there are many other ways in which the media can bring you to grief and both Stephen and I have good reason to recall the occasion when a local newspaper misprinted (albeit, just by one digit) the telephone number on one of Stephen's adverts. This resulted in a lady called Joan Robinson being bombarded by dozens of calls from people who wanted to book for "an evening of clairvoyance with Stephen Holbrook."

Now Joan had never heard of Stephen Holbrook but she had heard something about this "clairvoyance thing" and what she had heard had done little to impress her. Both her parents had been staunch Presbyterians and they had brought her up with a great respect for God and a fear of anything that went against the teachings of the bible. This was compounded by a thirty two year marriage to a man who was dismissive of all religions, and especially "that psychic lot who are all candidates for the funny farm". On the odd occasions when Joan had postulated the thought that there might be something in the idea of an afterlife, her parents, while they were alive, had assured her that there was, but only in the form of a very stylised Christian heaven (and only then if she was very very good) while her husband had pooh poohed the idea out of hand, and with such vehemence that she'd learned to let the subject drop for the sake of a quiet life. While she was dedicated to her marriage, by her own admission her husband Rodney was not always an easy man to live with.

Rodney passed over after a long and distressing illness in 1999 and the following two years were curiously isolated years for Joan. She missed her husband, but at the same time felt guilty about enjoying a new sense of freedom and independence. She also felt restless and frustrated about not quite knowing what to do with that freedom and independence. Certainly, she'd decorated the house more to her own chintz taste, getting rid of some of the sombre and sober shades that Rodney had seemed to appreciate, and she'd started going to the theatre to see the occasional play. She was fifty seven years old and had been married to her husband since she was nineteen, and now that he was gone, she realised that her life seemed awfully empty. With few friends, no surviving family and few real hobbies, her life revolved around the TV set, the theatre club (just once a month) and occasional voluntary shifts for the WRVS.

After an angry letter to the newspaper the bombardment of telephone calls diminished then disappeared, but her feathers had been ruffled and she was unaccountably cross about the whole affair. This story might have ended there were it not for one other phone call she received half way through the following week. This was Stephen ringing to apologise for all the trouble she'd been caused. 'He sounded very ordinary, just like the lad next door, and I suppose I was surprised by how young he sounded and the fact that he'd gone to the trouble to ring me up, when really it wasn't his fault that the paper got the advert wrong.'

Over the following weekend Joan found herself thinking about all the calls she'd had – her phone had never been busier, and in a way, she quietly admitted, it had seemed just a little bit exciting because certainly nothing like this had ever happened while Rodney had been alive. She found herself wondering what Mr Holbrook would be like in the flesh, and on the Monday, she made what was for her, a very impulsive decision, and donning her hat and coat walked through the November frost to the Morley Town Hall to see for herself what this clairvoyance stuff was all about.

She was amazed, first of all by the numbers of people milling around the building and once inside she was amazed again by the diversity of the crowd. There were many young people there, more girls than men, but there were men too, and there were many people around her own age group as well. At one and the same time she felt separate from and alienated from this throng, and also warmed and welcomed and protected by it. Taking a seat about as far away from the front as she could find, she sat back and waited. She was not, after all, there to take part in the evening, merely to observe.

She was surprised when Stephen walked out onto the stage... 'Not at all what I'd expected,' but she was even more surprised when, after the preamble, he'd wanted to know if the 9th of April meant anything, not just to anybody in the audience, but to a lady who had lost her husband in the last three years. Nobody in the room seemed to know what he was talking about but his words certainly meant something to Joan because Rodney had died on April 9th, and well within the three years' time framework. Nonetheless she steadfastly remained silent, determined not to be drawn into these proceedings.

The young man on the stage was quite adamant that someone in the room knew what he was talking about and Joan's blood ran cold when he went on to say that he had a gentleman with him who had passed over with prostate cancer who desperately wanted to talk to his wife, and the lady would know it was him if he mentioned "bangers and mash with brown sauce".

Well, Rodney had passed over with prostate cancer and for all the years she'd known him he had been quite obsessive about his favourite meal, namely bangers and mashed potatoes topped with dollops of HP sauce – frequently dashing her hopes of a night out in a nice restaurant because they wouldn't have sausages (not the way he liked *his* sausages) on the menu.

Joan's resolve began to waver, but still she sat silent. 'Mr Holbrook became quite agitated,' she recalls, 'and then he said something so specific that I finally gave in and put my hand up.'

'What did he say?' I asked.

'He said that he had Rodney with him and that he was drawing a big love heart around the letter J and saying sorry he didn't say anything about the four thousand pounds. And would the lady who understood exactly what he was talking about *please* put her hand up because if she didn't he was in danger of losing the message altogether. Well, I knew exactly what he meant because after Rodney had died and I was going through his things I found this brown envelope in the bottom of his sock draw stuffed with twenty pound notes, and there was exactly four thousand pounds. I never knew he had it, and if I had, I'd have been very cross because we weren't always awash with money and four thousand pounds could have paid an awful lot of bills.'

'What happened,' I asked, 'after you put your hand up and claimed the message?'

'Mr Holbrook said that Rodney was thankful for all the help I'd given him, especially in the last months of his life, and he said he was sorry too for the way he behaved sometimes. That he loved me very much, but didn't always show it. He said that I shouldn't feel guilty about anything and that I should get on with my life and enjoy it as much as I could. He said he's seen the new furniture and the new kitchen and that he likes it very much, and that he'd seen Marjorie and Ted and that they were fine over on the other side, up at head office... Marjorie and Ted are my parents' names, by the way. He also said that he was very surprised to see me in a place like a spiritualist meeting, but that he was even more surprised to be there himself because when he was down here he thought it was all a load of rubbish, but now he's over there he can see how wrong he was... and that's about it, really.'

'Will you go to another of Stephen's meetings?' I asked.

Joan Robinson gave me what I can only describe as a coquettish little smile. 'Definitely yes,' she said. 'In fact I've already booked my ticket!'

There's a line of thought here that is worthy of some exploration, that has a lot to do with Stephen's belief that if spirit wants you, they'll go all the way to get you, no matter what you do to avoid them.'

Was everything that happened to Joan Robinson just a coincidence, or was the hand of spirit at work here, causing the typesetter down at the local paper to misprint Steve's phone number by one digit, so that Joan would get not one, but forty seven wake up calls, that would in turn peak her latent curiosity and bring her through the ice and snow to Morley Town Hall to receive a message of conviction, love and encouragement from her late husband?

The sceptic will say the former but Steve and I firmly believe it to be the latter. Joan has an open mind on this point, but she is in no doubt at all that Rodney did communicate with her, giving more than adequate proof that he *was* Rodney, and that she would not have gone to see the demonstration had there not been the barrage of telephone calls.

Look, you're reading this, so what do *you* think? Answers please on a postcard c/o the website.

CHAPTER TEN

Foray Into Scotland

As a promoter it was (and still is) my brief to expand Stephen's circle of audiences and introduce him to areas where he's never been before and where people have never heard of him. When we first met back in the spring of '99 he was extremely well known with a wide following in the north of England (particularly in his native Yorkshire) and also down in the west country where his good friends Roger and Jill Prior had done a lot of promoting and trail blazing on his behalf. Pretty well the rest of Britain was virgin territory for me.

Of all the places we could have gone to, Scotland was the most obvious choice insofar as my wife has relatives living quite close to Glasgow, which would provide us with overnight accommodation, and our market research indicated that Scotland would provide fertile fields for Stephen's gifts. Furthermore I had fond memories of Scotland from my show business days; the Scottish audiences I had encountered in the 60's and 70's had always impressed me with their warmth and welcome, and I figured that if we could form a bridgehead in, say, Glasgow, this would give us an essential jumping off point from which we could conquer the rest of Scotland. That was the plan, anyway…

Duly, we did some more market research, found an excellent venue in the form of The Swallow Hotel on Paisley Road West, placed a lot of adverts in just about every newspaper we could find, then hit the road to do two nights back to back in September of 2000.

Initially the advance bookings were somewhat disheartening, but we nonetheless managed to drum up an audience of about a hundred and sixty for the Sunday night. Selling the books in the half hour before the demonstration began enabled me to tune into the audience's vibration, and I have to say that it was very tense and twitchy – a far cry from the warmth I had expected and an even further far cry from the buzz of excitement and expectancy we'd become accustomed to when working on our home turf.

70

In places such as Leeds, Hull, or Sheffield, or the Retford Little Theatre, there's always an electric atmosphere of anticipation, usually with a cacophony of conversation interspersed with disparate bursts of laughter. The Scottish crowd, however, sat there almost in silence and there were quite a few stony faces that seemed to say "prove it if you can!" In short, it was a dour low-key vibration and I had an inkling that Stephen might just be in for a bit of a rough night.

This impression was confirmed in the first five minutes of the demonstration.

As usual, Stephen strode out in front of the crowd, pacing up and down as he always does, trying to explain in a few short words what he does and how he does it. He was mid-stride and mid-speech when this elderly Scottish lady on the second row suddenly stood up and called out in a raucous voice – 'For God's sake man, will ye stop walking up an' down! Ah dunno what anyone else thinks, but yer makin' me feel dizzy!'

In any of the home turf venues this would either have brought a gale of laughter or scornful calls of condemnation, but the Glasgow audience shifted uncomfortably in their seats and hardly batted an eyelid.

Stephen, totally unphased, looked at the old lady bemusedly and said 'Oh, all right my love,' and then carried on as normal before drifting into his first link of the evening.

Jo and I were standing on the bar side of the double doors that led into the function room, watching the proceedings through the jar of the door as Stephen developed his link with an attractive young lady with short brown hair who was sitting a few rows back on our side of the room.

'I've got your Mum's Dad here,' he said, 'who's telling me that he and you had a very special relationship. He was special to you and you were certainly very special to him, and that when he passed over, all of the sunshine seemed to go out of your world...'

Stephen's tendency to make reference to "your Mum's Mum or your Dad's Dad, or your Dad's Mum, Mum's Dad" can initially sound confusing, but it's the way that spirit gives it to him, and as he says – 'it removes any ambiguity. We all have grandparents, but we've got two sets of them, one for each side of the family. I could say "I've got your Grandad here" and if

71

both grandfathers are over in head office, the person getting the message can be forgiven for wondering which one is trying to get through. If I tell them that it's their Dad's Dad, then at least it's tying it down to a specific.'

The Scottish girl is nodding her head emphatically. 'Och yes, mah Gran'ad an' me was real pals. There was no one else to look after me when ah was a wee bairn apart from him so he was kinda like a mother an' father an' a Gran'ad all rolled into one.'

'And he's telling me,' Stephen continues, 'that he had no time to say goodbye, that he passed over without any kind of warning and that he'd gone before his body hit the floor…'

'Aye, that's right, that's right.'

'And I'm getting massive chest pains…' Stephen clutches at his own chest to emphasise the point.

'Yes, he had this huge heart attack!' There's an open sob in the young girl's voice.

'And he's giving me the name of Karen – Karen or Sharon – Karen, Sharon, Karen…?'

'Mah name's Sharon but it's spelt with a Ch, so people call me Karen sometimes, especially when they're hearing mah name for the first time.'

'And he's telling me about the 13th of March. Do you understand?'

'He died on the 13th of March,' the girl gasps.

'And what does half past two mean? He's telling me half past two. Did he die at half past two or was the funeral timed for half past two?'

'The funeral was at half past two,' Charon whispers. 'It was supposed to be at two o'clock, but we were half an hour late getting started.'

'And,' Stephen slows right down, searching for the right words, 'did you, and please don't be nice to me, did you put something in the coffin with him before they closed the lid for the last time?'

'I did!'

'He's showing me a white rose. A single white rose. Do you know what this means, my love? He's saying thank you so much for all your love and care over the years and he's saying a very special thank you for the white rose.'

'Oh Christ,' the girl bursts into a wail of tears and jumps up from her chair. 'That's what I put in the coffin. Just a single white rose!' – and with that she forces her way through the rows of chairs and runs full tilt out of the crowded room, banging through the double doors and all but falling into my waiting arms.

Up close the girl called Charon looks totally shocked and dazed. Her eyes are flying everywhere, there is spittle at the corner of her mouth and her lips are literally quivering. She looks up at me with mute appeal, seeing me, but not seeing me at all.

'How does he know those things?' she murmurs in disbelief. 'How does he know *all* those things?'

Joanna took over at this point, steering the upset Scottish lass to the bar for a stiff drink. I knew she'd give her the standard "this is how it works" talk, and it allowed me to concentrate on what Stephen was doing. I don't mean that to sound casual or callous, but the fact of the matter is that a number people do make an exit from Stephen's demonstrations in some state of shock and distress (granted, not quite so dramatically) and in some ways this is very understandable. They are, after all, being presented with something incredible: in many cases, their preconceptions and well established beliefs are destroyed in an instant and they are left floundering without foundation. New foundations have to be built that incorporate the unassailable fact that their loved ones are not really dead, but have simply passed over into another realm of existence. Even for someone who has a firm belief in an afterlife, it can still be a deeply emotional experience to have that belief confirmed, and it can be more shocking still for the sceptics who do not have any such belief, to reconcile themselves to this new state of affairs.

Later, once the demonstration was over, we all went out to dinner with my brother-in-law. Special effects artist Tony Steers and his attractive actress wife Nikki Fury hosted a fabulous Chinese banquet in one of Glasgow's finest oriental restaurants. Tony and Nikki, who had attended the demonstration as our guests and who had experienced the Holbrook phenomenon for the first time, were full of praise and enthusiasm and bombarded Stephen with questions as he devoured his way through the late supper.

Stephen, who eats nothing for several hours before a demonstration, is always voraciously hungry afterwards, frequently eating a four or five course meal to compensate for the lost energy and depleted adrenalin. He answered their questions as best he could between mouthfuls of spare ribs and chicken curry, but watching from my corner of the round table I could see just how desperately tired he was. The weariness fell off him in waves of spent energy and I suspected that what he really wanted was to eat his dinner in peace before collapsing into a soft bed and sleeping the sleep of the dead for a dozen hours.

It had been an incredibly tough demonstration, and although his evidence had been solid and full of detail, he'd had to fight hard to connect the links. The audience's hesitance and reticence to respond had stilted the natural flow of events and the somewhat dramatic start to the evening with the heckling woman and the fleeing girl had ruffled what little atmosphere there was to begin with. The 'spikiness' I had sensed at the start of the night had never totally dissipated and the audience had never completely relaxed.

I write of this dinner party, however, because one chance remark made by my brother-in-law made a very important connection for me, that enabled me to gain a modicum of fresh insight into Stephen's work

We were laughing about the lady who had told Stephen to stop pacing up and down because he was making her feel dizzy, and Tony remarked that ' – When you're walking up and down the way that you do, you seem to be creating tremendous vibrations of energy, and I'm assuming that this acts as a platform for your spiritual contacts?'

…And I thought *My God, that's exactly what is happening! That's exactly what he's doing, whether he knows it or not!* And for me, this was a very important connection because in any kind of paranormal work the creation of the appropriate energy is paramount to the success of that work.

For example, something as innocuous as a Tarot reading needs an element of calmness of focus if the cards are to be interpreted correctly. Equally if a master of magick is seeking to craft a healing spell of love, he must suffuse his soul with those loving emotions of care and kindness that can 'carry' the spell across the ether to its intended destination. Any kind of anger,

74

angst, jealousy or ulterior motive will inevitably be detrimental to its efficacy. On the other hand, the black magician, seeking to ply his craft in search of revenge or his own selfish (and destructive) desires, must first work to focus all his anger and rage against his adversary. In other words, and in very simplistic terms, it is not the sticking of the pin in the doll which is the key, but the thought behind this action and the feelings and emotions behind the thought!

The fakirs of northern India cannot lie on their beds of nails until their minds are empowered by the necessary mental disciplines, nor can the firewalkers of Indonesia stride across red hot coals without damaging their feet until they have created the 'power' within their minds that tells them they can do this without getting hurt. In any kind of 'occult' practice then, there is a process whereby the practitioner must work to build a cone of power, and although Stephen would recoil at the thought of being labelled as an occultist, we must remind ourselves that this word 'occult' simply means 'that which is hidden' and Stephen most certainly does have dealings with something that by and large is hidden from the rest of us.

In his typical pacing up and down across the stage in front of the gathered audience, Stephen is creating serious waves of energy, both physical and metaphysical, and I never really made the connection until Tony's casual remark found its unintended target in my psyche.

As I've said before, Stephen is a totally natural medium. He does not question the source or the accuracy of his gift. This doesn't mean that he takes it for granted, but he is content to accept the gift at its face value, to go where it takes him and to allow himself to be used by the gift to help other people whenever and wherever he can.

In the same way that he is moved by spirit to make the right connections with the various members of his audiences, I now see that he may well also be physically moved by spirit in his pre-dem pacings to build the cone of power energy that spirit needs to manifest itself in his presence.

The following day presented Jo and I with an opportunity to see a somewhat different side of Stephen's personality. We were scheduled to be back at The Swallow Hotel for Monday evening, but this gave Steve a whole day in which to recuperate and relax. Normally Steve's alarm clock would go off at five thirty so that he could be at the hairdressing salon for no later than seven to start his ten hour day, so it was a rare luxury for him to sleep in well past nine o'clock and sit down to a hearty five course Scottish breakfast that included porridge and pancakes and the ubiquitous fry up, which in this neck of the woods included black pudding and beans, followed by racks of toast and litres of tea and coffee.

We managed to get out of the house sometime before noon and took a short drive through the spectacular Scottish scenery to a local garden centre of some repute. Here Stephen became rather like a cat with two tales and it was a good job we didn't have too much space in the back of the car or he'd have spent a small fortune on plants and pots and all of the other stuff that is associated with the garden.

To tell the truth, I'd forgotten that Stephen was an avidly obsessive gardener. It's supposed to be a Taurean thing, but like Steve, I'm also a Taurean and gardening leaves me stone cold! Great to sit in and look around occasionally, but God forbid I should get my nails dirty! Jo, on the other hand, is very knowledgeable and interested, so while these two were in some state of seventh heaven rushing from plant to pot and pot to plant, I mooched along behind carrying their purchases and stifling yawns of boredom. But it was a nice day and the sun was shining, so I made the best of it, happy to see that they were making the most of this rare opportunity to have some fun.

For lunch we ended up in the attractive coastal town of Largs and spent a marvellous hour pigging out on excessive portions of exotic ice cream in Nardini's famous emporium – a place where time has stood still since 1949. Between the ever present interruptions from the mobile phone, we were having a good old joke about nothing awfully important, when prompted by something inconsequential that one of us had said, the conversation came around to the latest offer from one of the TV companies that were trying to get Stephen on to the box. Stephen was quite open with regard to what was on the table financially, and quite frankly the figures were so staggeringly favourable that I simply didn't see how he could turn this latest offer down – and I said as much in no uncertain terms.

'Yes, well,' Stephen said thoughtfully, 'I'm still not so sure. I can't quite explain it, but I hate all the hype and I just don't feel ready for this kind of exposure just yet – and besides...' he fumbled to light a very rare cigarette ' ...did I tell you what happened when I was working in the garden the other day?'

Jo and I shook our heads in unison.

'Well, there I was, mowing the lawn, thinking about all this TV stuff. I'd just had Henrik on the phone telling me all about the London demonstration, and he was saying how certain he was that it would lead to something very big, very very quickly, and I was wondering what I should do about it all, because I'm not daft and I do know that opportunities like these don't come along every day. Then all of a sudden I got this feeling of glowing warmth all around me, everything became very still and calm, and the garden seemed to shift into a sort of un-focused state, and I heard my Grandad's voice saying "Take your time Steve. There's no competition. You're not in a race!" Then everything shifted back to normal.

'I know it wasn't my imagination playing tricks on me. The voice that I heard was definitely my Grandfather's and I heard it in my ear rather than in my head, so I'm taking this as a straight and genuine message from the spirit world that's telling me to slow down and take things at my own speed. Because–' at that point the mobile phone went and Steve calmly reached across the table and switched it off without answering it '–because I'm *not* in a race, am I? If these TV people want to do programmes about me, well, they'll just have to wait a bit, maybe a year or two, even four or five, until I'm ready in myself to have a go at it.'

I didn't doubt for a minute that Stephen's Grandfather had given him a message, but I couldn't help but wonder if it had been little more than a message of encouragement, in the sense that it was telling Steve what deep down inside he wanted to hear. I admired Stephen's principles and understood his reasons for holding back, but I also knew the world of television, and I did just wonder if the offers and the interest would still be there four or five years down the line. However this was obviously not the time to push forwards in the face of such opposition, but I do remember thinking that if someone had offered me thirty grand for five nights work, I'd have bitten their hand off faster than you could say BBC – but certain little Taureans can be a bit like that, I'm afraid.

Our second night in Glasgow went off reasonably well. We had a slightly larger audience, and none of the histrionics that had opened the demonstration on the Sunday. Even so, this Monday night audience was just as spiky, and after talking to the duty manager of the hotel, we put it down to the fact that public demonstrations of clairvoyance were not awfully common north of the border, and many people coming to see Stephen at the Swallow Hotel were not entirely certain of what they were coming to see. Indeed, there was quite a high percentage of folk who seemed a bit disappointed that they were coming to a public demonstration and that they were not going to get an in-depth one to one personal appointment.

Stephen battled hard to bring over some very strong evidence, and I'm pleased to say that he won the crowd over in the end, but it was flaming hard work!

We spent another pleasant evening in the company of Tony and Nikki, and on the following morning, after another long and leisurely breakfast, we hit the road for the next port of call in our whistle stop tour of Britain.

CHAPTER ELEVEN
A Bright Star In Sheffield

After the two tough nights in Glasgow we drove south on September 19th for Stephen's demonstration at the Sheffield City Hall with fellow medium Sue Cunningham. With the easing of the petrol crisis that had caused a lot of people a lot of problems in the Autumn of 2000, the traffic on the roads was particularly heavy – as was the rain which teamed in torrents from stormtossed skies – and by the time we reached the venue, all three of us were more than a bit tired and tense. This tension increased when we realised that the very expensive posters advertising the event were nowhere to be seen, despite the fact that Sue had delivered them to the city hall a number of weeks previously. With premonitions of disaster, probably based on tiredness rather than fear, we hauled ourselves into the venue, fingers crossed and hoping for the best.

We needn't have worried because four hundred of Sheffield's finest trudged through the downpour huddled beneath their umbrellas and wrapped in raincoats. They queued at the box office for their precious tickets then filed into the waiting auditorium with that palpable air of excitement that had been so absent in Scotland. Sheffield City Hall frequently hosts evenings of clairvoyance staged by many of the country's top mediums, but nights featuring Stephen Holbrook and Sue Cunningham (who, as a Sheffield lady, is working in her own back yard) are always immensely popular.

After the intense intimacy of The Swallow Hotel it was refreshing to see Stephen in a large hall with some space in which to move and breathe, and it was only as he went on stage to start the second half of the evening that I realised how tiring and frustrating the two awkward nights in Scotland must have been for him. I suppose this awareness dawned by degrees, the catalyst being the relaxed way in which he dealt with his audience and the easy fluidity of the messages as they came through. The clairvoyance in Scotland had been stilted and erratic, but now, back on his native Yorkshire soil, everything flowed with spontaneous ease and afterwards, when we were talking in the dressing room, I could see that he was clearly elated by the results of his mediumship.

There were a dozen links that night, all of them accurate, all of them good, but one particular message sticks in my mind, and for a couple of odd reasons.

We had stopped for coffee and a loo break at Scotch Corner on the drive down from Glasgow, and I'd taken the opportunity to mention my thoughts of Sunday evening – about Stephen creating his 'cone of power' in the pre-dem warm ups. He recognised that this was a possibility which had never really crossed his own mind, and this led to us talking about metaphysics and the paranormal (something which, by his own admission, he knows absolutely nothing about) and how I felt that some understanding of metaphysical symbolism could be of great benefit to his spiritual work. Here I lost him, and he asked me to give him an example of what I was getting at.

Being put on the spot like this placed me in a position where I had to do a bit of thinking because although it is easy to talk about parapsychological codes in an abstract sense, in truth it is a very subjective thing and each pathworker will acquire and develop their own set of symbols.

Occasionally, in my work as a psychic, if I am doing a reading for somebody, I may see a bottle of port superimposed over a map of the Iberian peninsular. Nominally I might make mention of a link with this part of the world, or I might mention the initial letter D or come out with the name of Don, because the label on the bottle that I am seeing in my mind's eye predominantly features the famous Don, which is, of course, the Sandeman trade mark.

If I see Mickey Mouse I might mention the initial letter M or make reference to a Mick or a Michael, or again I might make reference to the USA – America, of course, being the home of Mickey Mouse.

I presented these as examples to show Steve where I was coming from, and then went on to illustrate some rather more *objective* and ubiquitously recognised code symbols, using as an example for this, the motif of the star.

80

The star is a particularly potent symbol, so much so that different nations have adopted it as a mark of national identity; the white pentangle of the USA, the red star of the now defunct USSR, the six pointed Star of David, forever associated with national Jewry and the state of Israel. On a more personal and parochial level the star is imprinted into our human consciousness as a symbol of power – an elevated position to which we all aspire; we refer to highly talented people as being "stars", we place stars upon the tops of our Christmas trees, we have a wish fulfilment mantra manifesting itself in songs such as "When You Wish Upon A Star".

Consequently, the vision of the star in a psychic sense can logically be associated with some form of spiritual awakening, some striving towards (or indeed the acquisition of) a degree of elevation above the norm. It represents a moving on and a moving upwards towards some state of transcendence.

Stephen had looked extremely thoughtful at this point. 'Ummm,' he'd mused. 'It's funny you should mention a star of all things, because this has always been a very positive image in my mind, and I know the same is true for Jane McDonald because she always uses a star or a cluster of stars in all of her publicity material and her new book cover has got stars all over it... And when I come to think about it, when I started using a star border on all my newspaper adverts the numbers of people coming to my demonstrations almost seemed to double overnight... I know that it can't have been like that exactly, but it just seemed that way. Having said that, I've got to confess that I've never thought of the star having any particular meaning where my actual clairvoyance is concerned.'

'Well,' I'd reached for my pipe, earning a black look from my wife. 'It might be something to watch out for, and if something to do with a star comes through in a message, it may well be a sign of something of special importance.'

We'd gone on to talk about a load of other things and during the last hundred miles down to Sheffield we both forgot about stars and metaphysical symbolism as we did battle with tempests and twenty ton lorries which, between them, made the driving conditions absolutely abominable.

It was somewhere towards the end of the demonstration that my ears pricked up. Stephen opened the link by asking if there was a mother in the audience who had lost a daughter to the spirit world, and immediately a dozen hands went up in various parts of the hall.

'Oh quite a few of you,' he said, 'but let's see if I can narrow this down a bit, so listen in… I'm talking about a little girl here, I'm not sure of her age, but she would have been under ten.'

Half of the hands went begrudgingly down.

'I'm getting the month of January. I'm not sure if this little girl passed over in January or whether she had a birthday in January… So does anyone understand January?'

Another four hands went down, leaving only two, one at either side of the auditorium. Stephen turned to the lady on his left. 'My love, does the initial L mean anything to you?'

The late middle-aged lady looked disappointed and lowered her hand. 'No, not really,' she said.

Stephen then turned to the lady on his right, a younger fair-haired woman in her early thirties. 'In that case, does the initial letter L mean anything to *you*, my love?'

'Yes, definitely!' the fair-haired woman called back in a loud clear voice. 'My little girl was called Lisa and she died in January!'

'What do sixes and sevens mean, then?' Stephen asked. 'She's telling me all about the sixes and the sevens!'

'She was six years old when she died. She was borne on the 6th of January and she died on the 7th of January!'

It was a funny thing, quite odd really, but at this point a sigh seemed to ripple around the room, almost as though the audience was being touched in some holistic way by the sensitivity of the information coming through. Stephen must certainly have felt it because he moved over to the woman's side of the stage and went down on one knee, leaning forwards into the auditorium. His voice dropped in volume to what could only be described as a personal tone – he was talking directly to this one lady, and yet such were the acoustics of the hall and that curious God given gift that enables Steve's voice to carry where others fail to reach, that even on the very back rows we could hear every word that he said.

'My love, she's telling me that she didn't die straight away. That she'd been poorly for quite a long time and that you came to visit her every day in the hospital and that you'd play games together while she was propped up in bed. She's telling me that she knew you were very upset about her hair...' Stephen unconsciously brushed his fingers through his own golden waves, 'but she's telling you not to worry or be upset because all her hair has grown back now, as long and as thick and as silky as ever it was, and here's the strangest thing, she's drawing me a picture of a big silver star...' Something kicked me in the pit of my solar plexus. 'My love, don't be nice to me, just yes or no, do you understand what she's trying to tell me with the star?'

I don't want to be melodramatic but there was a genuine note of awe in the woman's voice when she said 'Oh yes, I know *exactly* what she means about the star.' And then almost as an afterthought... 'Oh my God!'

'No love,' Steve said very gently. 'It's just Stephen Holbrook!'

This produced some lovely laughter from the audience and it did much to alleviate the pin-dropping aura of tension that was so tangibly present throughout the packed Sheffield City Hall.

'She's telling me about... I'm not sure if she means Diane or Diana, but either way, she seems very excited about it, and she's saying that even though Diana was killed...' My ears twitched again because the word "killed" does not often crop up in Stephen's vocabulary. '...that even though she was killed, she's happy now in heaven. Just yes or no, my love, but do you know what she's on about?'

'Yes!'

'Who's Ted?'

'My father – Lisa's Grandad.'

'Passed over?'

'Yes.'

'And who's Nick or Mick?'

'My brother – Lisa's uncle.'

'Still living? Down here?'

'Yes.'

'Who's Chris or Christine?' *

'That's me.'

'Who's Frank?'

'I'm sorry, I don't know.'

'All right my love, I think I'm moving now, but just know that your little Lisa is sending you all the love in the world, all wrapped up in a big silver star, and that she's grown all her hair back – and *was* it particularly long and silky before she was so poorly?'

'Yes it was!'

'...And that she's with Diane or Diana and she's holding hands with Grandad Ted...'

Stephen brought through another two messages and then the evening of clairvoyance came to a close. There was the most awful crush around the stage area as people queued, first of all to buy Steve's book, and then queued in another line to have it signed.

On that particular night I was also selling Sue Cunningham's book, and for a while it was total bedlam. I did notice, however, that Lisa's Mum was hanging around at the fringe of the crowd, trying desperately to have a private word with Stephen and later, after I'd sold the last book, I looked up to find the blond mother and Stephen locked in conversation.

He beckoned me over and as I joined them I could see that he was very elated about something. 'Do me a favour, will you,' he said to the lady, 'and just tell James what you've been telling me, because if nothing else, it will make a fantastic chapter for our next book!'

There were half a dozen other people clamouring for Stephen's attention, and inevitably he became distracted and then absorbed while I found myself crammed into a noisy corner with the bereaved mother, trying to take notes on the back of a crumpled serviette.

Some journalist! – And it gets worse, because within twenty four hours I'd lost the bloody serviette with the relevant dates and telephone numbers which is why I have asterisked *Christine's name. I *think* her name was Christine and I *think* her lovely little girl was called Lisa, but if I have cocked-up and made a mistake, then it's my fault and nobody else's, and I apologise unreservedly to all concerned. I *do* recall that Stephen and I were given permission to use the story and because, for me, this story is particularly important, I've gone ahead and used it rather than lose it!

Anyway, Christine's story is incredibly poignant.

Her little girl arrived at her 5th birthday being the healthiest kid on the street. However as winter turned to spring Lisa started feeling unwell – she couldn't eat anything without feeling sick – and after exhaustive medical tests she was diagnosed as having leukaemia, and it was assessed to be in quite an advanced state of malignancy. She was subjected to chemotherapy and later on radiotherapy, which caused her lustrous long hair to fall out in great clumps until the poor little mite was completely bald. This caused Christine incredible distress but throughout it all Lisa remained ever cheerful, showing far more stoicism and confidence than the rest of her family put together.

Christine would visit the hospital every day and together they would play a variety of games spread across the bed sheets. One of Lisa's favourite pastimes was to look through her scrapbooks that contained all manner of cuttings and press reports concerning the late Diana Princess of Wales. It's fair to say that Lisa was quite obsessive about her heroine, and also very knowledgeable, even to the extent of being able to tell you what coloured dress she was wearing for which state occasion, and she had the chronology of Diana's eventful life off pat.

Christine started referring to Lisa as "My Little Star" and with Christmas beckoning, the nurses, at Lisa's insistence, hung a big silver star above her bed.

As Christmas approached Lisa became more and more poorly and on December 15th the doctors confirmed Christine's worst fears. Lisa's condition was terminal and it could only be a matter of weeks, a couple of months at the most, before she would die.

Although for very obvious reasons this information was kept from Lisa, the little girl must have sensed something had changed in the atmosphere around her (and let us not forget that all children are far more psychically sensitive than we give them credit for being) and on Christmas Eve, half way through a game of snakes and ladders, she suddenly looked up and caught her mother unprepared and unawares.

'Mummy, I'm going to die, aren't I?' – and there was something in Lisa's voice that challenged Christine not to lie…

something that said this was a rhetorical question anyway... that Lisa already knew the answer, and she was only looking to her mother for some honest confirmation.

How, I wonder, would any parent deal with this one?

To her credit, and reflecting the very special relationship she had with her daughter, Christine handled it remarkably well.

'Well darling, that's what some of the doctors think might happen, but you mustn't give up fighting to get better, and you mustn't give up hoping.'

'No I wouldn't do that...' Lisa looked sombrely down at the snakes and ladders game, and then looked up at Christine with a radiantly bright smile written across her face. 'But *I* think I'm probably going to die, and you mustn't worry or be upset, because I'll be with Princess Diana, and we'll be able to look after each other up in heaven.'

So, that's the story behind the incredible link Stephen brought through at Sheffield City Hall in September of 2000, and it sticks in my mind for one other reason, namely that through Stephen, Lisa referred to Diana as having been "killed" rather than having died or passed over. You might choose to put this down to the simplicity of childish dialogue, but I have to say that I do not know of a psychic or clairvoyant anywhere in the world that does not firmly believe that Diana, Princess of Wales, *was* killed on that fateful night in Paris, and that she didn't just die in a car accident.

The Wife's Tale

From Caroline Holbrook

Robbie, our eldest child of eight years, is just like his dad, and in more ways than one. He eats, sleeps, and walks like his father and he has Stephen's same untidy ways, ie. putting empty cereal packets back in the cupboard (they even like the same cereals), making a cup of tea and leaving the tea bag dripping on the worktop, no lids put back on the milk or sugar jar – I have to laugh because it is so uncanny. Robbie even makes his presence known to everyone in the room, no matter if it's just our family or a room full of strangers, but he has a gift of loveliness, and being loved by everyone, a real charmer but genuine and caring, just like his wonderful father.

In 1994, Robbie was six months old and my great Aunty May sadly passed over. She was adorable. She was ill towards the end of her life and spent the last few weeks in a hospice, but six months previously, on the 4th of June 1994 she visited her first great great nephew, Robbie, in Pinderfields Hospital. It was a magical feeling and I know when she held him in her arms, she was so proud.

A year later when Robbie was at the tender age of eighteen months, he had just started talking, saying quite a few words and, needless to say, once he knew he could talk, he never stopped. He was and still is so old fashioned. But one day, whilst playing in the conservatory, he just stopped in his tracks and walked straight over to my Aunty May's photograph and said to Stephen and I, "That's Aunty May". We just looked at each other, even though Aunty May was with us in mind and we knew she looked down on us, we had never actually spoken to Robbie about her and he was only six months old when she'd passed over, so he couldn't possibly remember her and the photograph had only just been put there the day before. So we put two and two together and made, yes, "another Stephen Holbrook". But it didn't stop there, Robbie would stand at the bottom of the staircase and I would be in the kitchen and I'd hear him talking (as I thought to himself) until I asked... "Robbie, who are you talking to?" "Oh, just Aunty May, mummy" he replied, and that happened several times. It was lovely to know she was there and that there was a kind of magical connection between Robbie and his Aunt.

Shortly after in 1995, Robbie started at a private nursery "The Willows Kindergarten", as I had to go back to work. Angela, who manages the nursery, asked me on several occasions who Emily was, because he kept talking to a girl at nursery called Emily, but they didn't have an Emily in nursery at all. Angela knew what Stephen did and asked me if Robbie was the same and I briefed Angela about the Aunty May episode and she just looked at me and said, "say no more". And then a few months later it was discovered (whilst the children were on a nature walk) that in an overgrown part of the Willows there were several old gravestones and, yes, as you can probably guess, one of them bore the name of Emily!

And I can remember another incident at the nursery... Angela had a secret about an infestation of spiders that had made a home in the kitchen of the Willows. She had kept this to herself, telling no one, not even her fellow staff, but had the problem sorted out without any one being any the wiser. A few weeks later in the schoolroom, at story time, Robbie piped up (his mind everywhere other than listening to the story) "Angela all those little spiders have all gone now"!

All I can say is that if, when he gets to be a bit older, Robbie turns out to be like Stephen, I wouldn't be at all surprised... In fact I'd be very pleased and proud.

Stephen has an incredible workload and his work means that he has to spend a lot of time away from myself and our children... and at times it becomes very lonely. I miss him tremendously and so do the children – "Mummy, is daddy coming home tonight – well, if he's not back tonight will I see him tomorrow – I want to see my daddy" – they all miss him so much. But Stephen makes sure that when he does have some time, he does spend it with myself, Robbie, Bradley and Ellie May. We have a wonderful relationship, and as a family we are all very happy. I sometimes take a step back and look at my life with Stephen and our three wonderful children and thank my lucky stars that we are all healthy and happy.

Stephen will come in late at night and brief me sometimes of his night's work. Some of the messages he tells me about are so *devastating. People are so brave to go along knowing that there's only a chance that they're going to get a message but when Stephen with his wonderful gift does manage to give a message it gives those people proof of life after death and maybe they can go home with some comfort and peace of mind knowing that their loved ones are safe.*

Stephen is pulled in many directions, not just by me and our children, but by so many people all wanting a piece of him... just a quick chat here (which ends up being a two hour conversation) or a short phone call there (which can become a fifty minute conference!).

I sometimes feel as though I just want to scream – "He's my husband and the father of my children, so just leave us alone and give us some time together!" We can't go out for a meal or go shopping together without Stephen being stopped in the street at least half a dozen times. It does get very tiresome, but at the end of the day, I suppose it's become part of our life now. And I love to know that when he is out working, he is helping so many people out there, and that makes up for everything. I mean at the end of the day, Stephen is only happy when he is busy and helping other people.

They say there is no such thing as a perfect person, but Stephen definitely is very very close. I'm sure all of you who have seen him or had the pleasure of meeting him would agree... He is a wonderful, caring, entertaining man and I'm so proud to be his wife!

CHAPTER TWELVE

Jane McDonald

One of the most frequently asked questions Stephen has to contend with is "Do you do private readings?" – and invariably the answer is no. There are some fairly obvious reasons for this, not least of which is a factor of time. Here is a man on the road four or five nights a week, who, until relatively recently, worked ten and twelve hour shifts as a hairdresser during the day, and who has a wife and three small children under eight who are worthy of as much of his spare time as he can possibly give them.

This is not to say that Stephen *never* does private sittings, because occasionally he will if it is a reading for a friend in need, and indeed, during his early training in the spiritualist church, he cut his teeth doing one-to-one sessions. But this is a far cry from doing private readings for the public at large and on any kind of commercial basis.

Another reason is that, by his own admission, he dislikes the intensity of doing one-to-ones.

In his own words – 'When I'm on the public platform, I get a great charge of energy from the audience that lifts me up and gives me the inspiration to do what I do, but that energy isn't there when you're just sitting across the table from one other person. When there's two hundred people sitting in a hall, there are plenty of candidates for a spiritual link and spirit can more or less make a choice… But if it's just me and that one other person I feel a great pressure and a great responsibility, and neither of those emotions are good for natural clairvoyance.

'Even when I started out at Peterson Road with Una Pierce and Janet Ferguson, I used to hate doing personal sittings because I knew that who ever I was reading was always expecting so much more than I could possibly deliver.

'And another thing – when you think about it, if someone gets a message from the public platform I'm usually with that person for no more than five or ten minutes before I'm being moved on to somebody else, but if I was sitting with them privately they'd be pretty fed up with me if after only ten minutes

I was saying "thank you very much, but your time's up." But apart from anything else, James, it *is* just the time factor. Do you know, there are even days when I've got to look in my diary just to figure out when I can wash my hair and take a bath!'

I can sympathise with where he's coming from on all counts, but there are some folk out there who are not so charitable and I remember well the lady who came up to me at one of the demonstrations and asked if she could book in for a private sitting. I politely told her, in effect, what I've just told you – 'Sorry madam, but Stephen doesn't do private readings' – to which she replied, very sarcastically, 'He does if you happen to be Jane McDonald!'

This lady was making reference to the well publicised friendship between Jane and Steve, and it is no secret that Stephen *has* done private readings for Jane over the years – but I must stress again, that this has not been on a commercial or a formal basis, but more on the vibration of friendship and spontaneous inspiration.

Back in 1982 Stephen was still only sixteen years old. The year had been a traumatic one for him inasmuch as the voices in his head that had plagued him all through his adolescence had got so bad that he'd finally plucked up the courage to go and see his doctor... And some courage was required for this because Stephen felt sure that the doctor was going to tell him that he was going mad and was a candidate for certification under section D.

As it happened, the doctor, a particularly enlightened practitioner, referred Stephen to the local spiritualist church (with the request that Stephen should never tell anyone of this piece of advice) and duly, with an even greater degree of trepidation, Stephen crossed the threshold of his closest spiritualist centre at Peterson Road – and in effect, he never looked back, for here he met a wonderful and caring congregation of people to whom "voices in the head and coming out of the ether" was a totally natural phenomenon!

Two people in particular took Stephen under their wings and helped him on the pathway towards developing his skills as a clairaudient medium. One was the worldly-wise doyenne of the spiritualist movement in the north of England, Una Pierce, while the other was a very gentle lady called Janet Ferguson. Together these two women not only saved Stephen's sanity, but introduced him to a whole new world of spiritual thought and dimension.

During the late 1980s Stephen's father worked as the manager of the Wakefield Theatre Club (at that time one of the most prestigious venues anywhere in the country) and naturally Steve was a regular visitor. As such he was privileged to see all of the top line acts that visited the venue including Cilla Black and Shirley Bassey, and he even made tea for The Three Degrees! As such, he reckoned he knew a "good turn" when he saw one.

There was a particular night in 1987 when he and a friend called Chris went out on the town and ended up gate crashing the VIP lounge at Mr Craig's – another famous night club of its day, situated in Leeds. As they cruised through the club Steve heard the song Lilac Wine, which was one of his favourite songs by one of his favourite singers, Elkie Brooks, and he actually thought it *was* Elkie Brooks until he heard an unfamiliar laugh half way through one of the stanzas. Going in pursuit of the singer, he turned a corner and discovered a very pretty young girl doing a cabaret set in the early part of the evening. Not only captivated by her voice – *Honestly James, there was so much depth and raw power there, it made all the hairs stand up on the back of my neck and it gave me goose bumps* – but also by the charisma of her personality which exuded over the footlights. Caught spellbound, he found himself rooted to the spot, listening as the singer did wonderful things with the Lilac Wine number (*not an easy song to sing! JC)* and, of course, the talented young vocalist turned out to be none other than Jane McDonald!

Now, ladies and gentlemen, for those of you who haven't met her, let me tell you that our girl Jane is not just a remarkably beautiful woman (much more so close up and in the flesh than the image which is projected from a television screen) she is also incredibly sexy and sensual and has that rare Munroe-esque quality that makes any male between fourteen and ninety four sit up and take notice with more than a passing twitch of interest! And yet for Steve (who is as hot blooded a male as you're ever likely to meet) there was a very different reaction.

He says 'I realised that she was very attractive but for me it wasn't a sexual thing... I didn't find myself looking up at this girl and thinking ooh I fancy you love, or anything like that... It was more of a psychic experience, and I found myself thinking this girl has really got talent... There's something very special about her, but I bet you that "off" stage she'd turn out to be a really nice person. At the time, bearing in mind that I'd only been "in training" for a few years, I didn't realise it for what it was, but looking back on it now, I see that this was some kind of psychic flash of recognition... That I was coming into contact, even though we were separated by the stage and footlights, with a kindred spirit.'

A couple of days later Stephen walked into Peterson Road church and was totally gob smacked to find Jane in attendance. Bearing in mind that *'we were the only two people in the building under the age of fifty'* it was quite natural for them to fall into conversation and when Steve asked her what she was doing there, Jane pointed out that she had every right to be there because her mother was the treasurer of the church, and an even greater surprise, that Janet Ferguson who had been Steve's mentor for the past few years, turned out to be none other than Jane's grandmother.

This first meeting created a natural rapport and led to a long ongoing friendship. Their common bond of interest was always spiritualism, and although Stephen's early experiences had freaked him out and had caused no small degree of distress, Jane had grown up with it in a very natural way and was used to 'seeing ghosts and hearing things go bump in the night.' Jane doesn't tell many people about her spiritualistic beliefs, but over the years she's had her own fair share of experiences and evidence to indicate beyond all shadow of a doubt that there is an afterlife.

Enjoying the bond of a very close friendship but never living in each other's pockets, Jane was always there for Stephen if he had problems and anxieties that he needed to get off his chest and, naturally, he was always there for Jane... but just as a friend and certainly not as some kind of psychic guru. Indeed, Stephen's flashes of clairvoyance for Jane have been relatively few and far between.

Stephen: 'My first glimpse of Jane's future came at Torry Road WMC in Leeds. She was singing her heart out up on the stage and then quite gradually I noticed that the curtain behind her had seemed to turn into the American flag. When she came off, I remember telling her that America was going to figure prominently in her future, and that one day she'd play in one of the world's most prestigious venues... I remember that she said "oh yeah?" with more than just a bit of 'I'll believe it when it happens' in her voice. However, twenty years later she did play to a packed house at the MGM Grand in Las Vegas, actually selling all the seats in two days, would you believe, and of course, America had already become important to her long before then, bearing in mind the cruise ships she used to work on would frequently sail from Florida.'

Like all highly talented and sensitive people Jane has had her fair share of emotional turmoil over the years and one day, while he was cutting hair in his salon, Stephen had a phone call from her requesting a lunch time meeting for a cup of coffee and a chat. Knowing that "something was up" Steve booked himself out for a dinner hour and the two friends met in a Leeds restaurant. It didn't take too long to discover what it was about... Jane, who had been very unhappy for quite a while, had just found a new man in her life, and was desperate to find out what Stephen thought about this new relationship with Danish Viking, Henrik Brixen.

Stephen: 'I really didn't know what to say... I remember staring at the white tablecloth and fiddling with my chips, and then something did start falling into place, although it wasn't particularly about Henrik. I told her that she and Henrik would be okay together, which is, I suppose, basically what she needed to hear, but the other stuff that came through... Well, I told her that I could see her in front of TV cameras, that she'd be being filmed with six or seven other people, but that she would emerge as the star of the show, really standing out from the crowd, and that it would all be happening on board a big ship. Also I told her that this would be just the beginning for her and that she would go on to have her own prime time TV show... It took fourteen months to start happening, but fourteen months later I did get a phone call from Jane's Mum saying that it was all coming true just like I said that it would and, a few weeks after that, The Cruise went out on the telly, and the rest, you could say, is history. Jane got her prime time slot with Star For A Night which turned out to be so incredibly successful.'

As we drive up and down the motorways of Britain, night after night to venue after venue, we invariably find ourselves playing one of Jane's tapes and, on more than one occasion, she becomes the topic of conversation. Both Steve and I think that she is a highly talented singer who has not yet reached the peak of her prowess. We both feel that she is under-rated as a musician (her voice has a rare precision and accuracy... It goes where she sends it, and stays there with incredible resonance and sustenance) and we both feel that much of Jane's long term future destiny revolves around the subject of spiritualism. I have had the pleasure of meeting the lady on a couple of occasions, and can vouch for the fact that she carries with her a phenomenal psychic vibration which explains much of the sister/brother relationship she enjoys with Stephen. Although Stephen never breaks confidence with his friend, he does have this to say...

'I've always admired Jane for her determination and her incredible charisma. She has a "presence" that is hard to describe. Even after all the success she's had, she remains unchanged... No, no, I've got that wrong! Actually, she has changed, and for the better! These days she believes in herself a lot more and knows what we're all going on about... Jane has a mysterious quality that fascinates me and there are a multitude of different voices hidden away that send tingles down your spine when she brings them out into the open occasionally. She still hasn't got the recognition she deserves, but I'll tell you this, she will get it sooner or later! She's got this fantastic writing ability and I've been going on at her for ages about writing a lot more of her own songs, and she actually phoned me the other day to tell me that she's taking two months out of this year's schedule just to concentrate on the writing, and I remember thinking that this was fantastic because it opens the door to a whole new pathway and one day people will be singing Jane McDonald songs! During the sittings I've had with her there have been a lot of other startling revelations, but that is for her to tell you about, not me. Knowing someone famous like Jane has taught me a lesson about keeping my trap shut, especially if there's a press reporter within earshot!

'Jane and I are two very similar people... In our own ways we're always in the public eye and yet we're both quite shy. We both love food, especially Chinese and Indian and Italian; oh what the hell, as long as it's food, food and food, we're both happy!

On more than one occasion recently I've told Jane about work in films, and I understand that there is something in the pipeline, but we'll all have to wait a little while to see just what it is exactly, although I'd be lying if I said I didn't have a good idea. We speak every couple of days on the phone and we're always giving each other advice. When we're not on tour, we go out for meals with my wife Caroline and Jane's husband Henrik, and we always have a load of laughs.

'The other thing I'm convinced about is that The Spirit World has a roll for Jane to play, and this is something that, for her, has only just begun!'

An appropriate note upon which to close this chapter is to quote from a recently published article in The Observer, some of the things Jane had to say about Stephen. In an interview with Kate Mikhail she said: 'There are so many charlatans out there, I can spot one a mile away. Steve is the most accurate medium I've ever known. He predicted the whole Cruise thing for me. He's fascinating to watch and I've seen a row of grown men sob their hearts out. He's not my best friend because he's clairaudient. He just has a wise way about him and I trust his judgement. He's like my big brother. He's like a tornado when he comes into a room – just lights it up and everyone focuses on him. He looks like a rock star and is always so full of fun. He's always got a story – he has me in fits of laughter! He has loads of energy – I wish I could bottle it up and keep some for myself. No matter how bad you feel, he always manages to cheer you up!'

Steve and Caroline
Christmas 2001

Top – Steve with Jane
Bottom – Steve with JC in La Miranda

JC and Steve in book planning session

Steve demonstrating to a packed house at Sheffield City Hall on the
night of the contact with Lisa and Princess Diana

Top – Steve in an intimate moment of communication with the photograph clearly showing the left arm paralysis
Bottom – Steve with Joanna in Nardini's getting fat on ice cream.

Top left – Steve aged 2 picking his nose
Top right – with his mother Margaret.

Recent wedding group showing left to right, Steve's sister Joanne, Margaret, Neil and Adele, Steve's other sister. Then to the right of the photograph Ellie May, Steve, Caroline and the two boys Robbie and Bradley.

Top left – Pat Johnson AKA "The Rottweiler".
Top right–Steve presenting a cheque for £15000 to the Wakefield
Hospice. This is the amount gathered by bucket collections and raffles
at Steve's demonstrations over an 18 month period.

Steve enjoying a casual moment.

Top – Steve in pre-show conference at the Cochrane Theatre

Bottom – Steve at large in London's West End with the ever ringing mobile phone.

Top – before the demonstration, "is there anybody there"
Middle – Mid evening, mid flow.
Bottom – The total exhaustion at the end of the night.

CHAPTER THIRTEEN

London In The Middle

'You cannot die – not for the very life of you!'

Jo and I watched, holding hands nervously in the darkened theatre. We were both aware that Stephen looked somehow different up there on that West End stage. Perhaps it was the unusually formal jacket that he was wearing or it could have been the quality of the stage lighting, but to our eyes he seemed straighter and taller and his whole manner exuded a confidence that certainly had not been there half an hour earlier in The Holborn Hotel. Normally he would have been charged with nervous energy, pacing up and down and building the power matrix, but this night, although he was mobile across the stage, he walked in measured strides, moving with a languidity that was alien to his nature. Also, another thing which struck us was the brevity of his introduction: in most circumstances Stephen will speak for a good ten minutes or so, setting the scene and creating some terms of reference before launching into the actual clairvoyance – he will tell an amusing story or two, just to put the audience at its ease – but on this occasion he virtually went straight in without any preamble.

'You cannot die for the life of you – and I want to go straight to a gentleman somewhere over here on the right of the auditorium, a gentleman who has lost his father quite recently, just within the last few months...'

A young man with fine fair hair tentatively puts up his hand.

'Thank you, sir. Can I just have your voice, just a straight yes or no... you have lost your father in the last six months?'

'Yes.'

'And is the 11th of August in any way significant?'

'Yes.'

'Why is that date significant?'

'He died on 11th of August.'

'And do the numbers ten and two mean anything to you.'

'Yes, he died at ten minutes to two.'

'And who is Derek?'

'That's my father's name.'

'And who, please, is Simon?'

'That's me. That's my name.'

'Fine. Who's Nancy?'

'That's my mother.'

'And why is your father showing me a picture of a big black jackdaw? It isn't a rook or a crow or a magpie, it's definitely a jackdaw.'

'He ran a pub called The Jackdaw for twenty years...'

'And can I ask, does Tuesday mean anything special to you, and this Tuesday that I'm getting would be in connection with someone who passed away quite recently, not your father but someone else, as a result of a car accident?'

'Yes.'

'And I've got someone here who is drawing me a big initial letter N... Sir, can I just ask you, and don't be nice to me, does the name of Nigel mean anything to you?'

'Yes it does.'

'Sir, who was Nigel?'

'Nigel was killed in a car crash – on a Tuesday.'

'The impression I'm getting is of being thrown forwards with a great force and hitting my head against something hard and sharp.'

'He went through the windscreen.'

'And who was Nigel?'

'Nigel was...' there's a half sob in the young man's voice that gives something of the game away. '...Nigel was a friend – a very special friend of mine.'

'And was there a white car involved in all of this?'

'Yes, Nigel was driving a white car.'

'And I'm getting another name here... Brent or Kent, or something that sounds like that... Went, Brent, Kent, something -ent, -ent, -ent.'

'Nigel's last name was Kent.'

'...And he's telling me that although he suffered this huge impact to his head, he didn't die straight away. He's telling me he can remember being in the ambulance and then being taken into an operating theatre and that he passed over while he was asleep under the anaesthetic?'

'Yes, that's right. All that is right.'

'Sir, he's showing me a photograph and it's a photograph you've only recently been looking at yourself. You're both in the picture, but there's a load of other blokes as well, and it's almost as though it's a team photograph of some sort, but it's not like a football team or a rugby team, and at the same time as all this he's shouting at me about Oxford... something to do with Oxford?'

'We both rowed for Oxford when we were at university together, and yes, we both had copies of the photograph.'

'And there's something about a tattoo? Did either you or him have a tattoo, and I won't say where I think it might be, and it would be a cartoony type of tattoo... something to do with a television character or something like that?'

'Yes, he had a Captain Pugwash tattoo on his...'

A ripple of laughter echoes around the pin-dropping silence of the theatre and nobody actually hears where the aforementioned tattoo was emblazoned.

'Sir, this is a bit strange, but why is he showing me a teddy bear... a big fluffy teddy bear?'

'I don't know.'

'Just think for a moment because I'm sure it means something important... a big teddy bear?'

'No, I don't know.' At this point a gentleman sitting next to him leans over and whispers something in his ear. 'Oh... yes, I suppose... the car crash happened in Paddington?'

'That'll do. Sir, I'm thinking this is all very recent. We're not talking here about something that happened months ago, or even weeks ago, are we?'

'No.'

'Sir, I've told you this happened on a Tuesday – was this only *last* Tuesday?'

This is the straw which breaks the camel's back of self control and Simon bursts into an open flurry of tears. 'Yes it was last Tuesday!'

This was Stephen's first link of a ninety minute presentation. I have neither exaggerated nor added to it, and I have recorded it as faithfully as my scribbled shorthand will allow. To me it is shocking in its accuracy and yet at the same time, throughout the whole encounter, Stephen seemed cool and aloof without any of the usual emotion or humour creeping into his delivery. To be sure, the emotion finally broke through with 'Simon's' tears, but that was on his part and not on Stephen's. He went on to forge another dozen links and as the evening progressed he increasingly became his softer, more humane self. Jo seemed to think that he went from strength to strength, but from my own memory that first message was the most dramatic.

Overall, however, I was deeply deeply impressed. I'd never seen Stephen so confident and so much in control, and I'd never known him be so specifically accurate with his evidence. It rolled off his tongue like peas falling off the edge of a knife – names, dates, times, a plethora of personal detail, even down to the name (Shanky) of someone's pet pig. He didn't – seemingly couldn't – put a foot wrong and when the audience finally filed out of the theatre at the end of the presentation, it did so in something of a daze. The boisterous "ooh hello darling" repartee at the beginning of the evening as the audience had filed *into* the Cochrane Theatre was replaced by quiet sober conversations held in rather mute and subdued tones as people huddled into little groups to discuss and dissect what they had just experienced. Tuning into several different conversations at the same time isn't easy even for the most well trained eavesdropper, but I kept picking up words like – *incredible – unbelievable – fantastic – amazing* – and even from one quarter – *gorgeous!* There was little doubt in my mind that Stephen had cracked one of the toughest audiences he was ever likely to encounter, but then, as now, I don't believe that he did it all on his own.

I suspect that being aware (a) of the challenge and (b) of the opportunity, The Spirit World channelled an unusual degree of energy into Stephen that night to get him through the "trial by media". To me this was not only evident by the intensity of his evidence, but also by the man's stature and persona as he worked from the Cochrane stage: there was an entirely different aura about him which is very difficult to describe, but suffice to say I'll recognise it when I see it again.

Prizing Stephen out of the theatre was quite arduous and took some ingenuity. Everyone wanted to talk to him, in depth and detail, and in the case of some of Simon's friends *in private!* We could see that while on a high, he was nonetheless shattered with tiredness!

In the end we managed to succeed and we ran around the corner in the pouring rain (it was still siling down) in search of something to eat. Amazing, but at ten o'clock in our part of central London there wasn't that much choice, and we crowded into the first pizzeria that we came to. As we munched our way through a trio of rather ordinary pizzas we talked about the demonstration in some depth, and Stephen confirmed something of what I'd already surmised.

'I was standing in the wings,' he said, 'waiting for the stage manager to tell me when to go on, and I was feeling – well, quite frankly, I was feeling totally terrified! Then I thought, hang on a minute, I shouldn't be feeling this way at all and I said a little prayer to the spirit world asking them to make it all right – and immediately something deliciously cool seemed to wrap itself around me... all the heat and the nerves and the tension just evaporated and I thought, let me get at 'em! If it's proof they're looking for, I'm damn well going to give it to them. Then it was time to go on and it was almost like I was floating rather than standing on the stage, and to tell you the truth I don't remember much of the messages or what I said to anybody in particular, but I just *knew* I was doing a good job.'

'D'you remember the first message you gave to the young guy called Simon?' I asked.

'No, not really,' he mused. 'Why? Was it all right?'

'Yeah, it was fine...'

'Do you remember the message about Shanky the pet pig?' Jo cut in.

'Oh yes, I do remember that!' Stephen grinned. 'Yes that *was* a lovely message for that lady, wasn't it...'

And so the conversation went around and around. Eventually we paid the bill, ran back to the car park through the rain, and as Big Ben started to chime midnight somewhere in the distance, I navigated the big old Volvo out of London heading north towards our native Yorkshire. Long before we hit the M1 Steve was fast asleep on the back seat, cocooned in a travelling rug and with a sheepskin over his briefcase acting as pillow. Eventually Jo dozed off in the left hand seat, leaving me alone with my thoughts.

As the motorway unfurled before me, the windscreen wipers danced their repetitive duet against the deluge, and my mind freewheeled backwards not only over the events of what had been an incredibly long day, but also over what had been an incredibly eventful year.

The association with Steve Holbrook had done a great deal to change my life, especially my working life. Gone were the routine days of sitting at a small table staring intently at patterns of lines on upturned hands of anxious clients and at spreads of Tarot cards as they cascaded their life stories across the purple velvet of the reading cloth... Gone were the days of booking dubious folk acts into dimly lit venues in the back street of North Yorkshire, and gone too (sadly) was the burning ambition to find a publisher for either one of the potentially best selling novels that sat gathering dust in the filing cabinet under the stairs. Instead, my life had become a series of journeys to venues all over the country as I tried to bring Stephen to the attention of a greater audience. My writing hours no longer told tales of vampires and creatures that lived in another space and time continuum, but rather tried to explain and chronicle the exploits and experiences of this extraordinary man whom both I and my wife had come to love and respect so much. At one point in time, I had been able to cast a cautious glance into my own future and see how it might well be that, putting it very crudely, Stephen may well become my meal ticket for the next few years... but now I was more circumspect.

Now, through the good graces of Henrik Brixen and his contacts in the industry, Stephen had been exposed to the crème de la crème of the British media: his demonstration and his evidence had been quite mind blowing, and I simply couldn't see how those invited VIP's in the audience could fail to take notice of, and respond favourably to his incredible gifts and powerful persona.

The way I saw it, there would have to be a massive media response with newspaper articles and radio shows et al and, whether he wanted it or not, I felt that Steve would now have to bow to the inevitability of television exposure. On the strength of his performance at The Cochrane, the doors of celebrity status would inevitably start creaking open, and before too much longer he would start to become the household name he so very much deserved to be.

The fact that this would put me out of a job did, I must confess, cause me some disquiet... but that was my business and, as far as I was concerned, I would keep it to myself.

CHAPTER FOURTEEN
Summer Solstice

The summer of 2001 was an extremely eventful time for both Stephen and myself. For my part, I went in for my long awaited heart surgery in May and I was out of it for quite a while afterwards. Jo ran the business whilst I did my best to recover from a double heart by-pass, and those people who talk to you about being up and about in a few weeks and walking three miles a day (and you hear this from without and within the medical profession) are talking through their funny bones!

If you use those much bandied words "heart by-pass" it sounds like a fairly routine procedure, but as a friend of mine observed, talk about "deeply invasive open heart surgery" and it puts it into an entirely different context. Suffice to say I was not up and about within a few weeks and I was not walking three miles a day... never walked three miles a day before the op and certainly have never been able to in the period after it either, so what else is new?

In all fairness, there were a few complications and after being discharged from Castle Hills in Hull I was hauled back into York District Hospital a fortnight later to allow a very nice Doctor called Dan Burrows to drain two and a half litres of fluid out of my left lung. Lovely!

Be that as it may, with Jo in attendance every step of the way, I was determined not to fall into the invalid mentality and I forced myself to get up and out on the road as much as I could, and although I had wisely placed Jo in charge of everything, I did make the effort to do my favourite zombie impression at half a dozen of Steve's demonstrations up and down the country, notably in Norwich and York. Needless to say (and against the concerned advice of my wife!), I tried to do too much too soon and set myself back rather than propelling myself forwards.

However that was then, and this is now, and although there are still a few aches and pains and unexpected twinges (Jo says not twinges but whinges) I guess I am back to being as fit as I'm ever likely to be.

On Stephen's part, he made a number of decisions that have had far reaching consequences.

Inevitably, after his night at The Cochrane, the offers came flooding in, and quietly and with no small degree of deliberation, he turned each and every one of them down. Yes, there were a couple of newspaper articles, and yes there was a chat show, but he came down with a resounding "no" against the (very lucrative) television offers that were presented to him. His reasons were the same as they have always been... he places great value on his privacy, and more importantly the privacy of his family and, in himself, he simply didn't feel ready to take this irrevocable step.

Two things did happen in the summer of 2001, one, I believe, being the direct result of the other. He first of all gave up his hairdressing salon, which had been the mainstay of his income for the better part of fifteen years, and on the strength of that singular action, his clairvoyance began to improve by leaps and bounds. In my eyes Steve was always "the best" and now the best started getting even better.

The decision to give up the salon did not come lightly. He knew something had to go, and instead of working six ten hour shifts, he tried working just four days a week, which was fine, but then he realised that he was working thirteen hour shifts. He cut it down to three days a week, and found he was working fifteen hour shifts... and all the time, he was still trying to function as a husband and a father and a professional clairvoyant.

The lease for the salon came up for renewal in June, and there was some hassle with the landlords who wanted to hike up the rent to an astronomical figure and in the end Stephen just walked away. Deeply sorry to be the cause of so much disappointment to his scores of loyal customers, but quite determined to carve out a better quality of life both for himself and for his family.

He started swimming every morning at his local pool, and took to jogging whenever he had a spare half hour. To alleviate the constant bombardment of telephone calls that invaded every five minutes of his waking day, he set up an informal answering service employing his mother to run the booking office for his various demonstrations (it seems incredible that some people think it's quite alright to phone at 8 o'clock on a Sunday morning or 11 o'clock any night of the week). He also converted the spare bedroom in his Wakefield home into a small office, where he usually puts in four or five hours every day arranging the adverts and press releases and making the scores of outgoing calls that are necessary to run such a business. He still works on average ten or twelve hours a day, but many of those hours are now spent in the home within a family environment, and although his workload is still quite outrageous compared to what many people have to contend with, it's a damn sight better than it was, and from all angles it was a very wise move to have made.

One of the things that pleasantly surprised us was the continuing popularity of our book "The Light In The Darkness". Most people seemed to like it, and it certainly stimulated a lot of response to Stephen's website and my post bag became bulkier by the week with readers writing in, not only with their stories of how Stephen had helped them with his messages from The Spirit World, but also with their own spiritual experiences as well. Work was tentatively begun on this, its sister and sequel.

Some of our venues went from strength to strength, while others never properly worked, no matter how hard we plugged away at them and regardless of how much money we threw at them. Sadly, lovely places like Shrewsbury and Cambridge were dropped from our schedule, and our Tyneside venue was relocated from Gateshead to Sunderland. Scotland has been put on hold for the time being for although we love both the place and the people, the sheer expense of staging events so far north has simply got the better of us.

Some people might look at the packed crowds that flock to Steve's demos and think that we're making a mint from them... but really, it doesn't work like that at all. For example, two hundred people pay, say, seven and a half quid each for their ticket, which means there's a gross take of fifteen hundred pounds – but then deduct two hundred pounds for the hire of the hall, eight hundred pounds for a month's advertising, say another forty pounds for petrol, another thirty pounds for the printing of flyers and posters, and say another twenty pounds to cover assorted telephone calls and postage... and that doesn't leave much profit to be split between two people when you take into consideration the thirty or forty man hours it has taken to stage the event. In short it means that we're frequently working for something less than four pounds an hour, and always taking the calculated risk (because there are never any guarantees) that we're not even going to earn that much! Believe me, wealthy men we are not!

Why then do we do the work? Well obviously we're *trying* to earn a living, but there is another agenda. Stephen, while not evangelical about either spiritualism or the spiritualist church, is genuinely sincere in trying to prove to people that because there is life after death, there need be no fear of death itself. I suppose I share that quest, and if Steve does what he can do through demonstrating and I do what I can do through writing these books, then it gives both of our lives some sense of meaning and purpose that is a long way removed from having to earn enough dosh to make the next mortgage payment!

During that summer, Steve and I had a number of casual conversations about a whole host of different things, and although they may have been casual in one sense, I did glean that some of his attitudes towards his own abilities were changing slightly. Once, a long time ago, I had asked his opinion on reincarnation and he said that he really wasn't too sure about it. Now he seemed to be more open to the acceptance of its possibility. Also he started looking, albeit tenuously, at the source of his gift... and, no, he hadn't come up with any definitive answers, but I thought that it was a healthy sign that he'd started to ask one or two key questions.

The really lovely thing that registered was his growing enthusiasm to collaborate on this book – which was a bloody marvel considering his reluctance to collaborate on the first one. "Light In The Darkness" was like getting blood out of a stone but with "Out Of This World" we haven't been able to shut him up! Indeed, he even came up with the title of the book and has had some very good ideas about what he wants to go in and what he wants to be left out.

We talked about this once in a transport café in downtown Castleford.

'So come on then,' I challenged, notebook at the ready, 'tell me a dozen things about yourself. You know, little personal things, that other people might find interesting, but at the same time gives some insight as to what kind of a guy you are.'

107

'Oh bloody hell, do I have to?' He looked at me appealingly over the rim of a ketchup-covered cheeseburger, hoping that I was going to tell him that I was only kidding.

'Yep, absolutely! Go for it!'

'But what sort of stuff do you mean?'

'Well,' I mused, 'how about that designer shirt you're wearing? How would you feel if everyone out there knew you'd just paid the fantastic sum of two quid for it down at the local charity shop?'

'Oh I wouldn't worry at all! You know that I love getting a bargain, and what's the point in paying fifty quid for a shirt when you can get one for a fiver if you look around? I mean this shirt's never been worn, and I think it's great. If I could get away with it I'd buy all my clothes in charity shops. I like the idea of putting my money where it can do a bit of good and it's a shame a few more people don't think like that.'

'Okay, so tell me something else. A dozen things!'

'Ummm, all right, well, I love good food and I love going to nice restaurants, I mean they don't have to be *good* restaurants as long as the food is good. On the other hand I don't like pubs and places where there's lots of noise and smoke. I don't worry too much about anything posh really, and I suppose the Peugeot we've just got is about the poshest car we've ever had, especially when you think about the last half dozen cars I've had which have all been Austin Montegos – you know, I think the Montego is a fabulous car... I mean the body work is a bit naff, but they've got super engines...

'Ummm, I love the sunshine and I love having a sun tan and I love going on holiday, although we don't get as many as we'd like. I love the Canary Islands but I can be just as chuffed being in a friend's old caravan out on the Norfolk coast – it's a bit of a crush with Caroline and the three kids but we always manage to have a good time.

'Ummm, I love Barbra Streisand and Shirley Bassey, and Jane McDonald of course, but I don't get too turned on by a lot of the modern music that's going around. I mean, I've listened to The Spice Girls but I wouldn't leave home for any one of 'em! Robbie Williams is okay, I quite like him, and Westlife sing some nice songs... but as for most of the other pop artists that are on the scene at the moment, well, I'm sorry, but I wouldn't know

Britney Spears if she came up and asked me for my autograph. I don't go to the movies all that often and when I do, it's usually to please the kids. I've seen Jurassic Park, Atlantis and Dr. Doolittle in the last few months and they were okay I suppose, but I'd rather have been sat in front of my own telly with Caroline and a bottle of red wine... Ummm, oh hell, that'll do, won't it?'

'Sure,' I grinned, 'for the time being.'

At that point the mobile phone started ringing like mad, so I guess you could say he was saved by the bell anyway.

'That,' he said after the phone call finished, 'was The Rottweiler!'

I laughed. 'One of these days, you're going to come a real cropper when she hears you calling her that.'

'Oh she knows!' Stephen exclaimed. 'It's been her nickname for years!'

Now for anyone who has been to Stephen's demonstrations over the years, especially those on his own turf, the chances are that you've already met the person we're talking about. She's the lady with the large chest and no-nonsense manner who has been doing "the door" for Steve ever since he started hiring halls eighteen years ago.

Pat Johnson AKA "The Rottweiler" is a lady of great character who, I suspect, secretly relishes the unofficial epithet and although she sometimes calls a spade a shovel with all the tact and diplomacy of a building brick, she really is the salt of the earth and her loyalty to Stephen and his family knows no bounds.

As a spiritual healer in her own right she and Stephen met quite often, just when Stephen was stretching his wings away from the constraints of the spiritualist church and she fitted Stephen's bill as someone who could hold her own under the pressure of "the door" and she fitted Stephen's wife's bill as being exactly the kind of person she wanted to keep Stephen out of trouble.

From what I can gather the Rottweiler tag originated from a night, many years ago in Knottingley, when a well endowed young female with lots of personality but very few clothes (well, it was mid-summer!) was desperately trying to persuade an embarrassed and reluctant Stephen to come back to her "party"... and Pat moved in like a Boadicean warrior armed with battle axe and bosom to extract Stephen from his plight. Steve says, 'She

109

was just like a Rotty going after a poodle and I suppose that's how she got Christened.'

The Rottweiler is an apt nickname, but it is used with love and humour. Pat has two sons of her own, Julian and Steven (who are both more or less Stephen's age) and she tends to see Stephen as one of the family. Over the years Pat has provided Stephen with invaluable service and companionship, frequently talking to him for hours on end, just to keep him awake at the wheel on the long miles home from any one of a hundred different demonstrations.

And it has to be said that manning a box office door for the frantic forty minutes it can take to get three hundred people into a venue designed to take only two hundred and forty is an art in itself. Jo, who does this job at the demos JCP arranges for Steve, will be the first to tell you how stressful and harrowing this task can be, and yet Pat takes it all in her stride, frequently ruffling the feathers of her customers by her direct manner, but always getting them in despite insurmountable odds... and sometimes a direct manner is an absolute necessity.

Pat recalls the occasion when a lady presented her with a fifty pound note.

'Thank you, Madam,' Pat said politely, 'but what's this for, exactly?'

'My tickets, of course,' the lady replied haughtily.

'Yes, madam, but how *many* tickets? Stephen's clairvoyant, but unfortunately I am not!'

Both Stephen and Pat recall an evening at Richmond Town Hall when Pat crossed swords with "the lady with the green hair". It was a very small venue with only a hundred seats and it had been sold out many weeks in advance. This particular lady, green hair, gold earrings and Doc Martins, arrived at the door five minutes after the demonstration had begun, demanding to be given access because "the advert said you could pay on the door".

'Yes, Madam,' Pat said, 'that advert *did* say pay on the door, but it also said "reservations advised" and everyone in that room *did* reserve their seat, but you *didn't* and we're full, so you're *not* coming in!'

When Pat crosses her arms and draws herself up to her full height of five feet one and throws out her chest (also five feet

one) and when she looks at you full in the eye, you do not –
believe me, you do not – argue with this mother of Valkyries! PR
expert she may not be, but as Steve says and has said many times
'I owe her so much and I'd be lost without her. She's been with
me since the very early days when, if we had twenty people in the
audience, we felt that we had a major success on our hands.'

The days of twenty in the audience are long since past, and
for a very long time now audiences of 200 have been nearer the
norm... at least, they were in the summer of 2001. However,
over the autumn and winter ahead much was to happen that
would double those audience figures and send us scurrying in
search of bigger venues.

The café door opened with a clatter as two young mothers with
pushchairs forced an entrance. I saw that it was raining again
outside, but at least the waft of fresh air did something to blow
away the smell of burnt milk, cheap cigarettes and frying onions.

'Okay,' I said, referring to the note book, 'tell me about
some of the things that really annoy you and irritate you.'

Steve threw back his head and laughed. 'You're joking
aren't you?'

'No, why should I be?'

'Because it's a long list!'

Ah, I thought, some of the juicy bits at last!

'No problem,' I said smoothly, all sweetness and light, 'just
give me a few examples.'

'All right... well, I absolutely hate it when, for example, I'm
in one of the local shops, and I'm asking the assistant if they've
got any of this or that, and they come out with the old chestnut
"oh you're the clairvoyant, so don't you know already?" Lord, if
I've heard that once over the years I've heard it a thousand times,
and I tend to just smile and say something like "oh yes, right..."
but the humour, if there was ever any there in the first place, is
beginning to wear a bit thin...

'And something that always irritates the hell out of me is
when I'm walking down the road, usually with the kids in tow,
and someone stops me and wants to talk about a message I gave
them two years ago, and along with it, their whole life story...
This happened only a week or so back when I was taking Robbie
and Bradley to the swimming pool; they were pulling on my arms

as if to say "Daddy come *on!*" but this lady simply wouldn't let me go, and I was with her for about half an hour on the street corner. I suppose I should have been tougher but I hate being rude to people, but then again, I felt really cheesed off that she was barging in on my time taking up the very precious time I have with the kids.

'It's the same kind of situation you get at the end of a demonstration. There are always loads of people hanging around wanting to talk to you, and there's always one person who wants to hog the conversation. All I want to do at that time is get my face into a plate of food and then get my head down on a pillow... I know you've got to talk to people, it's an essential part of the job, and if you can spend just a couple of minutes with everyone, well that's fine, but you *can't* spend a couple of minutes with everyone if there's one person who is hell bent on telling you the most intimate secrets of their family life of a generation ago. On the other hand, you can't just say "Thank you, madam, your time is up! Next please!"

'When I'm on the door people will come up and say to me "Is he any good?" They haven't a clue it's me they're talking to. Then they don't know where to put themselves when I say something like "well I think so love, because it's me!"

'And I hate it when people think that if they tell me something about themselves at the door, it will help them get a message, because it simply doesn't work like that – if anything it works against them because there's no way I could take advantage of anything like that.

'Another thing that makes me wonder whether or not I'm doing something wrong is when somebody comes up to me and says, usually in a conspiratorial sort of whisper, as though they're doing me a great favour, "Ooh Steve, I can get a house party together of at least ten people" – and I find myself thinking don't be silly love, I talk to 10,000 people or more every year, and for the umpteenth time, I don't do private consultations.

'I suppose I get irritated with people who either expect me to, or even want me to talk shop all the time. I know other clairvoyants grind their batteries down talking spirit, spirit, spirit all the time. They've only got one topic of conversation, namely the spirit world, and it's like a gramophone with the needle permanently stuck in one groove of the old record. For me each evening is like the first time, with the same adrenalin rush. I love brand new venues because this always brings some freshness into my working life.

'First thing in the morning, I love going out into my garden, even as early as 6.00-6.30am, watering the plants, just standing there in my boxer shorts in the cool morning air. This is so therapeutic, just the sound of the birds amid all the peace and quiet.

'Sometimes I get annoyed by all the offers I get to go abroad – "oh Steve you must come to America, Germany, Australia, Timbuk-flaming-tu – and it isn't that I'm not grateful for the interest, it's just that I've got my commitments to my family and I want to be around while the children are growing up. There'll be plenty of time to go globe trotting when the kids have flown the nest, that is, if spirit stills wants me too, of course.'

Stephen sat back in his chair, and eyed me with a gaze of shrewd mischief.

'But of course, James, there is one thing that really *really* gets up my nose!'

'Really?' I asked mildly. 'What's that?'

'It's talking to you, you crafty sod, when you've got me in the mood for talking, so you can put that flaming notebook away, and *you* can pay for lunch!'

The Neighbour's Tale

From Sue Marples

My name is Sue. My husband, Joe, and I live next door to Stephen, Caroline, Robbie, Bradley and Ellie. Our son, Gary, and his partner Rebbekah are also friendly with Stephen.

I met Stephen briefly a couple of times seven years ago before they moved in, but a third meeting is very vivid in my memory. Stephen and I were both in our front gardens. We discovered we were both Taureans and both loved gardening. Stephen was busy planting a variety of shrubs, including a treasured climbing rose that had belonged to his late, much-loved and missed grandfather. Having finished what I was doing I went inside, only to hear the doorbell and a distraught Stephen saying to Joe, "Is your wife there, please?"

I went to see what was the matter and Stephen said, "I think I've found a dead baby in the back garden, buried in the corner!" I tried to reassure Stephen and as we dashed through his gate I realised he had, in fact, dug up a small Sheltie dog that had belonged to the previous residents. "It's not a baby, Stephen, it's a dog. No baby could ever have teeth like that!" Stephen remained inconsolable. I removed the poor creature and buried her in my own garden. Stephen packed up his gardening things and went home.

Once Stephen, Caroline and Robbie moved in, I realised we all had a lot in common. Caroline and I, despite the age difference, are very good friends. We help each other whenever we can but do not live "in each other's pockets". In Stephen, I feel I have found a soul mate; we are very much alike in so many ways.

Our gardens are very different but we both love plants and often pass various things over the fence to each other. Stephen frequently arrives at the gate (often wearing nothing more than his boxer shorts) with presents for me or Joe – a bowl of strawberries, a plant, a jar of pickles or a cake.

I had known for some time that Stephen was a hairdresser but did not realise what else he did, until, one day, as we were both in our front gardens, he said, "Look at the time, I'd better

114

get ready for tonight, I'm working". "What, hairdressing?" I said. "No," said Stephen, "don't you know what I do?" I looked at him – his blond, streaked hair, all over the place and wearing scruffy shorts and his huge, unlaced garden boots. "You're not a male stripper, are you?" Stephen burst out laughing. "What, with legs like these, you must be joking! I'm a medium." I suddenly saw Stephen differently. He is a gentle, caring, sensitive young man, attractive, jolly, at times eccentric (sorry, Stephen!) and now I could see how he used all of this in his work as a medium to help people. Somehow, I was not surprised at what he had told me.

I have, since this revelation, seen Stephen at work. He puts people at ease, reassures them, makes them laugh and sometimes cry but never hurts them. I feel privileged to know Stephen. He has so much compassion and so much time for other people's feelings.

On my birthday this year, Robbie, Brad and Ellie turned up on my doorstep with a huge birthday cake, a card from each of them and a rather rude card from Caroline and Stephen. The children came in and Bradley said, "Do you like my card?" I said, "It's beautiful Brad, and you've written it yourself. I'm really proud of you!" "Good," said Brad, "can I have my piece of cake now?" The children sat and ate cake, all gave me a cuddle and went home. This is just another example of the caring neighbours we have.

I have so enjoyed having the 'seven years of good luck' since Stephen and Caroline moved in. Their children are all different, all lovely and all enjoy spending time with me. We, as a couple, have had some trauma over the years, which I won't go into (maybe I'll write my own book one day!) but Stephen, Caroline and their children have given us only pleasure and I hope – I know – this will continue for as long as we are neighbours, and beyond.

Thanks, Stephen, for making me laugh, for being my friend and for just being you – be happy!

Sue

X

CHAPTER FIFTEEN

Tenerife

The moment I set foot out of the plane my senses were assailed by the unique smell that said this was a Spanish airport and that this was Spain. It is a scent made up from kerosene and aviation fuel, wild jasmine and oleander, harsh black tobacco and carbolic disinfectant... It may be a distasteful smell to some, but to me it is always a heady mixture that does more for my senses and my soul than the headiest of exotic perfumes: it is the smell that says this is *Spanish* soil and that I am here, the expatriate wanderer returned, perhaps not to the land of his birth, but certainly to the land of his choice, the land of his *spiritual* home.

Tenerife may have been one of the furthest flung outposts of the Spanish nation, but it was still Spain, and as we disembarked from the 757 heading towards passport control, there was a lump of emotion in my throat and a sting in my eyes that said the magic was still there and the magic, more potent than ever, still worked.

It is hard to describe to someone not cursed by the same affliction, but in the space of twenty paces and a dozen heartbeats, all of the stress and cumulative tension that had been part of my life for many long months seemed to ease and evaporate: not only my spirit but also my physical body perceptibly lightened. My lungs drew deeper drafts of air, there was a chuckle in my heart and a widening Cheshire cat grin spreading across my face.

One day, of course, I will have to move back to Spain on a permanent basis – at least, I will if I want to avoid a premature death – but even if I don't make it, after I have passed to the world of spirit and my friends have mourned my passing (as an epitaph they might say "he wrote a few good poems") my wife, bless her, will scatter my ashes over the high hills of Southern Andalucia and the angels, should there be angels, will speak to me in Spanish voices.

Over the course of 2001 Stephen turned down opportunities to work in Australasia and the USA, and yet when the offer came in for a week's work in The Canary Islands, he thought about it for a while, then cautiously said yes, on condition that Jo and I went along with him as a security blanket and to act as manager/driver/chaperones. The week was scheduled for the end of January 2002, when he didn't have too much on anyway, and by virtue of the fact that it was only going to be for seven days rather than weeks on end, it meant he wouldn't be away from his wife and children for any great length of time. Furthermore, he was familiar with Tenerife as a holiday destination and being the sun bunny that he is, the idea of some mid-winter sunshine was not without appeal. Equally attractive was the fact that the three shows he would be doing were to be organised by a local British entrepreneur called Ken Fisher, so, in essence, all Steve would have to do is turn up for the demonstrations, then spend the rest of the time relaxing and soaking up the rays... It didn't quite work out like that, of course, but these were the thoughts and energies behind his acceptance of Ken Fisher's offer and, for our own part, Jo and I were delighted to go along for the ride.

We were met in the arrivals hall by Mr Fisher and incredibly also by a family from Devon who, after having seen the Tenerife trip posted on the website, had arranged their annual holiday around the event and had actually booked for all three of his demonstrations.

Ken seemed to be a quiet and quite charming sort of gentleman (not at all the flashy overconfident impresario Jo and I had imagined he might turn out to be) and very efficiently he organised ourselves and our baggage into the waiting minibus, and in the fading late afternoon light, we headed out along the motorway from Reina Sofia airport to our "digs" in Puerto de la Cruz.

The "digs" turned out to be a pair of adjacent four star apartments in the Club Martianez complex, right in the heart of the town. None of us had known what to expect and, as Steve had joked, for all we knew we might have been dumped in a couple of wooden huts down on the beach. Club Martianez gave a very favourable first impression of things to come and there was the added bonus of there being a private swimming pool, which left me cold, but as a dedicated swimmer, delighted Stephen no end.

117

We spent a minimal amount of time unpacking, then with Ken as our guide we went out to find some food, to take a look at one of the venues where Stephen would be working and to check out the town: we hadn't been there for an hour and Stephen was already talking about perfumes for Caroline and presents for the kids.

Following Ken and Stephen as we all strolled down Avenida de Generalisimo, I pondered on just how much Puerto de la Cruz had changed since I'd last visited the place back in 1976. Then it had been a rather tawdry little town, piled high with characterless concrete blocks of modern hotels and apartments that all but obliterated the quaint little fishing hamlet it had once been. But twenty five years had softened some of the harsh lines and rough edges and a patina of age had begun to touch the concrete canyons blending them in a little more sympathetically with the older buildings and elegant town houses. With the profusion of plants and mature palms (that twenty five years earlier had been mere saplings) and the scent of the sea counterpointing the scent of oleander and bougainvillea, the ambience was Spanish to the core and after the dreary perpetual bloody grey of England, it was like a breath of spiritual fresh air, reviving and intoxicating every fibre of my being. I was on an absolute high...

...But I came tumbling down rapidly when we walked into the club that was to be the second of Stephen's three venues on the island.

In all honesty, it was a very nice bar, with intimate alcoves and a clutter of small tables and stools, and there was a well equipped stage area at the far end with some expensive looking turn-tables and PA gear. The owners made us more than welcome, but with TV screens in four corners blasting out football match mayhem and a column of obtrusive pillars that ran right down the centre of the room, I could see straight away that it was completely the wrong kind of place in which to stage an evening of clairvoyance. For a cabaret act, a rock band, a country group or even a stripper, it was ideal, but for a medium both the layout and the atmosphere were all wrong.

I have to say, and I mean no disrespect to either the venue or the promoter, that I was heartily glad that I hadn't booked Stephen to demonstrate in such an unsuitable place, and I started worrying (a) about how he would cope with it and (b) what the other two venues might be like. One thing was for sure, if he

118

could work here, he could work anywhere, and in its own way it would be just as challenging as The Cochrane Theatre in London.

Ken was confident that Stephen would have a good night, and Stephen himself seemed curiously unperturbed – so I kept my worries and my concerns to myself.

We had an excellent late dinner in a Chinese restaurant and although I'd have preferred to dine Spanish, there wasn't much else open. It was amazing, but by eleven o'clock Puerto de la Cruz seemed to be closing down for the night, whereas in most of the places that were familiar to me from my time in Spain, eleven o'clock was about the time that things started opening and hotting up. I know it was a midweek night in the off season, but even so! Anyway, we all had what was to be the earliest night of the week's tour, and I suppose it did some of us some good.

Trying to condense that week in Tenerife into one concise and readable chapter is something of a literary challenge, so I'll tackle it in two sections, writing first of all about the demonstrations and the venues...

Steve's first outing was at The Gala Hotel in Playa de Las Americas and although that part of the island was, to my eyes, quite horrible, the hotel was really very magnificent, opulent and elegant, with a very good conference centre (which reminded Steve of a posh spiritualist church, complete with midnight blue flock wallpaper and a clear Perspex lectern). It was a sell-out evening, with not a spare seat in sight; about 97% of the audience was made up of ex-pats and holidaymakers, but there were a few Spanish residents, and we speculated as to what might happen should Stephen form a link with a member of this small but most welcome minority. If the messages came through in Spanish, he wouldn't understand a word and, not speaking Spanish, the passing on of any such message would be difficult if not down right impossible. Both Steve and I know mediums who claim to have worked to foreign language audiences using the services of an interpreter, and while Stephen is dubious about the possibility of such a system working, I'm more than dubious!

In any event, we never found out, for although the messages flew thick and fast, they all went to English speaking recipients. It was a solid session of good evidence, and to say that the audience was impressed has got to be something of an understatement. In fact, Stephen made so much of an impression that a high percentage of the audience made the long trek to the North of the island to see Stephen's next demonstration in the Puerto de la Cruz night club two evenings later.

Despite the fact that I had grave misgivings about the second venue, and although Stephen admitted that he was aware of the practical difficulties and wasn't really looking forward to it, he took it in his stride and in fact had a cracking good night. Once he had mastered a temperamental microphone, he soon broke the ice and having won the audience over, he settled down and really enjoyed himself. Perhaps because it was a difficult venue he put in some special effort (although he says not) but either way, some of the evidence was absolutely stunning, not least of which was a link that he forged with a truly marvellous lady called Adelaide Hanrahan. Rather than me telling you about this lovely message, I'm going to present you with the letter Adelaide sent me a few weeks ago, and she can tell the tale in her own words:

"Dear James – I hope you don't mind me contacting you but it's the only way I can send my thanks to Stephen and to tell him of my feelings and thoughts about the evening in Tenerife. My name is Adelaide, and it was a mind-blowing experience for me as I'd never been to such a gathering before. I certainly didn't expect anything to happen to me!

Stephen was reading for a lady across the room from me, on the far side where the book table was... This was about half way through the second part of the night. I'd been so absorbed with all the people who were getting messages, so I was surprised when Stephen excused himself from the lady he was talking to, saying that he had to talk to someone over where I was sitting with my friends. There were three tables all together with nine ladies and three guys, so no one was sure whom Stephen was talking about.

I thought, after he came nearer to our table, that he was looking at my sister-in-law so I moved slightly to one side, turned to her and said 'It's you' but then Stephen pointed directly at me and said 'It's your husband here and he says I've got to talk to you'.

I was just taken aback, then Stephen returned to the stage and asked me to confirm that my husband had passed over – and

120

obviously I said yes, then he said 'Your husband is crying! This guy is really crying!' and I thought Oh My God what is he going to tell me, then Stephen looked across at me and saw my reaction, and assured me that my husband's tears were tears of joy at getting through to me.

Stephen told everyone that my husband said 'she didn't just kiss me on the forehead after I'd died, or on my cheek, but she actually kissed me on my lips and she held me in her arms and hugged me and hugged me!'

Then I grabbed my sister-in-law's hand, as I couldn't believe what I was hearing as no one on God's earth knew that what Stephen was saying was a true fact! Then Eddie (my husband) told Stephen to tell me about the flower that I put in his coffin – he said 'tell her it's wilted so she can have it back!' We all laughed a bit at that, because that's just how Eddie was.

Stephen then mentioned a couple of names, but I could only relate to one, James, who was a neighbour's son. He was only twelve years old when his own dad passed on, so he started looking at Eddie as a father figure. He went on to university, reading physics, and he took Eddie's death very badly indeed because it was like losing two dad's in one lifetime.

The climax was when Stephen said he could hear a Jack Russell dog barking. The three of us on our table cried out in disbelief! They (the dog and Eddie) were together! As I told Eddie during his last week on this earth, he would soon meet up with Whiskey, our Jack Russell and he would be able to take him for walks again – but not too far, as they had to wait for me! Stephen also said that John was with Eddie, John being his older brother who died in 1996... James, while all this was happening I felt as though my body didn't belong to me!

Then Stephen asked me who was Marshall? I took it to be a Christian name, but then he asked who the old lady was who walked with a stick and I realised it was the surname of Marshall, which I knew, but I also knew that the Marshall family was in the audience so I just shook my head, and Stephen went on to talk about the lights in my home, asking if there'd been problems with them flashing on and off, and when I said yes this was true he just laughed and said that it was just Eddie letting me know that he was there.

121

"Then Stephen asked who Marshall was again, and the lady's family took the message and confirmed that she'd walked with a stick. I'd met her on three occasions and she really was a sweet old lady, but sadly I hadn't even realised that she'd passed away a couple of months before. Stephen made reference to February, and February was very special because it had been her 100th birthday. We all knew her as Aunty Dolly and Stephen kept using the name of Molly or Dolly...

PS Sorry for the scrawly writing but I'm waiting to have an operation on my eyes for cataracts so hopefully when I 'see' you next year it will be a clearer vision. PPS. I read and enjoyed your book immensely. It opens up a new world of insight to which most of us refuse to think about. Eddie and I always thought there was more to this life and we always believed that the spirit went on to another plane – one that we can look forward to.

Thank God and peace be with you and yours, Adelaide."

Thank you Adelaide for your letter, your good wishes and your evidence... and I've published the letter pretty well in its entirety, not just because Adelaide has given her own slant on the proceedings of the evening, but also because it reflects a growing mailbag of other letters that keep coming into the Mage office in response to Stephen's demonstrations.

After the evening in the nightclub we had another two days off before tackling our last venue, which was The British Club – a haven for long-term British ex-pats. Like the other two venues the British Club was packed to its rattan rafters and swirling Raffles fans, but the audience was much older and significantly more reserved. Blue rinsed perms rubbed shoulders with starched white shirts and yellow bow ties: there was even one elderly gentleman who boasted a straw boater, spats and a Malacca cane. Posh frocks and plummy voices quaffed copious quantities of gin and tonic and 'dray whate wane', and although as individuals most of them were probably very lovely people, as an audience they were like the kiss of the spider woman, and this was undoubtedly one of Stephen's most difficult demonstrations... ever!

'Worse than Knottingley?' I asked afterwards.

'No James, I keep telling you, nothing could be worse than that night in Knottingley!'

The British Club demonstration got off to a bad start when the club's chairman or MC announced 'Ladies and gentlemen, we have a young man who has come all the way from England to entertain us this evening, so let's have a big round of applause for Stephen Holbrook.'

A somewhat bemused Stephen walked out in front of the audience. 'Er, hello everybody, I don't know what you're expecting but I've got to tell you that I'm not an entertainer, and although I hope you find aspects of this evening entertaining, it certainly isn't an entertainment...'

And now the audience was as baffled as he was, so God alone knew what The British Club had told its members about the evening's proceedings. Certainly no one had bothered to tell the Spanish bar staff that they needed to be quiet, and Steve had to be very firm in his request for a bit of hush. Poor lad, he'd only been on stage for five minutes and things were not going well.

The situation improved marginally when he began to develop his first links. I say marginally, for the audience was very slow to respond to the link energies as they came through. For example, Stephen was going on about a gentleman called Gordon who had died in the last twelve months with multiple strokes, not just one, but two or three all within the space of a day or so, and the date of January 19th would have to be very significant.

A middle aged lady in designer clothes and diamonds claimed the message and confirmed its authenticity, even down to the fact that January 19th had been the date of her husband's funeral, but when Stephen asked her who Mary was, she shook her head and said she didn't know anyone called Mary.

Stephen looked at her with some exasperation. 'You're sure you don't know who Mary is?'

'No, I'm sorry but I don't.'

Other mediums might have passed on at this point... a lot of them do when they keep getting "no's" from the person they're talking to, but Stephen, being Stephen, was loathe to let it go.

'Are you absolutely positive, because this gentleman is yelling in my ear Mary! Mary! Mary! I know what I'm hearing and I know it's got to be right.'

'No, I'm sorry – ' and then the penny, or in this case the peseta or the euro finally dropped with a very loud clink. 'Oh, er, my *Mother's* name is Mary... does that count?'

As Steve said later it was like platting fog or pushing rain up-hill.

Towards the end of the first half he developed a very strong link with a youngish man in his early thirties, who seemed to be in the audience under some sufferance. Nonetheless Steve brought this guy's grandfather through, named him accurately as George, diagnosed his passing through heart failure, got most of the passing date right (April '88) and said that he was sending his love to three people, John, June and Frank. John was the recipient's name and the other two names were the names of his parents. Stephen went on to say that George was well and happy on the other side, and that he was reunited with his faithful Alsatian dog, who's name had been Prince, and who had died only a few weeks after George himself had passed over.

John was able to confirm the accuracy of all this information, apart from the name of the dog. But in the interval he put a long distance call through to his father in the UK who was able to confirm that the dog's name was Prince.

John caught Stephen just before he was about to go on for the second half to pass on the corroborative evidence concerning Prince and also to say that he had been approached by three people during the interval who'd wanted to know whether or not he was a "plant" that Stephen had surreptitiously placed in the audience.

'I'm so sorry, Mr Holbrook,' he said. 'I told them that I wasn't, but I'm not sure whether they believed me.'

Now if there is one thing guaranteed to raise Stephen's ire it is this recurring accusation of there being "plants" in his audiences. It's something he's battled with for most of his working life as a medium, and although he knows (and I know) that it is a totally preposterous idea completely without foundation, it is still a deeply hurtful thing to have to contend with. Stephen takes it very personally and it truly upsets him. 'Hell James, if I go out there and I get it wrong, they say I'm rubbish, but when I go out there and get it right, they accuse me of cheating! Sometimes I just can't win, can I?'

124

Actually, Stephen's bleat is itself without much foundation because (a) this accusation of planting people in the audience does not crop up all that often and (b) very seldom does he get it wrong anyway. Be that as it may be, he was really more than just a bit miffed by the accusation at The British Club – he was downright angry.

To be taken into consideration is the fact that we'd been in Tenerife for almost a week and he was missing his wife and children most acutely – it was the longest they'd ever been separated – and although the week had been a successful one, it had not been without its pitfalls and tensions. To add insult to injury, that particular night he was suffering a bit from having had a touch too much sun, and although not feeling ill or anything, he was uncomfortable in his own body.

I suspect all of these factors combined to push Stephen into starting the second half by telling the audience in no uncertain terms that he did not use "plants" and he did it in such a way that there could be little doubt in the audience's mind about what he thought of them and how deeply offended he was. He didn't lose his temper, but he allowed his anger to be seen, or, as Jo put it – 'He wiped the floor with them!'

It was tough, Stephen later admitted, to slip back into the roll of being a spiritual medium, but he managed it well enough and certainly he seemed to acquire more respect and attention from the crowd in the second part of the evening than he'd got in the first.

I've often seen Stephen looking drained and exhausted after a demonstration, especially after the audience has gone home and he's coming down from the heights of the adrenalin rush, but on that particular evening he was completely wrung out and Jo and I almost had to shovel him into the taxi that took us back to down town Puerto and our favourite restaurant for a late night supper. In many ways he was almost too tired to eat, but in the end his appetite got the better of him and he found a degree of equilibrium by dining lightly on some grilled fish and salad. Normally Steve doesn't eat for five or six hours before a demonstration and therefore he's usually ravenous immediately afterwards. A typical after dinner supper will be a three or four course affair with two or three side dishes, and the fact that he was barely able to get through the swordfish and salad is some indication of just how far gone he was. As ever, he was an amiable companion, but he was subdued, still smarting, I guessed, at the accusation that had been levelled, albeit indirectly, against him. For my own part I was saddened that our wonderful week in Tenerife seemed to be ending on such a low note.

Having said that it is a mark of his spiritual resilience that by the following morning it had all been put behind him and he was back to his usual cheerful self, packing away the presents for his wife and kids and racing around what had become familiar haunts in search of duty free bargains and last minute gifts for other members of his family. After a hectic morning we climbed into the clapped out hire car for the last time and enjoyed a leisurely drive across the island to the airport and our flight home.

Looking back on that week now, with the rain and sleet rattling against the windows of my draughty little cottage, although I remember the demonstrations well enough, the things which stick out in my mind revolve around the social aspects of our visit, and those seven days are a wonderful kaleidoscope of happy fun filled memories...

For example, our frequent visits to a harbourside restaurant called Casa La Miranda, the exquisite and very authentic Spanish food we ate there, the wonderful wines we drank, and Stephen's delight at sampling a proper sangria for the first time. I remember also the very attentive ministrations of our regular waiter called Bernardo (possibly the only Tarot reading camarero in Tenerife) who took an obvious shine to Stephen, and Stephen was very pleased and impressed until Jo tactfully pointed out that Bernardo was obviously gay and that there was undoubtedly an ulterior motive behind the great service that we got. But we *did* get great service and both Bernardo and La Miranda are to be praised and commended.

I wouldn't describe Steve as a gourmet, but he is a man who does love his food and one of the most pleasurable aspects of our working holiday was being able to introduce him to authentic Spanish cuisine rather than the rubbish that is dished out in the tourist trade cafes and fast food bars.

He loved the Spanish lamb, fell in love with tortilla, was amazed by the swordfish and marlin and went into gastronomic

126

delights over the salads, served with tuna, egg, anchovies, feta cheese, fresh asparagus and artichoke hearts. He purred like a cat over paella laden with chicken and king prawns, but drew the line at green octopus and freshly dressed whole squids served with salsa de mariscos.

There was inevitably a downside to all this culinary experimentation, and although he was in hysterics the night I bit into a green jalapeña pepper seed, the tables were turned the following evening when he made exactly the same mistake and had to quaff half a litre of water very quickly to prevent his head from parting company with the rest of his body. His already suntanned face turned five shades darker to deep crimson, and poor Jo took the brunt of it through ordering the peppers in the first place.

The other thing that gets you is, of course, the Spanish booze, and while Steve will enjoy an occasional glass of red wine he is by no means a heavy drinker. As I've already said, he acquired a taste for sangria, which can be fairly innocuous in its watered down tourist trap form, but can be absolutely lethal when you're dealing with the real McCoy.

Sangria recipes vary depending on the region, but it all revolves around a mixture of red wine, lemonade and fresh fruit. It is in the addition of the spirits and liqueurs that the distinctive flavours emerge and, of course, the levels of potency. A typical sangria will contain vodka, cointreau, (sometimes also brandy) and a unique Spanish liqueur called "43" which is concocted from fermented bananas and oranges. The only time in my life that I've been really paralytic was on a Christmas sangria binge many years ago on the island of Majorca, and I ended up trying to make love to a telegraph pole and rolling a hundred metres down the Playa de Palma in a big rubber dustbin – but that's another story for another book that will probably never get written and no one would believe a word of it even if it did!

Anyway, Steve got into the sangria with thirst and enthusiasm and because he couldn't identify all of the flavours, he tried a neat "43" on the rocks and then, because I couldn't finish it all, he grudgingly polished off a glass of my Rioja (which I admit, I did force on him). We finished our dinner with carajillos – thick espresso coffee laced with Spanish brandy – and staggered back up the hill to our apartments, very merry, but quite coherent. *Then* because it was such a beautiful night with Mount Teide glistening in the moonlit distance, we sat on our balcony and had stiff Stolichnaya vodkas with peach juice as a nightcap.

Steve turned in around one, and then woke up again at three o'clock in the morning realising that he was very drunk. Jo calls it the swirly pit syndrome, I call it an attack of the kamikazes and Steve calls it feeling just plain wretched. His home cure is to drink a litre of water and then to try sleeping with one leg out of the bed, foot on the floor – which seems to have worked for although he had a sorrowful morning and only managed to jog half a mile rather than his usual two or three miles, he was more or less back to normal by lunchtime – which is more than I can say for myself!

I have a delicious memory of Stephen sitting on a rock by the harbour on our first morning's exploration. The sun was shining brilliantly, baking all beneath its rays at a steady eighty degrees. None of us saw the huge wave breaking over the rocks and the first Steve knew about it was when five gallons of freezing cold sea water crashed into the middle of his sun warmed back. Jo and I (who remained perfectly dry) fell about laughing, not so much at what had happened, but at Steve's reaction to it. The look of astonishment and horror was a miracle to behold and although I am totally dedicated to my SLR and rangefinder camera systems I'd have swapped them willingly in that moment for a cine or a video camera that would have enabled me to capture that sequence of events, expletives and facial expressions. I did get one shot with the SLR of Stephen on his rock and was in the process of changing films when the rogue wave struck, so I guess it's a classic photographic version of the one that got away.

Another wonderful tale to tell concerns Stephen's remedy for sunburn.

It wasn't so much that he'd run out of after-sun, but more a case that there was a large pot of bio-yoghurt going to waste in the corner of his fridge... Stripping down to his swimming trunks, he liberally applied the aforementioned yoghurt all over his arms, legs, face and torso, and because there was a bit left he rubbed it into his scalp, which made his hair stand on end in more ways than one. He then caught sight of himself in the mirror and got the giggles as the rapidly drying yoghurt flaked and clung to his skin like wild Watussi war paint.

Being a wee bit of a practical joker, he pulled a small towel around his waist, slipped out into the corridor and rang on our apartment bell... I was dead to the world in the middle of a siesta, so Jo opened the door to find this mad masculine apparition standing before her. Her shriek of surprise and laughter hardly stirred me from my afternoon dreams, but Jo thought it was a fine old joke. Unfortunately, the two little old ladies who were walking down the corridor at the time did not.

Mount Teide, a volcano still disturbingly on the active list, dominates the island of Tenerife, and if you don't do anything else on the island, you really should take a drive into the hinterland and go up the mountain. It may take you half a day, but even with the tourists, it's half a day well spent. The views are magnificent and the air is so crystal clear it makes you wonder how we manage to survive living amid the smog and pollution that contaminates our ground level existence.

Steve and Jo declined the (very safe) cable car ride that hauls you up the last three thousand feet to the crater, but we all appreciated the stunning scenery and Steve marvelled at how you could be freezing cold (seven thousand feet above sea level) and yet still feel warm and catch the best tan in the world from the sun which belted down out of a cloudless blue sky.

A couple of miles beyond the cable car station is one of Spain's marvellous paradores and half a mile to the east of that there is a staggering rock formation called Las Roquetas. Huge monolithic stalagmite shapes of ancient lava, each weighing thousands of tons, force their skeletal fingers skywards in tortured supplication to unknown gods – almost like a Spanish Stonehenge, but one raised by the hands of heaven rather than by the hands of men.

The visual impact of the place is quite awesome, its spiritual vibration of age and tranquillity more insidiously subtle. It is a landscape photographer's dream come true, so while Steve busied himself scrambling around boulders and Jo wandered off to explore the far side of the site, out came my camera and for a while we all did our own thing.

Time passed and I was on my third roll of Fuji. I bumped into Steve coming down from the crag, and together we set about looking for Jo – except that Jo was not to be found. We wandered around the rocks, even drove the half-mile back to the parador in case we'd missed her, but still there was no sign. After about forty minutes I was beginning to get, well, not exactly worried, but certainly a bit fretful.

'Where the blazes can she be?' I asked, not particularly addressing Steve, although he was well within earshot, but more talking out loud to myself.

Steve obviously heard the question and without thinking what he was saying, he replied 'Dunno James, but she must be still alive somewhere otherwise she'd be on the phone by now for a conversation!'

We both had a chuckle at that, and if nothing else it did do something to break the little cord of tension that was beginning to build up inside.

Jo rolled up five minutes later, serenely and dreamily, after having gone Aboriginal walkabouts on the far side of the hill. She'd been caught up in the ethereality and timelessness of the silence that prevailed once she was off the beaten track and her own time-space continuum had become distorted.... At least, that was what she said, but I guess that what really happened was that she'd got caught up in her own little world and forgot that Steve and I existed for a while.

Mount Teide gave us all many treasured memories and for me, if you'll pardon the pun, our expedition up the mountain was definitely one of the high points of our week in Tenerife.

CHAPTER SIXTEEN

Premonition & Prophecy

It was our last day in Tenerife. I'd gone down to the harbour with my cameras whilst Jo and Steve were tidying up some business details with Ken Fisher at his bookshop. They'd just stepped out of the shop, discussing the itinerary of our homeward journey, when Steve suddenly paused mid-sentence, cocked his head to one side, and stared with unfocused eyes into the middle distance.

'Jo,' he said. 'I'm getting this really strong feeling that there's going to be a death in the royal family, and very very soon!'

'Do you think it might be the Queen Mother,' Jo asked, not in the least perturbed by this sudden shift in the conversation. After living with me for ten years and having been associated with Stephen for two, she's used to this sort of thing.

'No, not the Queen Mum… not just yet. She'll go a bit later on with the daffodils. It's someone else, but I know it'll be a senior royal, and not just someone on the edges.'

'So what are you saying, that there'll be two royal passings within the next few months?'

'Yes, that's what it feels like and I'm sure I'm right, although I hope to goodness that I'm wrong.'

But, of course, he wasn't wrong, for within the next few days Princess Margaret passed over and two months later, as the spring daffodils were blooming their hearts out (and most curiously, just as we were coming out of a bookshop) we learned that Queen Elizabeth, The Queen Mother, had passed over to join her daughter.

Stephen does not have that many premonitions, but when he does, they seem to be the portent of great things. Like a lot of people, myself included, Stephen has had a number of premonitions which have been invalidated because they have not been confided to a third party before the event, and it's easy to sneer when someone says "I knew that was going to happen" *after* the event. Jo was with him on the 4th of February 2002 when he spoke of the royal deaths and will bear testimony to his prophecy.

Another premonition Stephen had, this one shared by many psychics across the world, began to filter into his consciousness on September 9th 2001.

Stephen recalls: 'I woke up in the early hours of Sunday morning, I don't know what time it was but it was still dark, and I was in a hot sweat... I don't know whether I'd been dreaming or not, but I had this awful impression of some sort of terrorist attack coming down, and it had something to do with the word "center" but I couldn't understand the spelling of the word because it should have been "centre". Anyway I had a drink, then dozed off again.

'The following evening, and this would have been Monday the 10th at about half past eleven, I was just dozing off in bed. Caroline was glancing through a magazine, talking about plans for her birthday on the 13th and trying to figure out how we could work it in with my demonstration at Morley, and this dreadful sick feeling came over me and I told Caroline that I thought something very bad was about to happen that would make massive headlines and that it had something to do with this word "center" – Caroline wondered if it might be something to do with the IRA planting a bomb on the central line in the London underground, but I just didn't know.

'Anyway, the next day, September 11th, I was around at Jane McDonald's house, cutting her hair, and she was showing me the video of her performance in Las Vegas. We were talking about America and all of a sudden my left arm went cold and stiff, just like it does when I'm about to start demonstrating. We were both a bit bemused by this and noted the time as being 12.55 pm. Anyway, I couldn't dawdle because I had a telephone interview scheduled with Radio Sheffield for 2.15. We were only a few minutes into the interview when I was cut off mid-sentence by an urgent bulletin to say that an aircraft had crashed in New York... I was kept hanging around and I could hear all the pandemonium going on in the background and in the end I phoned the radio station on my mobile and asked them to let me go. Just as I'd done that, Caroline started shouting up the stairs telling me to come down QUICKLY! I wondered what the hell was wrong until I walked into our living room and saw the TV screen...

there was this burning tower block with the words "World Trade Center" flashing across the bottom, and the newsreader was going on about both towers being taken out by terrorists who had hi-jacked these planes. I focused on that one word "Center" and I just sat down in a state of shock. That same sick feeling was with me again, but it was twenty times worse than before as I realised the significance of what I'd been picking up on a psychic level for two days before that horrible attack took place.'

Stephen is far from unique in his ability to experience premonitions. It is a gift that most of us have on one level or another, although true to say, most of us experience in minor ways. We find ourselves thinking of an old friend whom we haven't heard from for ages and, lo and behold, there's a letter in the post the following week. Or the phone goes and automatically we know who's on the other end of the line even before they draw breath to speak. We feel "uneasy" about some of the people we meet, and although they may be all "hail fellow and well met" we sense in some way that they are not to be trusted and (if we trust our senses) we keep our distance.

We experience sequences of events that put us on our guard about the outcome of a given venture or idea, and I am reminded of a recent situation involving two good friends who were planning a long weekend in Madrid. Nothing went right from the beginning... first of all the bookings got muddled up, then the flight had to be cancelled and re-arranged, and then at the last minute the plane had to be re-routed via Amsterdam. As my friend said "it was almost as though something was trying to tell us not to go and that we'd be better off cancelling the whole thing!" However, they persevered and had a miserable weekend in appalling weather and ended up being robbed by a couple of pick-pockets who got away with a wallet full of credit cards and all of their holiday cash!

It is when we put our premonition into words that it becomes a prophecy but here the concept divides into two distinct streams of meaning. If I prophesy that it will take me twenty minutes to get to the railway station from my home it is either based on foreknowledge born of experience, or an estimate gleaned from studying a road map. If I prophesy that the Houses of Parliament will burn to the ground some time within the next twelve months, then this prophecy knowledge must come from some different source entirely, given that I don't know anybody called Fawkes and have no plans of my own to go playing with matches. Should Parliament burn, then strike one for Christie's prophecy, but should Parliament *not* burn, well the silly old duffer has got it wrong again.

But assume, just for a moment, that there *is* a fire in The Houses of Parliament... this now begs askance of a key question, namely, where did the information come from?

Stephen would be the first to tell you that his premonitions do not come directly from spirit. There is no discarnate entity whispering "Trade Center" in his ear and from what I can glean, he and I work from the same vibration when it comes to prophecy, insofar as we feel and sense something that wells up from our subconscious: we do not get the whole picture but only the vague shape, sometimes like a jigsaw with two thirds of the pieces missing, putting us at task to guess the rest.

Steve's premonition with regard to September 11th was far from complete, but he did hit on some key aspects. A terrorist attack that would make massive world headlines involving the word "center". His arm went stiff at 12.55 pm on the 11th which, if you work out the time differential, was just about the time that the first aircraft struck its unprotected and unsuspecting target... Had he remained silent on these matters, only claiming precognition after the event, then he would be exposing himself to all manner of ridicule, but as it is, he has me, Jane McDonald and his wife Caroline who can confirm his claim. We may not be totally dispassionate or uninterested witnesses, but we do exist!

The concept of prophecy and premonition is as old as language (and probably older than that if the truth be known) and history has given us some classical prophets ranging from Old Testament archetypes to Cassandra and Nostradamus, Mother Shipton to modernists like Hubbard and Crowley, but if you asked any of the aforementioned where their premonitions and prophecies actually came from, they'd be as hard pressed to tell you as we are.

For my own part I could say that much of my own prophecy comes from dreams, but that doesn't tell you (or me) where the dream comes from or what provokes the dream. One could say that the dream reflects one's own subconscious awareness, but there is no true clarity in such an answer and indeed, the answer provokes even more questions.

Man has always sought to see into his future and fortunetellers still flourish in response to this need within the human psyche. However if one is to cast a spread of Tarot or construct a birthchart the whole process is premeditated and a premeditated prediction is not the same as a natural premonition.

We are not splitting hairs in defining the difference between prophecy and premonition for clearly there *is* a difference – although to be sure, we are treading a fine line, and it is a line that is even finer when we consider the difference between prophecy and prediction. The difference stems from the source. As we have said, Tarot cards and birthcharts etc. can offer both prediction *and* prophecy but if premonition emanates from a *different* source, one that is intangible, an extra sensory perception locked away in the psyche and sensitivity of the individual (who may have absolutely no knowledge at all about the Tarot or astrology or any of the other divinational disciplines) then we must consider the very nature of that source.

To attain a glimmering of understanding as to how it might work, we need to look very closely at the concept of time. Most mediums, including Stephen, will confirm that time does not work quite the same way on the spiritual planes as it does down here on a temporal level, and as any psychic will tell you (if they are going to tell you the truth) getting the "what" of something right is far easier than getting the "when" of that something right – and so much so that many psychics I know will leave the "when" completely out of the equation!

In support of this we must never forget that (a) time is subjective to an individual's experience of it and that (b) the measurement of time is very much a man made invention. There might be an atomic clock in Greenwich which can measure the passage of time in nanoseconds, but you try telling that clock that five minutes in the dentist's chair is the same as five minutes of making love, or that the second week of a marvellous holiday lasts as long as the first week, and I dare say the clock would boing a spring in – well, in a nanosecond!

One can measure the passing of a year by the seasons and the phases of the moon, but we must ask, are there *always* twenty four hours in a day or seven days in one week? Not if we measure time subjectively, there aren't!

We conceptualise time as being linear – the past runs into the present, and the present, with its passing, becomes both the past and the future. However if we could look at time in a non-linear way, seeing it as layered rather than lined, might it then not be possible to get an occasional glimpse through the curtain?

This concept borders on science fiction but it is not only sci-fi writers who have had a field day with this subject, and some very serious minds such as Levi, Blavatsky, Neitche and Jung – and more recently our own Colin Wilson and Keith Ellis – have all postulated the possibility of seeing *through* and even metaphysically travelling through time. It was something that Albert Einstein thought he could prove by mathematic theory and he went to his grave trying. It may sound preposterous, but actually it is not a difficult theory to accept if we can refocus our perceptions of how time works.

If, just for one moment, we can accept the possibility of being able, just occasionally, to get a glimpse through the curtain (either consciously or subconsciously) it gives a credible explanation for the whole concept of premonition, déjà vu, and the phenomenon of the precognitive dream...

...And the dream must be seen as a particularly potent vehicle for premonition for while we are asleep our conscious minds are off the hook and the subconscious is very much in control – and Man knows more about the far reaches of outer space than he knows about the deeper, inner workings of the human mind.

Anyone working in the fields of the paranormal, especially if they are actively psychic or clairvoyant, must, I believe, be automatically more in tune with the subconscious than the rest of us. So it follows that someone like Stephen Holbrook will find it easier to get that occasional glimpse through the veil of time, even if he does not consciously go looking for it.

On the surface this appears to give credence to the belief that our lives are all mapped out in a pre-destined future and that therefore there is no point in trying to change anything if we are bound to an inevitable outcome, dictated by a fate and destiny over which we have no control. And yet there is ample evidence to suggest that this is *not* the case at all, and that we are able to exercise control through the simple mechanism of choice.

Consider this:

Sometime towards the end of 1987 I had a particularly vivid and horrendous dream. In this dream I was hovering about the smouldering wreck of a medium sized blue car. There were flames and smoke filtering out from beneath the crumpled bonnet, and lying amid shards of glass and twisted steel, there were three very broken and bloodstained bodies. All around me there were tall pine trees, and above the pines a canvas of midnight blue skies with a million stars twinkling in the heavens. I had no idea where I was and yet at the same time this little glade so full of death and carnage was strangely familiar. I levitated upwards towards the stars through the canopy of trees and realised that I was dead – that I'd been killed in the crash – and I was assailed by the most incredible feeling of sadness, so much so that I woke from the dream with tears streaming down my face.

This dream changed my life in two ways.

First of all, at that time, I was going through a very painful and unhappy chapter in my life and I'd more or less come to the conclusion that life was really not worth living. The dream gave me a massive kick in the seat of my pants and made me realise that life itself is worth the effort of living. From that day on I started fighting back against the clouds of nihilistic negativity that had been my constant companions for such a long time.

And I suppose I thought no more about the dream than that. I didn't own and had never owned a blue car and nor did I know anyone who did. I didn't recognise the location of the accident as any place that I knew, and although I "knew" the victims of the accident in my dream state I had no idea at all who they were in real life. The dream was extremely vivid and detailed and I certainly never forgot it, but was content to write it off as a "message" dream that said "come on lad, you're not dead yet, so get on with your life" – or some words to that effect.

Half a year later I'd packed all my worldly goods into the back of a twenty year old series three Land Rover and with just four hundred quid in my pocket I left England to find a new life in Spain. About a year after that, a good eighteen months after having had the dream, I was walking home from a late night party in a neighbouring village. I was very tired and weary and although I wasn't drunk (well, not by Spanish standards) I'd had far too much to drink. Even so, I'd still have driven myself home in the trusty old Land Rover but for a flat battery and no one around to give me a friendly push start at two o'clock in the morning.

I'd been walking for a good hour and was about half way between San Pablo and Jimena de la Frontera when a Ford Escort with English plates went hurtling past like the proverbial bat out of hell. The break lights came on and there was a squeal of skidding rubber, and then the car backed up to where I was walking. There were three English friends in the car and of course they threw open the back door and offered me a lift home. I was absolutely shattered and gratefully made to climb in and claim half of the back seat – then all of a sudden, a part of me was out of myself and the memory of the dream came flooding back. I couldn't define the colour of this car in the darkness but the car was well known around the villages (not many Escort XR3i's in Southern Andalucia) and I knew it to be bright blue.

Anyway, although I felt very stupid and foolish, I chose not to get into the car after all, saying that I'd had too much to drink and that it would be better for my head (and possibly the carpet and the upholstery of the car) if I walked back to Jimena. I admonished my friends to drive carefully, or better yet, park the car up and walk home with me – but Jimena was another five miles down the mountain and they thought I was nuts. The XR3 vroomed off down the road leaving me staring after it and wondering if I'd ever see my three friends alive again.

I didn't.

An hour later I came to the last bend in the road before the village, and there with the Guardia Civil crash truck in attendance, were the smouldering remains of the car. Looking down from where it had gone off the road, I was elevated above the scene, just as I'd been in the dream, and it looked as though the Guardia Civil had beaten me to it by only a few minutes, for there were the three broken bodies amid the wreckage just as I'd seen them eighteen months before. I hadn't known them then, but I knew them now, and although I'd driven past this glade in the pine forest at least a dozen times, I'd never recognised it as my dreamscape until that moment.

For quite a long time afterwards I felt a deep sense of remorse and guilt, berating myself for not having done more to stop them driving on down the mountain... But I wasn't sure of myself, I was acting on instinct and intuition, and if I'd said "look guys, I had this dream a year and a half ago about a car crash involving a blue vehicle and I really must insist you get out and walk to avert a disaster" then knowing that particular trio, they'd have thought I was drunker than they were – and, of course, had they got down the mountain in one piece after all, the story about this latest incident involving *el bruho canto* would be all over the village, and I was already living down the difficult reputation of being the mad English mystic and I was not eager to add fuel to the flames.

I do not think there is anything that I could have done to prevent the accident from occurring (short of throwing myself in front of the wheels of the car, that is) but I am acutely aware of the fact that my precognitive dream certainly saved my life that night. I believe that in my unconscious state my *subconscious* moved through a couple of layers of time and 'saw' one possible outcome of the journey from San Pablo to Jimena, and as one time stream caught up with the other (or vice versa) the subconscious connected immediately with the conscious and I had my warning by the roadside. A warning, thank God, that I listened to and exercised my choice of free will.

If Steve Holbrook had phoned the police on the night of 10th September and had said "look fellers, I've got a funny feeling there's going to be some sort of terrorist attack on some sort of centre that is spelt the American way, you know, c.e.n.t.e.r...." I wonder what the desk sergeant might have written in his report book and, whatever he wrote, it would not have altered anything that happened in New York on September 11th.

Whole books have been written on the subject of metaphysical time displacement and even more books have been written on the subjects of premonition and prophecy, so in this short section all we can do is draw some of the disparate threads together to reach a realistic and acceptable conclusion.

I take it as proven that Man *does* get occasional visions of the future and that by definition, when this phenomenon occurs he is looking through a window in time to a possible evolutionary projection of his present. In the case of personal premonitions

139

one can exercise choice (do I get into the car or don't I?) but in the case of non-personal premonitions the only choice is do we give voice to them or not. Ergo, some things can be averted (situations where we have the personal choice) while others cannot.

The ethos of spiritualism is not dominant here (for anyone of any faith can experience premonitions and make prophecies on the strength of them, should they so choose) but anyone travelling a spiritual or psychic pathway is more likely to make contact with precognitive energies than someone who is completely closed down and shut off from their own subconscious.

Stephen always has a choice to make. Does he give voice to his premonitions and risk ridicule if he is wrong, or does he remain silent and suffer remorse when things occur as he has seen them, frequently to the detriment and cost of other people? It is an awkward choice for on the one hand he does not set out his stall as either a seer or a prophet but on the other hand he simply cannot ignore the information he acquires through this process of channelling. On the public platform, for example, *he* will not give out predictions for the sake of gratifying himself with an eager audience, but if spirit is telling someone on the fifth row that they're going to be pregnant within the next eighteen months, Steve is duty bound to pass the message on, for he cannot and will not act as censor in this respect.

Over the years Stephen has found some safe and sensible middle ground insofar as he will not court public acclaim or condemnation by phoning The Daily Mirror every time he gets a premonition about something, but he *will* confide in a very tight circle of family and close friends who will act both as witnesses and judges to the veracity of his prophecies. I consider myself honoured to be part of this circle and I am more than happy to bare witness with regard to his uncanny accuracy in predicting the royal deaths and also to the salient facts concerning September 11th.

I make special reference to these two events because they were both world events that had international impact. However there are dozens of other incidents I could list, all of which are parochial and personal to private individuals. In themselves they may not be life changing issues '…James, you're going to change your car soon – Jo, you won't really do much with your college

140

education because you'll be too busy helping James – No, Pat, that isn't the right house for you because you're going to live in a street named after a tree with a stream at the bottom of the garden...' But put it all together and you begin to get a very clear picture of a man who does have an extraordinary gift of prophecy, even though he does not use it in public or for any personal gain.

Some people, our sceptics perhaps, may scoff at all of this, but as a litmus test of how seriously he is taken in certain quarters, in response to a request from a major regional police force, Stephen is currently using his psychic skills to help solve a particularly nasty murder case that has had the police baffled for many months. As the whole thing is sub justice, no more can be said about the matter at this moment in time, but this is not the first occasion and nor, I suspect, will it be the last that a clairvoyant manages to crack the case for our boys in blue. What I *can* tell you is that the police didn't just say to themselves "Right lads, we're stumped, so let's have a look through Yellow Pages and see if there's a good clairvoyant in the area!"

Stephen was very carefully vetted. On three occasions police officers attended his demonstrations incognito and a number of people who received messages from Stephen at those demonstrations were discretely interviewed afterwards to ascertain the veracity of the information they had been given. It was only after this that Stephen was quietly approached by the Chief Constable of the regional crime squad concerned.

This degree of recognition and accreditation indicates that some serious thought is now being given by certain sections of the establishment to the potency and possible usefulness of clairvoyance. There is a long way to go before the concept is accepted openly into society in general and even further to go before the scientific fraternity begins to accept the existence of something it cannot see, measure, touch, feel or quantify – but at least, thanks to people like Stephen Holbrook, the process has started and a small snowball has begun to roll downwards from the top of the mountain.

CHAPTER SEVENTEEN

Cassie Lomax

Professor Cyril Lomax did not believe in life after death, nor did he believe in God, Jesus Christ, or any form of religion and as far as he was concerned "spirit" and "spirituality" were nothing more than symptoms of the human psychological condition. As a scientist, specialising in physics and aerodynamics, he believed entirely in that which could be seen, qualified, quantified and measured. As an advanced mathematician he admitted to a certain spiritual beauty in numbers and he was also aware, perhaps more so than most through being able to view it with some detached scientific objectivity, of the intense physical beauty of Planet Earth; he could be as moved as the rest of us by a beautiful sunset, a tranquil ocean, a range of high mountains and a golden dawn. He also saw beauty in family and the family ideal, and if there was any merit at all in the life after death theory it came only in the form of the continuation of bloodlines born as a result of progeny. He readily accepted that after his death his genes would carry on in the DNA of his sons and daughter. But as far as any spiritual life form continuum was concerned, this was unproven and unprovable, therefore unreasonable, intangible and, by definition, non-existent.

Born on the 9th of September 1930 of essentially middle class family stock, it didn't take long for his teachers to realise that they had something of a boy genius on their hands, especially when it came to maths and science. He won a scholarship to attend his local grammar school and earned another scholarship that got him into Cambridge. By the time he'd finished his university education he'd acquired a formidable reputation as a mathematician and physicist par excellence.

At the relatively early age of twenty one he met and married Mary Cartwright and in 1954 Mary gave birth to twin sons who were promptly named Robin and Jeremy. At this time Cyril was a senior aerodynamical engineer for BOAC (The British Overseas Airways Corporation) and it was he more than anyone else who discovered that the cause of so many of the infamous BOAC air crash disasters in the 1950's was precipitated by metal fatigue around the square windows of these still relatively new high flying jet airliners. A conversion to rounded windows solved the problem almost overnight, and although someone else got most of the credit, it was Cyril Lomax's team that had come up with the solution.

Twenty years later (Cyril was now with British Aerospace working on the Concorde project) Mary Lomax surprised everyone, not least her husband, by falling pregnant again and on 15th October 1974 Caroline Lomax (never to be called Caroline but always Cassie) entered the world with a cry of joy and exultation that reverberated along the walls of the Cambridge Royal Hospital.

Cassie did nothing to change Cyril's spiritual beliefs (or in this case, his lack of them) but she did melt his heart and a very strong father/daughter bond existed almost from day one.

In June of 1985 Mary Lomax was tragically killed in a road traffic accident and as by then both Robin and Jeremy had married and left England for, respectively, Canada and New Zealand, the full weight of fatherhood fell fairly and squarely on Cyril Lomax's shoulders – and the way that Cassie tells it, he did a damn fine job.

'My Mother died when I was still only eleven,' she narrates, 'and although I missed her terribly, Daddy was there to plug the gaps and he did all that he could to fill the void. I loved my mother very much, but I suppose I was always a Daddy's girl, and although it isn't an easy thing to admit, I loved him more. It would have been too awful to contemplate if, for example, things had happened the other way round – if, say, Daddy had been killed and it had been left to my Mother to bring me up. She was always a bit dippy, into her CND activities and avant-garde poetry; I suppose you could say that Mummy was one of the world's original hippies a good ten years before the term was invented by the media.

'Anyway, Daddy saw to it that I got a good education and right through all of my school years he was always there for me. We played chess together, had lovely long walks in the summer that always ended in a picnic somewhere nice down by the River Cam... We went to theatres and cinemas, had lovely long holidays in Wellington and Vancouver whenever Daddy could

143

take the time off work and although he was a dreadful workaholic, sometimes putting in eighteen hour days, especially when I was a bit older and was away at college, he did take time out to make sure that family links were maintained with Rob and Jerry.

'I remember we talked about politics, sex, art, drama and just about every subject under the sun and I seem to remember the only thing we didn't talk about was faith and religion or anything to do with spiritualism...' On my tape Cassie Lomax laughs liltingly. 'In fact I don't think my father would have even known that there is an organised religion of spiritualists, and if he did he would have pooh poohed the notion out of hand.'

'What about you?' I asked. 'I mean, given the absence of any kind of family background, where does your own interest in spiritualism come from?'

'Oh that didn't happen until much later on, long after daddy died, in fact.'

'Okay,' I prompted, 'tell me more about your father.'

'Well, we were coming back from Vancouver – this would have been back in 1994, I was just 21 and was half way through my third year at Oxford. We'd just celebrated Daddy's 64th birthday in Canada – he was coming up for retirement, but was fighting the idea all the way down the line. "I'm perfectly healthy," he would say "fit as a flea and strong as an ox, my mind's as bright as ever it was and I'm good for another twenty years yet!" – But the only thing is, he was looking his age by then, and to our eyes he was becoming a little bit tired and frail. Nothing to worry about, perhaps, but certainly something we'd all noticed and were all aware of.

'Anyway, as I say, we were flying back from Vancouver when Daddy started feeling ill, and by the time we landed at Heathrow he was only half conscious, slurring his words and unable to keep upright in his seat. There was an ambulance waiting when we landed that took us straight to Staines Hospital, and it transpired that daddy had had a stroke... The doctor was extremely kind and told me not to worry because they didn't think it was a big stroke and that with lots of care and rest, everything should be all right. That was in September. We got Daddy home by the middle of October, but he had another stroke on December 1st and this led to a heart attack on December 4th.

144

He was very very poorly throughout the whole of December and I was told that he wouldn't last through Christmas.

'I spent most of that time sitting with him on the edge of his bed. He slept a lot of the time, but he did have lucid moments of consciousness and in those times I would read to him and talk to him and tell him everything that was going on in the world... I remember, there was this one afternoon, just before he passed over, that I got very emotional and I said to him "Daddy, promise that you'll come back and visit me from Heaven when you get to the other side" and I remember so clearly what he said... he said "Listen darling, there isn't any heaven and there isn't any other side, but that's fine because I've had a wonderful life and you've been a wonderful daughter and I hope that if you have children of your own they will love you as much as you have loved me..."'

Thirty six hours later Cyril Lomax died in his daughter's arms. Cassie told me that she wept for quite a while before getting up from the bedside, and that before leaving the room, she leaned over her father and gave him three small kisses – one on his forehead, one on his cheek, and one on the end of his nose. This third kiss, Cassie tells me, was the important one because over the years she'd got into the habit of kissing her father's nose: it was a very large nose and Cyril was always a bit self conscious about it and it was Cassie's way of telling her father that "Big noses are cool, Daddy!"

Cassie married Malcolm Dowell in 1996 and in 1998 gave birth to a lovely little girl who was Christened Emily Jane. Sadly, Emily died in 1999 through what is commonly known as cot death syndrome and Cassie separated from her husband in 2000. It was at this point in time that she started to get interested in spiritualism, an interest that was intensified when she was taken to see medium Stephen O'Brien. When she saw that our Stephen, Stephen Holbrook, was visiting Cambridge in 2001, she immediately booked a seat for his demonstration at The Royal Cambridge Hotel.

Cassie: 'After Emily died I just seemed to lose my way in life. Nothing seemed to matter very much any more, not even Malcolm, and though he tried hard to bring me round, it simply wasn't there any more. Malcolm got a rotten deal out of me and

I'm really sorry about that, but there wasn't anything much I could do about it at the time.

'My friend Barbara is mad keen about the whole clairvoyancy thing so I let her drag me along to see Stephen O'Brien. I didn't expect to get anything out of it, but I was so desperate for *something* that I went along with a reasonably open mind.'

'So what did you think?' I asked, eager to learn what Cassie Lomax had thought of the O'Brien experience.

'I was really quite impressed. He comes over as a sincere and genuine gentleman, although I could have done without all the smoke and special lighting effects. I didn't get a message, of course, but I was sat next to a couple of people who did, and I suppose this was enough to start opening a few doors for me, so when Barbara suggested we go and see your Stephen in Cambridge, I was all for it. To tell you the truth I didn't realise it was a different Stephen till we got there and he walked out onto the stage.'

'How did you feel when he came to you with a message?' I asked.

Cassie smiled. 'I couldn't take it in really, not at first. He said he wanted to talk to me, the lady wearing the brown jumper, who knew something about May 19th and a little girl who'd gone over to the spirit world before her time. Well, I knew I was wearing a brown jumper and that Emily had died on 19th May and, my God, it *was* well before her time, but I still couldn't quite click that the message was actually for me. In the end Barbara put her hand up and Stephen found me through her. He asked if he could talk to me and I said yes, although I suppose it came out a bit like a muffled croak...

'Anyway, he said he had a little girl with him who had died when she was less than one year old and that she was drawing him a big letter E wrapped in a big love heart. He said that she had passed over in her sleep – which she did – and that she had lots of freckles – which she had. He said that September 2nd was important, which it was because that was Emily's birthday. He said that I had lots of overseas links, which obviously I had with Rob and Jerry, and he said that Canada was important to me because that was the last place that I'd been where I was truly happy. I had to think about that one for a while, but he wasn't

146

far wrong. He also asked me who Malcolm was and I told him that he was my husband.

'Then he said he had a gentleman with him who was very surprised to be talking to me through a medium and that he was just as surprised to find me in a place like this. He mentioned the initial letter C, which was obviously my father, and said that he hadn't thought he would die in the way in which he did and that it would have been better for everybody if he could have died while he was still up in the air – and did this mean anything to me? Well, it wasn't too difficult to work out what Daddy was saying, and I suppose from his point of view, it would have been better if he could have just fallen asleep with that first stroke on the flight back from Vancouver... that was so typical of Daddy. He absolutely hated being the cause of any kind of fuss.

'Anyway, Stephen actually told me that the gentleman he had with him was saying that he hadn't believed in life after death and that nobody was more surprised than he was to be proven wrong. Stephen told me that I'd sat with Daddy while he was dying and that after he'd passed over I'd kissed him three times, once on the forehead, and once on his cheek and once on the end of his nose. He even said that Daddy had a thing about the size of his nose, which of course, he did, all through his life. He gave me the number 23, which was right because daddy had died on 23rd December and he also said that September 9th was an important date, which it was because that was Daddy's birthday.

'Stephen also went on about wings and how the wings were so important for some reason. At first I thought he was talking about Paul McCartney and his band, and then I twigged what he was going on about because daddy had spent most of his life working with aeroplane wings and their design, so that had to be it. He also said that the last two years had been fairly awful for me, which they have been, believe me, but from that night onwards, things would start to get better. I've got some apologies to make and some humble pie to eat and a lot of ground to make up.'

'Did this make any sense to you?'

'Not right then, no, not really, but over the next few days I began to realise what he was talking about – and I'm meeting Malcolm for a drink on Saturday night.

147

'I suppose,' Cassie paused, floundering and fishing for the right words, 'I suppose the most important thing Stephen said to me that really turned things around in my head, was that the little girl who'd passed away while she was still so very young, was with my father and that he was looking after her, just the way he'd always tried to look after me. That's when I started crying – I just couldn't stop myself – and that's when I knew, absolutely *knew* that one day I'm going to be with Daddy and Emily again.'

Stephen Holbrook's evidence for Cassie Lomax and Cassie's unequivocal corroboration of that evidence is, I believe, vitally important for one single salient point.

Cyril Lomax was an agnostic sceptic who did not believe in any kind of post mortem survival other than through the progeny of DNA, and yet his spirit manages to find its way to a cramped hotel theatre in a provincial English city to admit that he was wrong and to provide hard factual evidence to prove that this is indeed the spirit of the said Professor Cyril Lomax, deceased. He backs this up with names, dates, times, places, which by necessity are meaningless to the medium, but which are poignantly meaningful to the recipient of the medium's message.

Extrapolate this line of thought and one arrives at a rather delicious conclusion.

It seems fairly obvious that even those sceptics, atheists and agnostics who have no belief in a spiritual afterlife are in for one very big surprise when they wake up from Death to a new life on the other side of their old lives left behind.

The Promoter's Tale

From Jo James-Yorke

*In his first biography, James uses the analogy of 'an onion' to
describe the process of getting to know Stephen; as each layer is
exposed yet another presents itself. He has indeed a many-
faceted personality. However, I think of him as a man of
contrasts. Whichever aspect of his character I care to think of,
seldom is it present without a balancing and often contradictory
shadow. This is the man who leaves a trail of crushed cigarette
packets, spilt sugar and empty sandwich wrappers behind him,
who works from a scrap of paper with unintelligible scrawls of
writing, but who rarely forgets to make a phone call, who chases
up his adverts, his press releases, his venue bookings with icy
determination and a cheery professionalism which I admire
through a green haze of jealousy. My only criticism of Stephen
is his habit (and I think it is only a habit) of knocking himself in
front of people, referring to himself as a bit dizzy or absent-
minded. Well, this couldn't be further from the truth, as any
misguided person who has tried to pull the wool over Steve's
eyes or take advantage of his generous spirit would tell you.*

*The Stephen Holbrook that you see bringing messages of
great clarity and compassion to audiences all over the country is
but one element of the man I have been privileged to spend time
with over the last few years. To say that I feel my life has been
enriched by this contact may sound a little over sentimental (I
can see Stephen cringing now), but it really has. Stephen, James
and I have one of those rare examples of an association that
stretches to encompass and accommodate business and
friendship – and successfully, too.*

*Steve's fickle relationship with popularity is one perverse
aspect of his personality. He responds to the encouragement of
his audience's attention and will always attract people to him
and glow in their reassurance, yet is almost obsessive about his
desire for privacy, and will shy away from excessive
compliments. Trying to wheedle out any personal information
about him to incorporate in the book has been a battle and only
when family, friends and neighbours have confirmed that readers*

149

want to feel that they know a little of the man behind the scenes, has he slowly come around to the idea. I've noticed a bull-like determination not to be dragged into something he isn't quite happy about, until he makes up his own mind or something clicks in his head and then try stopping him. It's exasperating to hear him enthusing at long last about an idea that you've been trying to encourage him about for ages.

As well as a lot of hard work in the preparation and coordination of the demonstrations that James and I set up, we do have an awful lot of fun too – Stephen sees to that! Whilst he may be totally committed to his work and his beliefs (and believe me he does work hard at it), I'd swear Steve can't get through a single day without at least one practical joke, three leg-pulls and half a dozen comments dropped innocently into the conversation and designed to shock and leave you speechless! Many's the time I've been on the mobile taking a reservation and trying to maintain a degree of professionalism when Steve's had me spluttering and coughing at a carefully placed and most inappropriate comment. When James and I are driving Stephen to one of his demonstrations, he will often sit in the back of the car with his pilot's case by his side using the time to make and take phone calls, and catch up with paperwork. One of his favourite wheezes is to prolong a telephone call after the person has said goodbye and terminated their call, initially quite sensibly and then he'll say something quite outrageous. He had me going the first few times, but I've cottoned on now and don't react, but he keeps trying to catch me out.

He's a little devil for finding your weak spots and teasing you. Steve knows I'm nervous if I have to speak in public or stand up in front of a crowd and he'll ask me just before he goes on stage to bring him out his jug of water in front of the audience, knowing my legs will be wobbling with nerves. In contrast, however, if you really need help with something, anything, Steve's your man. I've handled the box office on a few occasions when we've had an angry crowd of people who couldn't get in to see Steve, due to incorrect press releases or a shortfall in the number of seats we'd ordered, and under extreme pressure he remains calm, professional and good-natured. I've never had a sharp word from him – often a cheeky one – but nothing ever said in anger.

150

Another example of the contrast in his character is reflected in his taste for designer clothes. He is so clued up on designer labels, yet I've never seen him buy a garment at full price; they're mostly from charity shops. He is also a control freak; this is evident in his attitude to gardening. Steve and I often talk about gardening on our long drives around the country (James will either be asleep or feigning sleep). However, my idea of horticultural paradise is a semi-wild creation of orchards, rambling roses, bamboo mazes, softly dancing ornamental grasses and lawns sprinkled with daisies. Steve's idea is a regimented order of evergreen shrubs, clipped to within an inch of their lives, an ivy covered arbour without a hint of deciduous decay and a lawn of vibrant emerald green; lush, verdant and without a single weed – and I mean a single weed. I've never known anyone mow their lawn (and re-seed it) as often as Steve. I really think he'd be much happier with Astroturf!

Steve is a man of generous nature. He knows my love of quality chutneys and conserves and will search out specialist shops and present me with a jar of some expensive delicacy, yet will not hesitate to query a bill if he thinks we have been overcharged, be it for the price of a cup of coffee. On the subject of generosity, I can't remember a time when we have been away on a mini tour when he hasn't disappeared to the shops to find presents for Caroline and the children, taking time to find the right gift to suit their likes and dislikes.

Without doubt, Steve is a workaholic and I don't think I know anyone who puts in as many hours with such tenacious energy as he. All the more reason then to schedule some time for a little 'R and R' to recharge the batteries and allow himself to recuperate, but he finds it very difficult to do so without a measure of guilt. In the case of time taken out of his working day for himself – guilt that his time should be better spent back at his desk with an ever-growing intray. In the case of some leisure time whilst on tour in Tenerife – guilt that he should be back at his home/office and guilt that he is sitting having a cup of coffee in a boulevard café and his beloved Caroline and treasured children are not. The fact that he works all hours, all days and tries to be everything to everybody all of the time is sadly forgotten.

This man is a treasure.

151

CHAPTER EIGHTEEN
Clairvoyant to Clairvoyant

They say that you cannot choose your family but you can always choose your friends and it is not uncommon for a friendship to be more important to someone than a family relationship. Stephen frequently forges links between friends and just because a message isn't coming through from a mum or a dad or a son or a daughter should not diminish the validity and the intensity of the message. The "friendship" energy is carried by a unique vibration, and when that energy is linked by the power of clairvoyance and psychism it is frequently even more powerful.

I know that if I am doing a reading for someone, be it palmistry or with the cards, if that other person is also psychic, the reading is much more precise and direct: indeed there are times when all I have to do is take someone's hand, not looking at the lines and completely ignoring the pack of cards, and the information rushes through like a waterfall. The conjoining of two psychic energies acts as a natural bridge and removes many of the usual obstructions.

And so it is with Stephen as this testimony from fellow clairvoyant Donna Rathbone clearly indicates.

Donna: 'I had a wonderful friendship for a number of years with a fabulous lady called Sybil Burgon. She was a strong figure in our community and ran a local shop in Osmotherly with her husband Dave. Five years ago she was diagnosed with soft cell sarcoma. This is a very aggressive form of cancer that affected a lot of organs in her body. When one part of the growth was removed it weighed an incredible twelve pounds!

'Sybil asked me to help her get through the ordeal of the operation with some hands on healing, which I willingly did twice a week initially – but then when the cancer came back I was working with her every day, especially in the last three or four weeks prior to her death.

'It was a time of great spiritual growth for me – I developed clairvoyantly through my channelling link with Sybil. We became very close spiritually and we talked a lot about life after life.

'A good two or three months before Stephen Holbrook's demonstration at The Northallerton Community Centre on November 15th 2001, Sybil and I made a pact because we both knew she wouldn't be coming with me.'

The pact between the two friends was, that if there were any way possible, Sybil would "come through" at Stephen's meeting.

Sybil Burgon died on September 25th and on the evening of 15th November Donna, accompanied by Dave, Sybil's husband, duly attended Steve's demonstration. Dave hadn't a clue what to expect, but Donna, who had seen Stephen a couple of times before, was able to put his mind at rest.

Donna had been "told" by spirit to sit on the right hand side of the auditorium and about three rows back from the front. Unfortunately by the time they arrived all the seats close to the stage were taken so Donna and Dave had to be content to sit at the back. Curiously, as the evening progressed Donna noticed that a very high percentage of Stephen's messages were going to that area of the room in which she had been told to sit. Occasionally there are psychic hot-spots in a room, and this particular evening in Northallerton was a prime example.

As the evening was nearing the end, Donna felt that Sybil was around her but didn't know if she would push herself to the front of the crowd of spiritual presences that were trying to connect with their loved ones.

Donna: 'Then she came to me and said, "I'm next, Donna". I felt I should have had the courage of my convictions and told Dave what was going on, but I didn't want to raise his hopes or make any false promises, so I didn't. Anyway, and this was the strangest feeling, I felt Sybil step into and through me and then power her way towards the stage and over-shadow Stephen. It's hard to describe, but I was looking at Stephen but I was seeing Sybil. She was wearing one of her favourite dresses, one that I remember quite vividly...'

As Stephen went on to the next link, he asked if anyone could connect with 3rd August. This date was known by Donna and Sybil as a particularly traumatic date in Donna's history for

153

this was the date that Donna's husband officially left her with a divorce pending.

Donna put up her hand and accepted the link. 'Stephen told me that I was going through a period of great emotional turmoil and upheaval and he wanted to know if I could take a female energy? A lady who was confined to a wheelchair for the last days of her life and who had pain and paralysis in her right leg. Well, of course, the answer was yes because as Sybil's tumour had begun to grow it had started to press against the nerves in her leg: she could no longer use that right leg and she was in a lot of pain and discomfort. Stephen went on to describe other symptoms and said that she had had a longer illness, but that she had passed quickly in the end. This was all very true, as she only took to her bed two or three days before the end. He mentioned the cancer and spoke about just how invasive it had been.'

Donna, at this point, said that she had Sybil's husband sat next to her.

'Stephen said that Sybil had to come through me because Dave wouldn't have put his hand up if he'd been there on his own. Dave nodded quite vigorously and managed to say "yes" which enabled Stephen to make the link directly with Dave and he said that Sybil was talking about a three bedroomed house by water and that she had been there and gone through all the rooms and had stayed with Dave while he'd been there. She wanted him to know that now she was free of the body which had confined her for so many months, she would be as close to him as she had wanted to be in life.

'Dave said this was a cottage that had been booked for a family holiday that Sybil had hoped she would be able to go on, but unfortunately she hadn't been able to make it.

'Then Stephen said that she was talking about her face being stroked after she'd passed over and Dave nodded and confirmed that he had lain on the bed beside her and stroked her face for at least an hour after she'd gone. Through Stephen she also mentioned that she was with Dave all the time in the house he lived in and Stephen wanted to know what the number 15 meant to him? Well, the number 15 was 15 North End, Osmotherley, which was where Sybil and Dave had lived together. Stephen also made mention of a photograph of Dave in a black flip top leather purse. Dave couldn't recall this, but a few days after we'd

154

been to see Stephen he showed me a purse which flipped over and there were two pictures of Dave, one as he is now and one of him as a little boy. It's amazing that Sybil had carried these pictures of Dave around with her and he'd never known!

'Also, on a lighter note, because Sybil was a great person with a wonderful sense of humour and a laugh that carried far and wide, she talked about Dave bringing her a red rose one night. He'd only been able to buy an artificial rose from a petrol station on the way back up from work. He'd crawled into bed in the early hours of the morning and when he awoke, Sybil was downstairs complaining that he hadn't put the rose in water and ended up laughing at herself because she'd actually put an artificial rose in water. Stephen had spoken of a single flower being important and the connection with the flower was important because it was a story that they related quite a few times over dinner with friends.

'Stephen also made mention of constantly moving cushions on the bed before she had died, and this was so true because before she could find any comfort there was always a great shuffling and propping of pillows so that she could catch enough breath...'

Sybil Burgon is with Donna all the time and Donna will always be grateful to Sybil for helping her to develop as a medium. As far as Donna is concerned if anyone ever wanted proof of life after life, this story provides it. She remembers the pact that she and Sybil had made and knows that Sybil had to be strong to come through that night. She made a supreme effort and proved to her husband that as she was there for him in life, she is still there for him, guiding, guarding and protecting from the other side until his own time comes. Both Dave and Donna take great comfort from this thought and Donna hopes that anyone reading this story will know that when they pass from this dimension to the next, that everyone they knew and loved will be there waiting for them.

On a personal note there is one very interesting point that comes out of Donna's testimony. She speaks of looking up at the stage and seeing her friend Sybil superimpose herself upon Stephen. This phenomenon is called transfiguration and it is a relatively rare occurrence experienced by the very few. Many mediums, especially those on the salon and séance circuits of the early and mid twentieth century, strove hard to acquire this skill and many even boasted of being able to transfigure at will, but along with the equally famous phenomenon of ectoplasm (the concept of spirit drawing physical matter from the medium to provide a base for spirit taking on human form) this was strenuously investigated and huge shadows of doubt were cast upon the validity of both concepts. Stephen has no experience of either transfiguration or of ectoplasmatic build up, and if he were asked I suspect he'd say something like "Oh no, I don't want any of that kind of thing, thank you very much!" ...But personally, I am curious. On the one hand I do not entirely debunk the idea of ectoplasm, but I think that the concept is more in tune with myth and magick than with spiritualism, and I speak here as one who has had some evidence to suggest that the power of magick is not entirely mythological. With regard to transfiguration I have a far more receptive mind, for I believe that I did see this once, while sitting in a séance with my mentor Ossie Rae. I was still very young at the time and I accept that the passing of thirty years may well have clouded my objectivity, but I do remember it as a very real memory.

I have checked through Donna's story in some depth and under most circumstances would be prepared to leave it wide open with a question mark – maybe she did see transfiguration and maybe she didn't – but you'll note that I say *"under most circumstances"*. What persuades me to give her the benefit of the doubt is that night at The Cochrane Theatre in London, for the more I think about it, the more clear I am in my own mind that for the first half hour or so of that particular demonstration there was a very strong spiritual personality overshadowing Stephen and giving him the presence to rise to the challenge of the audience: certainly this wasn't transfiguration in the true sense of the word, for he was still visibly the Steve Holbrook we've come to know and love. It was his manner and personality that were so clearly different, and although you might say that this was just a natural response to the circumstances, ie. Steve drawing on some inner strength to tackle the difficult task ahead of him, I am quietly confident that it was something significantly more than this.

So the jury is out, but I'll tell you what – if *you* are attending one of Stephen's demonstrations and you see something odd, don't just put it down to your imagination! Please give *yourself* the benefit of the doubt, and share your experience by contacting us c/o the publishers.

The Son's Tale

The Everything Daddy from Robbie Holbrook (8½)

My name is Robbie and I was eight on the fourth of June. My dad is Stephen, he does everything with me.

He lets me help him in the garden. We work as a team; we cut the grass and cut back the bushes. Sometimes he lets me use the hosepipe.

We like to go to car boot sales. Once my dad got me my own garden shears. He got a great bike for himself once and we have bought lots of plants and toys.

We go swimming and take Brad with us. We like to go to Hemsworth Water Park, but we only paddle there.

We go on bike rides to Normanton. Dad goes in front, Brad is in the middle and I'm at the back to keep an eye on him.

I help dad wash the car but sometimes we go to the car wash. Once we were in the car wash and the door was not shut properly. Dad opened it to slam it and the brush came in the car and we all got soaked and soapy. We all laughed but it wasn't funny really.

Once we were washing the car on the drive and my dad threw a bucket of soapy water on the car and it all splattered back at him. We all laughed.

Sometimes my dad shouts, but not much, only if he gets really mad.

My dad is really nice and special. My friends think he's a magician because they don't know what a medium does, but I do. My dad talks about spirits. Spirits are ghosts but you can't see them because they're invisible. Spirits don't hurt you, they're only people who've died and gone to heaven, but sometimes their spirits visit us. They surround my dad and talk to him sometimes.

I love my daddy very much and my mum. Now you see why I call my dad Everything Daddy.

Hi, Robbie, first of all, can you tell me what your teachers at school say about your Daddy?

"They say he's really famous because he's always in the Wakefield Express."

What do you think about that?

"He works all over the country so he'll be famous there as well, I suppose."

What exactly does your Daddy do?

"Oh he does lots of things and he always tries his best."

How do you mean?

"Er... we go to model railway exhibitions... and he takes us swimming, and he brings us a lot of toys."

How do you feel when Daddy says he's got to go off on a journey?

"I get a bit down and think – oh my Dad's off away again."

Do you know what Daddy does when he's working at night?

"Yes, he talks about spirits in shows to a very lot of people on stage – in Wakefield and everywhere!"

What does Daddy say to people?

"He talks to them on the mobile a lot."

Your Mum says that you and your Dad are very alike, so what do you think?

"Yes – we eat the same food and we both make a bit of a mess. Bradley takes after my Mum but I take after my Dad."

What do your friends say about your Dad?

"Mostly they want to read his book. Every morning when I go to school all my mates crowd round asking questions and saying things like 'your Dad's the medium' – and I just say all right, whatever, whatever, and can we get in to the class... It gets on my nerves a bit after a while."

Does Daddy take you to school?

"Yes and we used to do reading together, but now he does that with Bradley, and I like to have the radio on but it gives Daddy a headache when he's tired."

What the best thing about Daddy?

"When he takes us on holiday. Bradley likes going to hotels in the Canaries but I like it better when we go to the caravan."

Why's that?

"Because we're all closer together."

Can you remember what happened on the beach when you were on holiday in Gran Canaria?

159

"Oh that, yes well, we were playing tag on the beach and then Daddy went swimming and was going to get cut off by the waves so I decided to go and find him. My Dad saw this boy and wondered who it was and then he saw it was me and he thought, oh no he's wandered off my from my Mum, and the next thing we saw was this jeep flying up and down the beach and there was this helicopter flying around, so I suppose just like my Dad I'd caused a bit of mayhem, and when we got back Mum thought we'd both drowned and she was very very very mad."

What do you think about Daddy's cars?

"Well what I hated about the Montego was in the back I didn't like all the bumps and rattles, and Daddy just goes on buying more Montegos without even telling me!"

Daddy's got a Mondeo now, so what do you think of that?

"Not much."

Do you like Mum's Peugeot better?

"Yes 'cos it's sportier."

Well what car do you think Daddy should have?

"A car called a Banshee, that's made in America, or, no, sorry James... a nice silver BMW!"

Thank you Robbie, that'll do nicely.

"Oh that's all right James. You're welcome."

CHAPTER NINETEEN
The Power Of Healing

For a number of years especially in my heyday as a professional psychic I moved through the world of new age healing and alternative medicines. I attended countless courses and festivals up and down the country as part of the body mind and spirit movement, and I came to a number of rather sad conclusions.

The first was that body mind and spirit should be called body mind and wallet.

The second was that although some alternative remedies were extremely effective and useful, others were absolute rubbish promoted by people with little or no knowledge of what they were doing.

The third was that for every individual who had a genuine gift for healing, there were a hundred who only thought they had but hadn't, and another thousand who wanted that gift so badly that they convinced themselves and many gullible members of the public that they did actually have it! Needless to say, always with disappointing and frequently disastrous results, and more commonly with no results at all!

And yet it is an indisputable fact that *some* people out there do have a very strong and potent gift for healing. Usually they do not resort to gimmicks or 'ologies' but simply act as a channel for an enigmatic and elusive energy that is extremely potent in its efficacy.

On two occasions in my life I have been on the receiving end of such healing, and therefore I know that it has worked for me. On one occasion a lady, who at the time was a total stranger to me, came over to the table where I was sitting. We were the only two people in the café and I was in absolute agony with bursitis. My knee was a throbbing mass of inflammation, swollen to twice its normal size, and I'd been unable to walk for three days. The ibuprofen was not even scratching the back of the condition and I was just about ready to perform an amputation!

This lady introduced herself as Liz Endrick. She said that she was a healer and that she'd felt my pain from the other side of the room. She asked very gently if she could have a go at taking some of the pain away, and I was so desperate for some relief that I was more than willing to let her have a bash.

All she did was kneel on the floor in front of me (God knows what any other customers would have thought if there'd been any body else in the café) and place her two hands either side of my swollen knee. She did not actually touch me – her hands were each about three inches from my leg – but within seconds, there was an icy tingling sensation, and in less than a minute all of the raging heat had departed and along with it the crippling pain. My knee was still swollen and quite weak *but all the pain had gone* and within half an hour I was walking unaided back across York to my office, marvelling at the miracle I had just experienced. This was the beginning of a long friendship with Liz and I shall always be grateful to her for plucking up the courage and approaching a complete stranger with her offer of healing help.

On another occasion a very special friend of mine called Bette Whittaker (who enjoys a formidable reputation in her home city of York as being a seer and mistress of runes) came to my aid at a very dark hour in my life. This time the pain I was suffering was mental rather than physical and for many weeks I had been living in a fugue: my head was not my own and I was out of it more often than I was in it. I'll spare you the details, but suffice to say I finally ended up at Bette's flat, whereupon she took me in, gave me a cup of tea, listened to my babblings and ravings, and then told me to sit still while she did some work on me.

Bette's "work" was to stand behind me for ten minutes or so with one hand resting lightly on the back of my head, while in the other hand she held a beautiful piece of clear crystal quartz. Again, as with Liz Endrick, I started to feel better within a very few minutes... all of the tension and stress seemed to drain out of my body, and ten minutes or so later I was fast asleep. I slept for a solid twelve hours and when I woke up, wrapped in a travel rug on Bette's sofa in front of the fire, my head was quite clear and my heart was calm. Certainly, all of the problems that had brought me to my friend's door were still there, but the point was, so was I, and in a fit state to start dealing with them rather than recoiling from them.

162

From the beginning of recorded history there have always been a chosen few who have had the ability to reach out and heal their fellow men. If you had suggested to Stephen Holbrook a year ago that he might be one of those people he would have laughed at you and denied it, but in this last year from 2001 to 2002 things have begun to change and rearrange themselves in Stephen's spiritual life.

As biographer and diarist I can trace his pattern of subtle change back to the time when he gave up the hairdressing salon and dedicated himself full time to his spiritual quest. The messages have become more detailed, his delivery has been more confident, and increasingly we are hearing reports of Stephen's ability to heal.

These "reports" come in the form of the many letters, emails and phone calls we receive from people who have attended the demonstrations and who want to share their thoughts and experiences with us. In all truth it must be said that until very recently Stephen has not been aware of any healing energy working through him, and therefore some of the letters we began to receive a few months ago came as quite a surprise to him.

For example, a letter from Dorothy Welbourne of Chesterfield, received in August of 2001...

Dear Mr Holbrook... I write to thank you for the wonderful message you gave me from my mother last week at The Winding Wheel. I can't tell you how much good it has done me. For years I've gone through life without any energy at all and the doctors have been thinking that I've got ME, but in this last week all the lethargy has blown away and although I'm not going to start climbing mountains or running a marathon, I've been able to walk down to the shops with a spring in my step and I can actually get through the day without falling asleep on the job and when I do go to bed at night, I'm able sleep properly for the first time since my mother passed away in 1997... You said in your message that my mother wanted to give me healing and she certainly seems to be doing a good job so far. I know she couldn't have done this without you acting as go-between so I just wanted to write and thank you so very much from the bottom of my heart... Love and best wishes from Dorothy.

It was this letter and maybe another half dozen letters along the same lines that alerted Steve to the fact that something was "happening" through his messages and in his subsequent demonstrations he deliberately tried to tune into this new vibration. As an objective observer at most of Steve's evenings I began to notice that the word "healing" cropped up ever more often and in the mailbag there were an increasing number of thank you letters that made reference to the healing aspect of Stephen's work. Stephen has not, does not and will not set out his stall as a healer but if there is a healing energy channelling through him he is more than delighted to make it welcome and to direct it where it wants to go.

We were sitting in a restaurant in Stratford-upon-Avon a little while ago, coming towards the end of a short tour that had taken us to Southend and Worcester before finishing off at Stratford's wonderful Falcon Hotel on Chapel Street – and yes, they deserve the plug because they do look after us well at The Falcon! We were talking about the contents of this book and inevitably the conversation came round to the subject of healing. I asked Steve if he could describe how he felt when this energy was channelling through him, and if he agreed with me that this new energy had really only begun to manifest itself after he'd closed the hairdressing salon.

'Well first of all, you're right about there being a difference since last July when I stopped hairdressing... Everything seems to have become a lot more focused and it's almost as though the spirit world is saying to me "right, now you're giving us 100%, we'll give you 100%." I've had a lot more energy, and although it took a bit of getting used to, I don't regret giving up the hairdressing. I always thought I *was* giving 100% to the spirit world, but looking at it from their point of few, I can't have been, can I, not if I was tearing my hair out and working forty hours a week in the salon.

'As for the healing, this isn't something that's just slapped me round the face all in one go, but something I've only become gradually aware of over the months. What does it feel like? Well you could best describe it as a cold tingling feeling that goes half way down my back and along my arms, or sometimes when it's particularly strong I'll feel it throughout my whole body. I've come to learn that if I'm feeling it, so is the person that I'm linking with, and I've proved this to myself simply by asking the person that I'm talking to whether or not they can feel the cold tingling and so far nobody has ever said no. Sometimes it's so strong that I can even see where the energy is going to.

'There was a lady in Huddersfield who had suffered with deafness in her left ear for more than thirteen years. I was aware of the bluey green energy flowing into the side of her head... I wasn't pushing it there, it was just going out of me and getting there on its own accord, and anyway, she phoned me three days later to say that she was hearing clearly for the first time in all of those thirteen years... I was a bit unsure, so I asked her to keep in touch, and she phoned two weeks later and then three months later after that to say that it wasn't just a fluke and that everything was still okay.

'Then there was this other lady who got a message from her brother who had died in Germany in a car accident. They'd had a very fiery relationship and hadn't always been the best of friends. Anyway, as I say, the brother came through with a load of information, including the fact that he'd been in the car crash with three friends and they'd all been killed. He named names and gave a load of different dates and even mentioned the names of the family pets. As a parting shot he said that he knew she was having a lot of pain with her back through a bad disc problem and to make up for some of the unbrotherly things he'd done while he was down here, he was going to send her some healing. Anyway, we had an email a few days later saying that *all* the pain had gone from her back for the first time in the last six years.

'As with the deaf lady in Huddersfield, I don't know how permanent this healing is... I mean, I really hope it lasts but I just don't know how it all works. But look, even if it only gives a bit of relief, at least it proves to me that the spirit world is trying to help.

'And there's another thing I can think of here which is quite important because there's more to healing than just taking away the pain from someone's bad back. There was a lady in Scunthorpe who'd had a terrible row with her husband and he'd stormed out of the house and had been killed on his way back from the take-away. This poor lady was in torment because despite the fact that their last words were so full of anger, it had actually been a loving and caring relationship, and she never forgave herself for having provoked the fight that in her words had "sent Mick out into the night and to his death". This lady was on loads of tranquillisers for years and suffered terribly from guilt...

'Anyway, at this demonstration, her husband Mick came through for her, and among other things told her to stop taking "all those bloody tablets because you don't need 'em any more" and he went on to say he was giving the "thumbs up for Andy and that he was okay" and also that the 16th was in some way a very important date. Which it was, because that was the date that the lady intended to get engaged to Mick's best mate Andy. Mick also brought through messages of love and support from the lady's mum, and both Mick and mum were telling this lady that she had to put the past behind her and get on with the business of living her life for the present and the future.

'Well, she came to see me after the demonstration and she was in tears, but they were really happy tears because she told me that this great weight that she'd been carrying on her shoulders ever since Mick had passed over had suddenly been lifted from her and she felt light in her heart. She wanted to know if it truly was Mick who had helped her or if it was me, and I told her straight out that I had nothing to do with it at all. I was just the messenger boy and it was all coming through from Mick.'

So, as we see, not only is there a physical healing energy at work here, there is an emotional energy also. I believe that Stephen is and has always been a natural healer, but that this gift has lain dormant for many long years until he has begun to find the time and strength to deal with it in a mature manner without any of the hype that usually goes hand in glove with this sort of thing. With Stephen it is a quiet awareness, an increasing of the psychic envelope, something he has not gone looking for, but something that he will naturally accept as an added dimension to his ongoing work with the world of spirit.

CHAPTER TWENTY
For Dogs And Angels

Death hurts.

Sometimes it hurts the person passing over and it always hurts their loved ones left behind. Somehow, no matter how spiritually aware we might be and no matter how much we might believe in an afterlife, there is still a terrifying finality about death that skewers our guts with dread.

Man is not the only creature abroad on this planet with intelligence but he is the only creature to have reason and intellect as part of his psychological make-up, and the downside of this is that Man is the only creature born with the awareness of his own mortality. Other animals might acquire this knowledge – the gazelle learns to fear the lion and the lion learns to fear the long gun – but Man carries this disturbing knowledge in his psyche from day one!

Evidence from top mediums like Stephen Holbrook assures us that there *is* an afterlife and while intellectually we grasp at this with gratitude, in the deeper emotional recesses of our souls still we shiver with doubts and uncertainties, for there are still too many unanswered questions.

As a gentleman said to me recently after one of Stephen's demonstrations – 'Just because somebody on the front row has got a message from their dead father proving that their father's spirit lives on, what proof is there that this is also true of *my* father? What proof is there that the same rules will apply to me when it is *my* time to die?'

Stephen would say that if one spirit transcends death, then so too, surely, do all spirits. There is reason and logic in this supposition, but for the fearful doubters this "reasonable and logical supposition" is just a supposition and does not constitute hard proof.

Reason tells us that there must be more for us than just one life, for what would be the point and purpose of life if, at the end of life there was nothing but a void? Our egos and identities grasp at this concept eagerly, but ego apart, it is still a reasonable concept. It makes sense and we know it makes sense, but many of us are Doubting Thomases at heart and we need proof before we can believe. We want to believe, we need to believe, we *long* to believe, for the prospect of there being nothing after death is too awful to contemplate – and therefore, to support and give foundation to our belief we search for evidence. It is no accident that over the last couple of years Stephen's audiences have steadily grown bigger and bigger as the word has gone out on the grapevine that here is someone who can provide that evidence.

It might not always be conclusive proof for everybody but it is hard evidence that cannot easily be ignored.

People do not just come to Stephen's demonstrations in the hope of receiving messages from loved ones passed away, they come also for a glimpse of heaven – an indication of what life might be like on the "other side".

Stephen is quite straightforward in his response to this expectation. He says 'I'm sorry to disappoint people, but I've got to tell the truth and say I've got no idea of what heaven might be like. I've never seen it, never been there and I've never talked to anyone who's been in a position to describe it to me. I know other mediums have come up with visions of summer gardens and mountains and streams, but I've no idea where they're getting their information from.'

'But,' I pointed out in a recent conversation, 'you've been a working medium for almost twenty years so surely you must have *some* idea of what it might be like, even if it's just an impression?'

'No, not really... there are some things that I *do* know with absolute conviction, like, for example, the fact that there are no penalties against suicides, that if you're sick and ill on this side you're healed and healthy on the other side, that all the pain is taken away, that children grow up on the other side – they don't just stay the age they were when they passed over. I know that if you were a grumpy old sod on this side you're likely to be a grumpy old sod on the other side, and I know that animals have spirits as well as human beings, because you know yourself James, never a night goes by without someone's pet coming through as part of a message, whether it's Prince the dog or Percy the parrot...'

168

There are a number of issues here that are worthy of further discussion.

We have already dealt with suicides in chapter seven, so let us look at the concept of healing on the "other side".

In everything I've ever read and confirmed by every spiritualist I've ever spoken to, there is a common belief that no matter how ill and broken you may be on this side of the veil, once on the other side there is a healing process that removes all pain and sickness from the soul. Stephen will frequently give messages from people who speak of their heart conditions or their lame legs, but they do this, we believe, only as a form of identification. How the healing process works, how long it takes and as to whether or not there are heavenly hospitals is anybody's guess, but the overall impression we get is that the healing process is fairly instantaneous. You are in agony. The body dies. The pain is immediately removed. Memories of the pain, and memories of mental and emotional pain may well remain but only as a memory, and a receding one at that.

When a friend who was badly mangled and killed in a car crash comes back to me in my dreams and psychic visions, he does so full of smiles and laughter and without a cut or bruise in sight. When my grandmother who passed over as a very frail and bed ridden ninety five year old makes her presence felt, she does so as a sprightly seventy year old, full of raw energy and rude good health.

We believe that the spirit transcends and grows, and remembering that there must be some free interpretation of the concept of time, perhaps each spirit transcends and grows when it is good and ready to!

A pivotal point of my own belief is the retention of identity after death, and therefore I worried slightly when Stephen first spoke of the grumpy old sod syndrome – for on the one hand I wanted to think that there was retention of the identity at the same time as there was also spiritual transcendency, but Stephen soon put my mind at rest on this one when he pointed out that again the "grumpy old sod" personality was only a vehicle of identification.

'What would be the point,' he said, 'of Uncle Arthur trying to come through for Auntie Jean as a calm and gentle spirit, full of love and enlightenment if, on this earthplane, he was a whinging old codger who never had a good word for anyone? Jean wouldn't recognise him, so he's got to use the personality Jean *would* recognise to forge the link.'

On the subject of animals I share Stephen's conviction that they, like us, have spirits and that those spirits, like ours, transcend to a higher state. I don't think there is an evolutionary process whereby the spirit of a dog can evolve to become a human spiritual being and it seems logical to assume that species will retain the identity of species. I could be completely wrong in this assumption, for at the end of the day there is no hard proof either way – but I am absolutely positive that when we get to the other side our animal friends will be there to greet us.

Truth is subjective and proof is personal to the individual, but I have my own truth and proof that comes from two different strands of evidence, and I am quite happy to share this with you.

Stephen believes that it is the vibration of love that generates the power behind the links he forges, and I think it can be generally accepted that many of us have as much love for our pets as we do for our human relatives. I was deeply saddened when my mother passed away, but I wept buckets when one of my cats was killed by a car. On the surface this makes little sense – unless you are privy to the relationship I had with my mother and unless you know how I feel about my cats!

Many people are able to forge stronger bonds with animals than with their fellow men, and the intensity of this love should not be diminished or disregarded. You might scoff at the man who feels more love for his dog than he does for his father and you may well question his character and moral fibre, but consider the implications of the father being a drunken wife beating pederast and the sad possibility that the only true love our man has ever received has come from faithful old Fido, his four legged friend! Puts it in a different light, doesn't it?

In all my years of psychic research I have never seen a ghost – that is, I've never seen the ghost of a human being, but on two occasions in my life I have been visited, haunted if you like, by the spirits of two cats that have passed over... and on a third occasion I once spent some time in an old house and kept tripping over a big black cat that wasn't there in the fur, but by God, he was certainly there in the spirit. As far as I am concerned, and I reckon I have enough experience to be objective, these catty visitations were not flights of imagination but very real occurrences of sufficient strength and intensity to give me *my* proof. If this were not enough, there is also the plethora of evidence that Stephen brings through that indicates beyond all shadow of doubt that wherever we go after death, our animals go too.

In Tenerife there was a detailed message about Prince the Alsatian, in Ossett Stephen identified Charlie... not a budgie or a parrot, but a bright yellow canary. In Huddersfield he spoke of Mickey, which was the landlady's code name for the large mouse which terrorised her bar and cellars and in York he spoke of Bernie and Bradley, two Jack Russells that had both been killed in a house fire. In Retford he brought through a crossbreed called Bruno and in Bournemouth he spoke at length one night about Tilly the Tortoise who had had her name painted on her back. Hardly a demonstration goes by without an animal making its presence felt somewhere in the course of an evening. Obviously dogs don't bark messages and cats don't demand Whiskas from beyond the grave – they are there to lend weight to the evidence Steve presents to his audiences and if he is giving a message to someone it is frequently the presence of the departed pet that acts as the clincher.

As one lady put it to me recently... 'I was sitting there in a state of shock while Stephen was telling me that my late husband was looking after our son on the other side, and I just couldn't take it in... God knows I wanted to think that Michael and David were together, but I just couldn't be sure... and then Stephen said something about my husband and son taking Brandy for long walks and that David in particular was so happy that he'd got Brandy back again. Brandy was our Golden Retriever and he'd died about a year before David got sick, and David really missed him quite dreadfully...'

And talking of the little boy called David who died with a brain tumour when he was only eight years old brings me to the last part of this chapter, for if we are to get any glimpse of heaven through Stephen Holbrook's work, it probably comes through most strongly in his links with children.

Messages involving children are always very poignant and I think there is good reason for this. We begrudgingly accept the

171

inevitability of death and we understand that death is the great leveller – prince or pauper we must all pay the ferryman sooner or later. When an elderly person passes over we are able to soften the blow by becoming philosophical and making reference to someone having had "a good innings"; when someone passes as a result of a protracted illness we think in terms of a release from suffering. When people die in war we may find it abhorrent but intellectually we understand that in wars people get killed. Tidal waves, earthquakes and volcanoes exact their toll but (especially in safe little Britain) we can rationalise nature's natural disasters with the collateral damage inflicted upon the poor people who are caught up in the calamity. In other words, we find death more acceptable when we can equate it with some obvious law of cause and effect.

However, when a child is taken from us there are other emotions released into the vortex of grief, not least of which is a raging feeling of anger that is usually supplemented by a profound sense of injustice. A baby dies in its cot, a six year old girl dies with leukaemia, an eight year old boy passes with a brain tumour – and we demand to know why these precious little lives are cut so short before their time. They have not had a "good innings", they are not combat veterans in a war zone and our sense of unfairness makes us question the existence of whatever God we worship. We demand answers but so very few are ever forthcoming.

There is a belief, not only held by a number of spiritualists but also accepted and tentatively investigated by mystics of all religions and spiritually aware people all over the world, which, if it is correct, makes some sense of something which to us seems nonsensical.

The belief is simply that in our spiritual state before we are born, we are given a clear vision of all that our life will be, all that it will contain, all that we will suffer and all that we will enjoy. That armed with this foreknowledge we accept the challenge of the life on offer to learn all that we need to learn from the experience. We recognise the significance of the interactivity between our own life and the lives of others we are destined to meet and have dealings with along the way, and before we take our first breath we know that we are not talking about just one life, but something more akin to a term at school. Spiritually we use our human lives for the purpose of learning and progressing along a pathway that brings us closer to God, and when you think about it in human terms greater learning comes from pain than comes from pleasure.

This introduces the subject of reincarnation, which is something that Stephen is rather dubious about, whereas I have no doubts at all about the veracity of the concept. Either way, if we choose life knowing that we must move on from life once we have learned or taught the lesson we have been incarnated to learn or teach, there is some logic and some reason for our arrival and our departure, no matter how premature that departure might seem to be, both in our own eyes and in the eyes of others.

It is given that as the spark of spirit acquires sentience within the new life born, all memories of previous spiritual existence are deleted from the consciousness and laid to rest deeply within the subconscious: life would not be a fair test for us if we could see the contents of the exam paper before the test began.

This is not just a theory, it is also a deeply albeit quietly held belief most precious to many who know far more about life's mysteries than I do. It crosses the boundaries of different faiths and in some quarters it is even regarded as an arcane or "secret" teaching revealed only to adepts once they have attained a certain degree of spiritual enlightenment. There is no hard *proof* of its veracity (that I know of anyway) but if one accepts the possibility of such a concept, it does offer an explanation of something that, to our human minds, seems inexplicable.

And I suppose if there is one truth I have learned along life's precipitous pathway it is that to every question "why?" there is always an answer – providing we're prepared to go looking for it with total self honesty. We might not like the answer when we get it, but it's there to be found for those who seek.

Stephen has told us that no matter what age a child is taken from us its spirit continues to grow and develop on the other side. Generally, although I can think of one odd exception to the rule, if a child has passed over at an age when it could speak for itself, the child itself will deliver the message through the medium. If, however, the child passed at a very early age, stillborn or even within the womb, it will use a third party as a spiritual intermediary.

173

Sometimes, as Stephen freely admits, there can be some initial confusion linking messages with children: he might be speaking of a seven year old and nobody in the audience is able to connect with this until Stephen recognises the problem and speaks instead of a child who would be seven years old if it were still alive down here on the earthplane – and then, usually, the message is immediately picked up.

Some of the messages from children can be tearfully sad, while others can be hilariously funny.

There was a wee boy who came through at one of the Glasgow demonstrations who told his mother and father that he liked the way they had decorated the bedroom and he liked the sound the bed springs made when they squeaked "two or three times a week" and I shall always remember the link with another little boy who came through for his mother in Tamworth.

He identified himself by describing his personality, bright and bouncy almost to the point of hyperactivity, and then by giving a host of dates – the date he passed over, his birthday, his mother's birthday – and he clinched the evidence for post mortem survival by telling us that his mother had a lock of his curly fair hair in a locket that she wore around her neck, and that she never ever *ever* took it off. Needless to say, the mother was overjoyed to learn that her little boy was alive and well on the other side, but she simply couldn't understand why he kept going on and on about a broken fridge. She admitted to the audience at large that she had, within the last few weeks, installed a new fridge in her kitchen, but that it certainly wasn't broken.

There wasn't much Stephen could do in the face of this denial, other than to reiterate what he was being told and to suggest that she have another look at the fridge as soon as she got home. An hour later, just as we were coming off the A38 onto the M1 the lady in question phoned Stephen on his mobile to say that as soon as she'd got back to her house she'd had a good look at her new fridge... and had found a long split in the seal on top of the freezer door. She was totally dumbfounded, Stephen was pleased that he'd been right, and I made my notes...

Another memorable link concerned a little boy who had passed over when he was still only four or five years old, and Stephen had some difficultly understanding what he was being told by spirit. 'He keeps saying Boo Boo – nothing else, just Boo

174

Boo! Boo Boo! Boo Boo... and the weirdest thing is I keep getting the word "lasagne" but I've got to admit I haven't got a clue what any of this means, except to say that while he was down here this little lad had lots of problems with his health, but now he's on the other side he wants you to know that he's absolutely perfect.'

This little boy's parents were able to explain things readily enough. Their son had been autistic and the only words he'd ever been able to utter were "Boo Boo" which he did repetitively all day and every day. He'd had such a passion for lasagne that it was the only food his parents could ever get him to eat – so it was lasagne three times a day, breakfast, dinner and tea – and both parents were deeply moved to tears to know that their son was "perfect" now that he had escaped from the trap of his earthly body.

Perhaps the most telling message Steve's ever channelled came through from a little girl at a demonstration in Plymouth. This link is worthy of special mention because although Stephen goes to great lengths to clarify the point that he is clair*audient* rather than clair*voyant*, on this occasion he says he saw the little tot quite clearly on the stage next to him. He accepts that this could have been a mental projection of his own mind's eye, but even now at the time of writing some weeks after the event and with the benefit of hindsight and objectivity, he's still not sure. Either way, this little girl, barely three years old and dressed in a sparkly party dress was with him in a very real sense and it is one of the very few occasions when Stephen has actually seen a spirit form. Or to be more accurate, *half* a spirit form.

As he looked to one side of the stage, he could see the bottom half of a little girl (roughly from the waist down) with little pasty legs. The girl was shouting 3rd of June and Stephen turned to the audience and asked if anyone could link with the 3rd of June. When there was no response Stephen kept repeating it, determined to find the link for this little girl. Then he heard her say "you daft brush, I'm *three* in June" and in passing this to the audience a lady at the back shouted "Me!" and put up her hand.

The little girl then gave information about the house where she lived and about certain items that had been put into her coffin; this was confirmed by the recipient of the message. She sent love to her mummy (who was not in the audience) and said that her mother had had to go to the doctors and was on tablets as she hadn't been able to come to terms with her daughter's death. The little girl also said that her Nana had said lots of angry swear words – and this the lady in the audience readily confirmed. The little girl then mentioned her daddy and tut-tutted, saying she didn't like him at all because he'd been "very very bad".

Later on at the end of the evening, the lady who was the recipient of this message and who turned out to be "Nana" the little girl's grandmother, approached Stephen and told him that the little girl's father had murdered her by stabbing her fourteen times and then had turned the knife on himself and had taken his own life. She confirmed that the little girl's Mum was on a life support system of Librium and Prozac and that she herself had been (and still was) so angry that she spent many hours in any given day cursing and swearing, sometimes out loud, but more frequently just under her breath. She wasn't too surprised that her granddaughter had heard her, for in life she'd been able to hear the twist of a toffee paper being unwrapped at five hundred yards.

Traumatic as this terrible message may have been Stephen recognises that there is usually some significance in a link of this nature and speculates as why he only saw the bottom half of the little girl. He wonders if this has something to do with the manner in which she was killed... For example, did the little girl not wish to show the top half of her body if she had been badly mutilated by the repeated stabbings? I know that this particular link upset Stephen badly for a long time, and even now he speaks of it with reticence and great sadness.

'The one thing I know for a fact,' he says quietly, 'is that when we get over to the other side we will be free of all the terrible things that hurt us and cause us so much pain and grief down here.'

There is an Andalucian folk proverb – *'gatos y peros van al cielo y nuestros niños seran angeles'* which loosely translated means 'cats and dogs all go to heaven and our children shall be angels.'

176

CHAPTER TWENTY ONE
"One Day At A Time"

"One day at a time, sweet Jesus, that's all I'm asking of you..."
The radio alarm started blaring the 1970's Kris Kristofferson hit
into Stephen's left ear. This piece of basic electronic wizardry
was a recent addition to the Holbrook household and like all
good Taureans, Steve hadn't a clue how the damn thing worked.
He reached over in a foggy daze of sleep to turn it off but instead
managed to hit the volume dial so that the next line of the song
punched even more raucously into his ear drums... *"Show me the
way and tell me today what I've got to do..."*

As Caroline stirred next to him Steve reached down and
pulled the radio plug from the wall, plunging the room into a state
of blessed silence. Propping himself on one elbow he stared
belligerently at his watch in a state of mild disbelief; it was 6.15,
and he could hardly believe that it was morning already. It
seemed as though his head had only just touched the pillow – but
that was back at one a.m. when he'd crawled into bed after a long
demonstration over in St Helens and an equally long drive home
along the M62 from Lancashire to Yorkshire.

For a moment he fell back on his pillow and closed his eyes,
trying to come to terms with the fact that after an eighteen hour
day he'd had a fraction over five hours sleep, and now here was
another eighteen hour day looming ahead of him. He sighed
ruefully, wondering where the hours went – he'd given up his
hairdressing salon the previous year so he would have more time
with his family, but instead of working eight hours a day in the
salon he now found that he was having to work those same eight
hours a day in the office just to keep on top of his work as a
clairvoyant!

With a groan of effort he pulled himself out of bed and
padded barefoot over to the window. The first grey green light
of the early morning threw the garden below him into a two-
dimensional base relief, but despite the shadow he still managed
to feel a small thrill of pride. The garden was coming on very

well, and the many months of love and labour were beginning to pay handsome dividends.

Steve's senses reached out through the silent house and touched the sleeping presences of his wife and three children, and a different sense of pride suffused through his being. *One day at a time, sweet Jesus...* The words of the song that had woken him echoed through his mind... that was the way it should be, wasn't it? Taking life one day at a time, celebrating each day for that day's own sake, and being ever thankful for what you had. Caroline had overcome her potentially fatal illness, his children were growing well, there was a little bit of money in the bank, his garden was an Eden to behold and this sense of well-being was worth every hour he had to work to create it.

He showered and dressed, then spent five minutes in his office checking through the day sheet to see what was on the agenda. It seemed like a pretty average day that revolved around getting the kids to school then spending several hours on the phone before picking the kids up again. He noted that Bradley, his youngest son, had a half day and that he'd promised that he'd take him out for an hour on a rowing boat after lunch, and then the rest of the afternoon would be spent getting ready to go to Northwich (back along the M62 into Lancashire) for the evening's demonstration. If he was lucky, he might be back home for midnight and back into bed for one o'clock again!

From his office he moved down into the kitchen and brewed a pot of tea, taking the tea up to Caroline, he went about the business of waking the children... Ellie, typically, reached up and gave her father a big kiss before scampering into the master bedroom to climb into bed with her mother. Robbie, his eldest son, looked at him accusingly, but stirred himself well enough. Bradley, the youngest son, still only four, opened one eye cautiously...

'Is this a *nice* day daddy, or is it a school day?'

Trying to keep a straight face Stephen told him that the first half of the day was a school day but that the second half of the day would be a "nice" day because they were going out on the lake in a rowing boat. This seemed to placate son number two, who dutifully followed son number one into the bathroom.

By eight o'clock Caroline was up and in charge of the children, releasing Stephen to make a start on the office work.

He'd no sooner picked up his landline to phone his Mother when the mobile started jangling with someone who wanted to make a booking for the evening demonstration. Steve duly made the reservation, trying hard to maintain a neutral tone of voice and resisting the temptation to tell the caller to phone back at nine o'clock or some more sensible hour of the day. Sadly so many people fail to show Stephen the same courtesy they would show their local cinema or theatre, and they seem to feel that it's absolutely fine to phone at eight a.m. or twenty minutes to midnight to book tickets.

At eight thirty Stephen was back on duty for the school run, and piling his sons into the back of the car, he started off on the five mile round trip. Robbie was in a particularly talkative mood that morning...

'Daddy?'

'Yes Robbie?'

'Are you famous or something?'

Steve laughed. 'No, of course not, Robbie. What put that idea into your head?'

'Well my teacher says you're famous. She's seen your picture in the paper and she says you're a media.'

'Does she really?' Stephen murmured, not quite knowing what else to say.

'Yes,' Robbie went on, 'and we've been talking about heaven at school, and I just wanted to know if you come back from heaven?'

Stephen was caught off guard and wasn't really ready for this kind of conversation, certainly not this early in the day and not with an eight year old boy. 'Robbie love, I'm really not sure...'

'Well,' Robbie persisted, 'do they have baths in heaven?'

'No, I don't think so. They don't need baths.'

Robbie's eyes opened wide in astonishment. 'But Daddy, I've got to have a bath every day!'

'Robbie, if I were you, I really wouldn't worry about it too much.'

'I'm not worried about it, but I'll get back from heaven to have a bath because I'll catch a plane!'

Stephen smiled at his son's delightfully simplistic logic. 'Robbie, *please* don't worry about this because we'll all be there

179

together and if you want to have a bath in heaven I'm sure we can sort something out…'

Between nine and nine thirty Steve made about a dozen calls to various newspapers checking that the adverts for the various demonstrations were all running to schedule, which might seem like excessive zeal, but things can so easily go wrong with an advert and unless you stay on top of the job things can go awry very quickly. One missed insertion can cost a lot of money and an advert with a wrong date or an incorrect telephone number can cause no end of confusion.

At nine thirty he was just about to put a call through to the next newspaper on his list when the jangling bell pre-empted him and he picked up the phone to find himself talking to Jo from the JCP office over in York. Glad of the opportunity to take a short break he leaned back in his chair, prepared to have a nice little chat… but he came to attention very quickly once he heard what Jo had to tell him.

'What,' she asked over the phone, 'is one of the worse case nightmare scenarios you can possibly imagine?'

It wasn't so much the words themselves that brought him to attention, for Jo's tone of voice told him that something was seriously amiss. With a sinking feeling in the pit of his stomach he knew that whatever this was about, it wasn't going to be good news.

'Go on,' he said, 'tell me what's happened.'

For ten minutes he sat in silence listening to the report he was receiving. 'Okay,' he said when Jo had finally finished, 'you make your calls and get back to me and I'll see what I can do from this end in the meantime. Give me this guy's number will you, and *I'll* have a talk to him, and if I can sort something out, I'll come straight back to you.'

'Okay Steve… Look, I'm sorry to burden you with this, but I thought you'd better be put in the picture.'

'Don't worry about it, and just tell James not to panic.'

'James isn't panicking,' Jo said, 'he's just getting ready to drive down to Southampton and throw a wobbly!'

Jo hung up and Stephen sat back in his chair frantically thinking what he should now do for the best. Instinctively he reached over and turned off his mobile phone and took the

180

landline receiver off its cradle. It was still early in the day, but he reached into his battered briefcase and pulled out a very rare cigarette, and went through the business of smoking it, hardly inhaling but nevertheless soothed by ritual, while he pondered the pros and cons.

When Jo had spoken of a worse case nightmare scenario she had not been exaggerating. An hotel in Southampton that had been booked for six months for a demonstration less than ten days away had suddenly discovered that it had double booked its function room and was now denying all knowledge of ever having had a reservation for Stephen's evening of clairvoyance. Jo had already spoken to the hotel manager on three separate occasions earlier that morning and his mood had been adamant and intransigent... there was no booking, there never had been any booking and there was certainly no room for the Stephen Holbrook function as advertised on May 20th. All this in the face of the evidence (fax transmission confirmations and email logs) that clearly proved that a booking *had* been made and that therefore the hotel had dropped a bollock from a very great height. Jo was now taking the matter up with the hotel chain's regional office and at the same time was looking for an alternative venue. The trouble was that there'd already been three expensive weeks of advertising with only one more week to go before the event was scheduled to happen.

Stephen chewed things over. The least favourable option was to cancel the demonstration and absorb the costs into the annual turnover. At this stage, that idea was completely unacceptable. The logical plan was to find another venue quickly and pay for some more advertising. But that was jumping the gun, for surely, Stephen reasoned, the original hotel had some responsibility in this matter?

With this thought in mind, he tentatively picked up the phone, still deliberating before he dialled the number of the Southampton hotel. On the one hand, he needed this distraction like he needed a hole in the head, apart from which this was not an event he had planned himself or was, therefore, in any way responsible for; it was JCP's responsibility. Yet, although he was reasonably sure that JCP would sort something out to salvage the situation one way or another, the people over at JCP were not just business colleagues, they were also good friends and he felt compelled to try and do something constructive to be helpful.

Taking the bull by the horns, he finally dialled the number and asked to be put through to the hotel manager. The gentleman subsequently came to the phone and gave Stephen the same story that he'd given Jo. There was definitely *no* booking on the 20th of May, or any other date for that matter, for either Stephen Holbrook or for JCP. The hotel, Stephen was informed, kept a careful log of *all* incoming and outgoing phone calls and faxes, and as far as he, the manager, was concerned, he'd never even heard of either Holbrook or JCP until a member of staff had drawn his attention to an advert in the local newspaper the previous evening.

Stephen very politely pointed out (as had Jo) that JCP also kept communications records and that there were copies of emails and faxes sent to the hotel, which, unfortunately, the manager dismissed out of hand saying that proof of dispatch was not proof of receipt.

Stephen was getting very cheesed off by the manager's attitude and very careless manner, but he managed to stay calm and tried another tack, pointing out that *someone* in the hotel must know something, especially as JCP had phoned less than a week ago to confirm arrangements and to enquire about wheelchair access. At this point the manager's tone hardened, and although he was not abusive he made it fairly clear to Stephen that as far as he was concerned the matter was closed.

At this point Stephen lost some of his patience. 'Look,' he snapped, 'clearly I'm not getting through *to* you and I'm not getting any help *from* you, so would you mind getting off the line and putting me through to your boss or to someone who *can* help me!'

'I'm afraid I don't like your tone,' the manager retorted superciliously 'so would you mind putting me through to *your* boss!'

At this point Stephen's patience went out of the window. 'Listen, you daft sod,' he yelled down the line, 'I *am* the flaming boss, so put me through to your chief executive *NOW!*'

The telephone calls between Stephen and the Southampton hotel were no more fruitful than JCP's phone conversations with the same organisation, so smoking another cigarette (my God, he thought, two in one morning! I'm becoming a chain smoker!) he tried another tack completely, and going through directory enquiries, got the number of the Southampton Hilton Hotel. Phoning their conference and banqueting department, he explained what had happened with the original hotel and then went on to point out that he worked regularly at other Hilton hotels up and down the country and so, therefore, was there anything at all that the Southampton Hilton could do to get him out from between the rock and the very hard place. "No problem, Mr Holbrook," came the polite and very positive response, "we've got a room available, and it's yours if you want it!" Steve then got on the line to JCP and told them that he'd fixed an alternative venue, albeit at twice the price, and what did they think? JCP agreed that they were not in a position to be fussy about the price and a deal was struck with the Hilton that very same day.

So, by lunchtime it had all been resolved, but it had cost Stephen four hours out of his busy schedule, leaving him way behind with the rest of his work.

On a positive note, the evening at the Southampton Hilton Hotel on Monday 20th of May was a resounding success with no small amount of thanks due to Stephen's intervention and the tremendous help and co-operation that we received from the hotel's management and staff.

After resolving the Southampton crisis Stephen finally managed to get out of the house by two thirty to do the banking and to pick Bradley up from school. As promised, father and son made their way to the local boating lake and Stephen ordered a skiff for an hour. Not wanting to leave his briefcase with the evening's float in the back of the car, he dumped it in the bottom of the boat and then followed a pleasant half hour in the early summer sunshine, sculling around the local pond.

You can't be with Stephen for any length of time without your conversation being interrupted by the ubiquitous mobile phone and, sure enough, the phone started ringing in the middle of the lake with a very nice lady from Huddersfield who wanted to reserve two seats for a forthcoming demonstration. With the oars at rest, Stephen had his bookings ledger on his knee and, pen in one hand, mobile in the other... and of course, this was when four year old Bradley spotted the fish swimming by the side of the boat and wanted to get a closer look. To *get* that closer look, he stood up and leaned over the edge of the boat, and would have toppled head first into the water if Stephen hadn't reached out and grabbed him. Unfortunately in the process of the rescue mission, the mobile phone went over one side of the skiff and the bookings ledger went over the other.

Stephen stared in disbelief, first of all at the phone, which floated for a few seconds, and then like some forlorn submarine after an argument with a destroyer, sank beneath the waves for evermore. His attention swiftly moved to the ledger, floating away on the ripple like a swan under sail. He started paddling after it in a full panic for the ledger contained every booking for every venue for the following three months and without it he would be like, well, he'd be up a creek (or a Wakefield boating lake) in a canoe (or in this case, a council rowing boat) without a paddle or an oar.

Ledgers... they were made of paper, right? Paper was made out of trees and trees are made out of wood... wood floats on water, right?

Wrong!

As Stephen came within finger grasp of the ledger the big green work book did its own version of the Titanic and sank beneath the surface of the lake to keep the mobile phone company for eternity.

Bradley was completely unshaken by the turn of events and couldn't– really couldn't understand why his lovely Daddy was quite so upset. The lovely Daddy in question didn't know whether to laugh or cry, and in the end, managed to do both at the same time, while he forlornly rowed the boat round in circles in some faint hope that phone and book might suddenly and miraculously re-emerge on the surface.

Needless to say, this did not happen... and then it started to rain... and then Bradley said he was hungry and wasn't feeling very well.

For three months Stephen did a juggling act with the numbers of people attending his evenings, never sure until the last person had arrived whether he was going to be grossly overbooked or underwhelmed, not knowing how much to spend on adverts, and having to ring around every single venue to remind himself of the booking terms and conditions and each venue's maximum numbers. The mobile phone was replaced easily enough but the loss of the ledger was a major disaster and caused quite a few nightmares.

It was only a good few months afterwards that he learned, in casual conversation, that the boating lake was only about two feet deep. If only he'd known that at the time... "I'd have rolled my trousers up and kicked around that flaming pond all day until I'd found the dratted book!"

By four o'clock Stephen had already been up and on the go for ten hours, but now it was time to go to work in earnest. Picking up The Rottweiler and Jo, he headed out through the busy tea time traffic towards Northwich – another laborious crawl and stop journey across the M62 with cars and lorries locked nose to tail and belching out exhaust fumes guaranteed to kill a planet within half a day.

The journey seemed to take forever, and whilst Jo and Pat were in talkative mood (Jo wanting to relate the further events concerning the Southampton debacle and Pat wanting to talk about her frustrations in completing a house purchase), Steve had a pounding headache and found himself longing for some peace and solitude: he was also incredibly tired and on more than one occasion he found he was nodding off. In the end, he opened the sunroof and deliberately engaged in conversation, just to keep himself awake, keeping the sanctified thought of being home and tucked up in bed with Caroline at the back of his mind. Those golden moments were still hours away, but they were closer than they'd been when he was talking to the hotel manager in Southampton, they were closer than they'd been when he'd been going around in circles in the middle of a boating lake looking for a sunken ledger and a torpedoed mobile phone!

Eventually, almost an hour later than scheduled, Stephen pulled the Mondeo into the car park of the Northwich Memorial Hall and even as he did so, he uttered a groan of dismay. For there, on one side of the street was a long queue of people waiting to go into his demonstration, while on the other side of the street a group of Christian zealots were staging a demonstration of their own.

185

'Oh no, not tonight,' he muttered. 'I am *not* in the mood for this *tonight!*'

Occasionally, and it is only very occasionally, a group of Christians, usually a splinter group from the main body of the church, takes it into their head to come and protest at Stephen's demonstrations. Their argument is that anything to do with clairvoyancy and spiritualism is supernatural, and that by definition it is Satanistic and the work of the Devil. If you read their tracts and pamphlets or question them you soon come to realise than *anything* that does not conform to their version of Jesus Christ and Christianity is also Satanistic and the work of the Devil!

This small crowd, less than a dozen strong, but nonetheless waving banners, playing guitars (badly) and chanting their slogans of hatred and intolerance, had already pamphleted the queue of Stephen's customers and were making a substantial din. Working beneath the banner of the Northwich Christian Fellowship they were members of the Pentecostal sect, and had gone to a lot of time and trouble to advertise their protest meeting – and it has to be said that a lot more people came to see Stephen than those who came to protest against his presence in their town.

'Let's just walk in quietly and not get into any arguments,' Steve said. 'We'll get the doors open as quickly as we can, and hope that this lot won't give us any trouble – but God, I do *hate* it when they start having a go at the people who've come to see me.'

Stephen and the ladies got into the building without any incident and had the doors open within a very few minutes. By and large the people who came into the hall fell into two camps; half of them were outraged by the arrogance of the Pentecostalists, while the others found their behaviour either very sad or very funny.

One young man, very big and burly but also quite gay, turned around to Jo and said 'I've half a mind to go out there and give their ringleader a punch on the nose... I'm already damned in their eyes anyway' while another gentleman quietly went down the queue of waiting people and collected up all the pamphlets and dumped them back over at the feet of the protesters.

One elderly lady, who wasn't attending Stephen's evening but who just wanted to come into the building and use the phone,

186

was told by one of the protestors that she shouldn't enter the building because she was about to be conned...

'I'm only going in to use the telephone, for heaven's sake,' she replied tartly.

'Oh but you'll still get conned if you talk to anyone in there' the evangelistic youth told her.

'My dear,' the elderly lady replied sadly, 'I don't think there is anyone *in there* who will try and con me!'

The only time it came close to getting nasty was when Stephen had to go outside to check the numbers of the queue against the numbers of spare seats still available in the building. It was at that time that he was approached by the ringleader of God's Gestapo, a modestly built man, clean shaven with thinning hair and glasses...

'You are *Satanistic!*' he screeched in Steve's face doing a fair impression of the Reverend Ian Paisley on a bad day in Belfast. 'You are the spawn of the Devil! You will go to *Hell* and there you will rot in the eternal flames of *Damnation!*'

Steve ignored him completely, and called out to the queue.

'Ooh hasn't it been a *lovely* day today... Look I'm *ever* so sorry about this long wait, but we'll have you all sorted out with seats in the next couple of minutes or so!'

He refused to be rattled and did not get rattled, but he was angry and simply chose not to let the anger show. By this time a local press cameraman had turned up and the Pentecostal host (by that time numbering eight) really started playing up to the camera; the Reverend Ringleader gave an on the spot interview consisting of several very long sentences of cant and rave, with his seven ardent followers filling in the gaps with an ongoing chorus of "Praise be" and "Jesus saves" except that it came out as praise beeeeee and Jeeeeeesus saves.

One of Stephen's customers, a lady called Amanda Johnson, decided that enough was quite enough, and she went over to this not so gentle man of the church and gave him a thoroughly good piece of her mind. She did not mince words, much to the delight of the photographer/reporter who got some excellent shots of the confrontation, which were plastered all across the local paper the following day. Whether the Reverend Rennie (this we learned later was the churchman's name) was dismayed by the publicity or was just glad of *any* publicity at all, we shall never know, but I think it's fair to share that his little picket backfired quite badly and he and his fanatical and misguided followers left the Memorial Hall with egg on their faces.

Stephen got on with his job and did a respectable demonstration. By the end of the night the zealots had all gone home and Steve and Jo and Pat drove gently back to Yorkshire.

After dropping off the ladies, Steve finally closed his front door behind him a little after midnight. Caroline and the children had gone to bed and so he had the house to himself. Sitting at the kitchen table he ate the supper Caroline had prepared for him – not really tasting it, but eating to take on fuel to balance out the energy loss and adrenaline rush. Normally he would have sorted out the box office, but that night he was too fazed and tired. Instead, he found himself looking through one of the pamphlets that had been thrust at him by the Northwich Christian group, and although Stephen is a reasonably well educated man, the pamphlet simply made no sense to him. Apart from being full of generalisations, it was also full of contradictions and wildly inaccurate assumptions: if the people who had written this pamphlet seriously believed in what they were writing, then by any standards they were either certifiably insane or arrogant beyond all credible belief!

"The variety of ways into the spiritual realm" he read *"actually divide into two basic routes. One way is a living, real and dynamic relationship with God through meeting Jesus Christ. The other is by way of the occult. These are the only two sources of spiritual power..."*

Stephen pulled back and re-read the section again, trying to understand what was being said here. It seemed that he was being told that you either believed that the only way to God was through Jesus Christ and if you followed any other pathway, that was the occult, governed by Satan and Lucifer, and therefore you were all damned and doomed!

Stephen was not an occultist – he recoiled from the thought – but he *was* a spiritualist and yet, according to this Northwich Christian Fellowship publication, he and all his fellow spiritualists, Hindus, Moslems, Buddhists, Sikhs, Bahais... all were doomed to eternal damnation. And according to the little man with the foaming mouth and angry words who had spat such

188

vitriol in his face earlier that night, so were the Catholics and any other protestants who didn't follow the Pentecostal pathway!

Surely, this could not be right?

Stephen made himself a cup of strong black coffee, splashed some cold water over his face, and sat down to read the pamphlet in earnest. Twenty minutes later after having read it twice (making three times in all) he pulled back in bemused amazement, for that was exactly what the pamphlet was saying!

Steve tore the pamphlet in half and threw it in the dustbin. Then, on impulse, instead of heading upstairs to the bedroom, he slipped out of the back door and went and stood in the middle of his garden. He was assailed by the scent of fresh grass and dew soaked evergreen plants: the perfume of summer stillness soothed his troubled spirit and he attuned to the stillness, revelling in the solitude and silence of the moment. Gone were aggressive evangelical words of no substance, gone was the dull head-searing roar of M62 traffic, gone were the nerves and the urgent cacophony of voices in his medium's head that urged him impatiently to forge links between two worlds... No children's voices, no harsh music, nothing but the stillness of the midnight and the silence of his thoughts.

He glanced up at his bedroom window. It seemed incredible that this day had started with him standing at the glass, looking down at this very garden, with Christian sentiment ringing in his ears. *"One day at a time, sweet Jesus!"*

'Well pardon me, Jesus,' he thought, 'but it has been one *hell* of a day, and now I'm going to bed! But before I go, for heaven's sake do something about that lot over in Northwich, and all the other "lots" like them all over the world. Because it's fairly obvious that they haven't got a clue what you're all about and they've shanghaied your name for their own nasty and spiteful little agendas. It's people like them that cause all the problems in places like Ireland and Pakistan, and just about everywhere else in the world where people go to war over religion. After all, Jesus is a name that's supposed to be associated with love and forgiveness, not persecution and hatred...'

And with that, Stephen closed the door on another day and went in search of his wife and another few hours of all too precious sleep.

189

CHAPTER TWENTY TWO
Hard Proof

What constitutes hard proof of life after death? Different people will give you different answers to this question depending upon their own personal belief and experience. The person who has had a message through Stephen at one of his demonstrations is likely to give a more positive response than someone who has not and I suppose that someone like myself who has not only attended scores of demonstrations but who has also investigated some of the messages in great depth, must have more conviction than the person who has never been to *any* demonstration of spiritual mediumship. One person can take their proof from a single message whereas I can take mine from the hundreds of messages I have been privy to over the last three years.

For some people just a few words are often enough. *"I've got a lady here who says she's your mum. She would have passed over in the last twelve months and she wants you to know that now that she's on the other side, she's got the use of her legs back!"* Others need a whole chronology of names and events before they can begin to believe. To his credit Stephen usually does provide the detail, and it is inevitably the inconsequential little details that deliver the coup de grace. *"You broke a milk jug this morning when you opened the fridge door"* or *"You tore a hole in your jeans last night on a rusty nail and your Gran's having a good laugh about it. She says you always were a clumsy kid!"*

The names of loved ones (on both sides of life) the names of pets, dates, times, health conditions, house numbers etc., all constitute highly persuasive evidence for life after death and for many this degree of evidence is proof enough; even the diehard disbeliever who claims that the evidence is circumstantial must review their opinion in the face of so *much* evidence coming through and, indeed, over such a sustained period of time. I mean, for God's sake, if smoke is billowing from every door and window of a house do you have to see the flames to know that the building is on fire?

Just as Doubting Thomas had to put his hand in the wound inflicted upon Christ by the spear of Longinus before he could allow himself to believe in the resurrection, there are individuals who cannot believe in the validity of Stephen's work until they have put him to the test.

It is no great surprise that eighty five percent of Stephen's audiences are women – females are generally more in tune with the psychic and spiritual sides of their natures and 'feminine intuition' isn't called that for nothing. And yet, rather curiously, some of the most devastatingly detailed and accurate messages seem to go to the small percentage of men that fill out the audience. I think of the young man called Simon at The Cochrane Theatre, I think of a chap called Dave Munroe from Knaresborough who had a chapter to himself in "Light In The Darkness" and more recently I think of a gentleman called Albert Ackerman from Ilford in Essex. It might not be accurate to say that Stephen changed Albert's life, but it would be accurate to say that Albert's life did change through his experience with Steve. Albert was looking for hard proof of life after death, and he'd searched in a number of different places before he found himself at the Holbrook door.

I met Albert for the first time in September of 2001 and again in the spring of 2002... There has been some correspondence between us, and Albert is not only happy that I tell you his story, he *insists* that I do so.

Ruth Feinstein was born in 1920, in the Polish City of Kraków. She was part of a strongly traditional Jewish family who failed to see that Europe was not a good place to be in those very turbulent times. Ignoring opportunities to leave, they left it too late and in 1941 the whole family (along with just about every other Jew in Kraków) were interned in the Birkenau concentration camp. In 1942, on the day of Ruth's 22nd birthday, what was left of the family was relocated to Auschwitz. Amazingly Ruth survived the holocaust – but she was the only member of her family who did. Through starvation, illness and the gas chambers, she lost her brother, her two sisters, her father and her mother, along with five cousins, two aunts and an uncle.

191

In 1947 she came to Britain and in 1949 she married a British soldier called Maurice Ackerman, who also came from very devout Jewish stock. In 1951 Ruth gave birth to her first and only child, who was named Albert, after Maurice's father and grandfather.

Maurice died in 1972 of heart failure leaving Ruth to struggle on alone, with only her son for company. At twenty one years old, Albert was a very shy and introverted young man, and lived a very sheltered life beneath his mother's matriarchal dominance. Albert says – *'She was certainly a very strong woman, and it's true that she was very demanding in her expectations of me ... very possessive and very protective, and yet we had an incredibly strong bond and I loved her to distraction. I was aware of all that she had been through and felt that it was my duty to be there for her, even if it meant there were times when I couldn't always do what I wanted to do ...'*

Steeped in the tradition of his background and bloodlines and seeking some degree of escape from the stringent parental control imposed upon him, Albert gravitated towards Hasidicism, and was accepted by this branch of the Judaic faith in 1979. Hasidic Jewry is a very strict branch of the faith, and generally one has to be born into the faith rather than converting to it, but Hasidicism ran throughout Ruth's family lines and Maurice's family also had a powerful strand of Hasidicism running through it. Thus Albert was welcomed with open arms, and much to Ruth's disdain (for her faith had been sorely tried over the years of the holocaust) he took to wearing the black hat and coat of the sect, and allowed his sideburns to grow into the distinctive curls that makes the members of this group of people so easily recognisable.

In moving closer to his church Albert was able to put some distance between his mother (and her increasing demands for attention) but nevertheless they shared the same house until Ruth passed over in March 2001 after a long and losing battle with lung cancer.

Albert: *'She was eighty one years old, bless her, and tough as old boot leather. Surviving the Nazis and smoking forty cigarettes a day has got to take its toll and it's amazing she lived as long as she did. She fought the cancer for three years, but one thing you've got to do if you're fighting that kind of fight, is to stop smoking, which was something she either wouldn't do or couldn't do. When the end came, it came quickly, but it was a long time coming and those last few years were not easy years.'*

Initially Albert took the passing of his mother very philosophically. She was, after all, an elderly lady who had had a long, if not always good or happy life. In fact, in the first few weeks Albert actually felt a profound sense of release. He had fulfilled his filial duties as a son, could look back with pride at the way he had always stood by Ruth, and now was prepared to admit to some feeling of relief. His mother had passed on and now he was free to get on with his own life and do what he wanted to do.

The only problem was that Albert was now fifty one, and what little fire and ambition there might have been while he was still a young man had dissipated over the years and he was left at a loose end. It was only after her passing that he began to realise just how much of his life had revolved around Ruth, and now that she had gone all he was left with was his religion and the prospect of empty years ahead.

'What woman in her right mind would be interested in a balding, pot-bellied, middle aged Jew with a very modest income and very little savings? All my life the only woman in my life had been my mother and I simply had no social graces, no experience and no confidence with women. In those early weeks after her death, the only one I could turn to was God!'

But during those spring and summer months of 2001 Albert became increasingly depressed and distraught. The hole left by Ruth's passing became an echoing empty cavern and Albert started asking questions, of himself, of his brethren in the faith and of his Rabbi. These were questions he had never asked before; had never been able to find the right words for... Questions like *'Why did my mother have to die? Why did she have to die of cancer? Why did I have to give her so many of my years? Why couldn't my father have lived longer? Why was there a holocaust? Where are my loved ones now? Why does God let all these awful things happen if he is so loving and omnipotent?'*

In short, Ruth's death precipitated a major crisis of faith, and the crisis deepened significantly when Albert failed to get any of the answers he was looking for, either from his own conscience or from his teachers and friends. The emptiness caused by Ruth's absence from his life became an increasingly heavy weight to carry, and by the mid summer of the year Albert was quite ill: his mental state was unstable and were it not for the Prozac prescribed by his GP he would have probably ended up in a mental hospital. *'There was so much anger in me. I was angry with my mother for dying, I was angry with myself for having not done more with my life. I was angry with myself for feeling so impotent and useless, I was angry with my Rabbi for not giving me the answers to what were, as far as I was concerned, very simple questions. All the time I felt on the brink of tears and I cannot begin to tell you how desperately lonely I was feeling.'*

In August of 2001 Albert happened to see an article in the local newspaper advertising the visit of a clairvoyant called Stephen Holbrook who, so the newspaper said, was able to prove that there was life after death and that he (Holbrook) could talk to the spirits of people who had died. Albert had absolutely no knowledge about spiritualism, but the thought that "messages" could be relayed between heaven and earth was both astounding and intoxicating. Even though Rabbi David told him that he should not even contemplate going to such a meeting, Albert (whose faith in the Rabbi was already seriously shaken) resolved to go anyway, and go he did.

'I went to the Essex County Hotel not knowing what to expect, and I sat through two hours of Mr Holbrook's demonstration totally bewildered and confused. He seemed to be an extremely ordinary young man, but here he was, talking to people about their dead relatives, and coming out with all kinds of information that he could not possibly have known about beforehand. His affirmation that you can't die went against all of my own experience, but when he went on to say that it is only the body that dies and that the spirit continues eternally, then this did make some sort of sense... I did not receive a message that night, I was not expecting one and I was sat right at the back of the room, so nobody could have seen me anyway, but I was given a lot of food for thought. When I spoke to my Rabbi about it the following day there was an awful argument and he got very very angry with me and told me that I had to make a choice between God and the devil and that if I were to go on any more about spiritualism it would be obvious to him that I was siding with the devil... So for the time being, I caved in and let

194

the matter drop, but I was uneasy about Rabbi David's attitude and the vehemence of his denials. Judaism had not answered my questions and, for that matter, neither had Mr Holbrook, but at least Mr Holbrook was addressing matters that seemed to be very important to me, even if they were taboo subjects to my own faith.'

Albert maintained his usual presence in the Hasidic congregation, but over the winter of 2001/2002 he started reading about spiritualism and acquired some terms of reference: the more he learned, the more he questioned his Judaism and the discipline demanded by Hasidicism. Early in March 2002 he again tried to broach the subject of spiritualism with his Rabbi, and again there was another altercation. This time, however, Albert was armed with more information and a lot more confidence than he'd had on the previous occasion, and was not prepared to be browbeaten into subjugation or submission. The result of this battle was that Albert left the synagogue in disgust, did nothing for a week, and then, with total premeditation, he built a large bonfire in his back garden and when the fire was well ablaze he threw his long coat and two black hats into the flames. Helped along with half a gallon of Esso's finest, they burned quite merrily.

'One part of me was totally horrified at what I was doing, but there was another half of me that felt an enormous sense of relief and justification. A lot of the anger seemed to lift out of me and as I stood there, watching the garments disintegrate in the flames, I thought of Mr Holbrook and I said to myself that if God was alive and if there was life after death I wanted some hard proof of this, and that the only proof I would settle for would be a message from my mother at Mr Holbrook's next meeting! If you like, I was putting God to the test, and in a funny kind of way, Mr Holbrook as well, I suppose...'

Albert duly booked his seat for Stephen's next visit to Southend, this time at the Rayleigh Mill Hall, and being one of the first to arrive, he chose his seat carefully. This time he did not want to be right at the back out of sight, but nor did he want to be prominent on one of the front rows. Thus, he placed himself fairly and squarely in the middle of the hall on the assumption that if Stephen did have a message for him, the clairvoyant would have to work to find him in the middle of the crowd.

The evening in Rayleigh got off to a good start with Stephen bringing messages through, first of all to a young mother who had lost her baby, and then to a mature lady who had recently lost her husband. Stephen's third message of the night connected with Albert.

'I want to talk to a gentleman,' Stephen said, 'who has recently lost his mother to the spirit world and who desperately wants to hear from her this evening…'

Albert almost put his hand up, but then pulled back from the action – after all, any one of a dozen men could have lost their mothers recently, and any one of them would be desperate to hear from them. No, better to be cautious and wait for a bit more proof that this really was a message for him. Even so, Albert was tingling all over, and he told me later that even then he knew that this message was going to be for him.

'I want to connect this lady's passing with the number seventeen… it's either a birthdate or an anniversary. I'm getting massive pressure in my chest, but it's not like a heart attack or anything like that, and I'm feeling that this lady would have passed over with cancer.'

Albert was perspiring and at the same time feeling slightly nauseous and dizzy. Now he had no choice other than to put his hand up, for had his mother not died on the 17th of March, and had she not died of cancer?

'Thank you sir,' Stephen honed in on him immediately. 'Now can I just have your voice – just a yes or no – this lady would have been a very strong lady and I don't want to accuse her of being bossy, but she was very set in her ideas and she liked to have her own way?'

'Yes.'

'And I'm getting the feeling that although she had been poorly for a long time, when the end did come, she deteriorated very quickly?'

'Yes.'

'And I know for a fact that this lady would have been very stubborn and it was hard to get her to do what she was supposed to do. She wouldn't take advice unless it suited her?'

Albert thought of the forty cigarettes his mother had smoked every day despite the dire warnings from the doctors and he nodded his head in agreement.

'She's drawing me a picture,' Steve continued, 'of a big star... a big six pointed star. Does this mean anything to you?'
Albert thought of the six-pointed Star of David, and confirmed that this emblem did hold some special significance for him.

'And she's writing a big letter 'A' in a love heart, and she's sending her love to this person...'

'Yes,' Albert croaked.

'Who is Albert?' Stephen asked.

'I'm Albert,' Albert answered.

Stephen paused, paced up and down the stage for a moment or so, cast an odd glance across his shoulder and said 'Yes I'll tell him' as though he were speaking to someone present that only he could see, and then... 'Sir, this lady is telling me that she's with Maurice and that she's got the rest of the family around her too, but she's specifically telling me to tell you about Maurice and that his heart is all right now. Do you understand?'

'Yes.' Albert could hardly speak through the lump that was forming in his throat. He wasn't sure about the rest of the family but he *was* sure about Maurice, for this was his father who had died before his time with premature heart failure.

'Who's Ruth?' Stephen called out.

'That's my mother's name,' Albert confirmed.

'And I've got Judith and Rebecca... your mum's sending love to you from Judith and Rebecca, and she's telling me that although you've never met them, you'll know who they are.'

'Yes, that's right.' Judith and Rebecca were his aunts – Ruth's two sisters who had perished in Auschwitz. Obviously he had never met them, but he certainly knew all about them from the stories his mother had told him time and time again.

'And,' Stephen continued, 'do you know who Vera is?'

'Yes.' Again he'd never met her, but he knew Vera to be his maternal grandmother, also lost in the holocaust.

'And who's Nathan or Nathaniel?'

'Yes.' Both these names held significance for Albert, for Nathan had been Ruth's father's name and Nathaniel was the name of her younger brother.

197

'Well, they're all here, and if we have any more, we'll be getting a coach party coming through!'

The audience laughed but Albert failed to see the joke.

'Your mum is telling me something that I don't understand... it's something to do with a tattoo or some tattoos, and she wants you to know that the tattoos have been taken off...'

Albert tells me that at this point his blood ran cold and he felt as though he was going to faint. He immediately knew the significance of tattoos for all his family would have had their forearms tattooed with their camp numbers and even his mother had never had her own tattoo removed. *"Have it taken off?"* she had said on more than one occasion. *"Why no, thank you. It can stay there as a reminder of the evil that men do and as a testament to my survival."* The thought that all the tattoos had gone made a truly profound impact on Albert's consciousness and, as he later admitted, this was the one piece of evidence that he took as hard proof. However there was more to follow.

Stephen stood in the middle of the stage, looking perplexed. 'Sir, I've got to ask you this, and please don't be nice to me, but have you recently burned some old clothes? Your mum's telling me that she watched you throwing some clothes onto a bonfire and she's saying good riddance to bad rubbish. And she's also telling me something about you getting your hair cut and she's saying she likes it a lot better now that it's shorter...'

Albert was stunned, for there was no way that either his mother or Stephen Holbrook could have known about the burning clothes and the cutting of the Hasidic locks, but obviously this information was available in the "spirit world" which had to be proof of *something*?

Stephen went on to say that Ruth was telling him that Albert had been under the weather for quite a few months, that he taken the death of his mother very badly, and had been in a state of mental confusion.

'She's telling me that you've been asking yourself lots of questions and that if you keep on asking them, sooner or later you'll start getting the answers. She's also saying that she was grateful for all the love and attention that you gave her and that she's sorry that she was sometimes very selfish about things. She says it isn't too late for you to get on with your own life but that you've got some work to do with your self-image. You've lost a

198

lot of confidence recently, but you mustn't worry because you are going to get it back and that things will look very different for you before the end of the year.'

Stephen then asked if he knew a John and a Mary and if he could make any connection with the 15th of August... Albert had to say that he didn't connect with either name and that the date was meaningless to him, at which point Stephen said it was time to move on to the next link. Albert didn't mind, for in his own mind, he had had his proof and it was proof a'plenty. Assessing the evidence later, he came to the conclusion that every single thing Stephen had told him had some specific relevance, and that he'd spoken of things that nobody could possibly have known about other than Ruth. He was one hundred percent convinced that Ruth had communicated with him from beyond the grave.

Five days after the Rayleigh demonstration Albert telephoned me to ask some questions of clarification and to tell me of the impact of Stephen's message from his mother. He also confirmed the accuracy of Stephen's information, at which time I asked him if he'd be willing to send me his story with a view to publication in this book. Within a month I received a forty page report, much of which I have narrated over these last few pages.

For me there are two key issues here; one is that Albert was looking for his hard proof and got it, and the second is that Stephen passed the test that Albert set him. On a happy note, Albert has found some inner peace of mind and has acquired some rekindled faith in his own religion. He no longer follows the Hasidic pathway, but is content to call himself a Jew and he takes pleasure in attending and working for his local synagogue, secure in the knowledge that even if Judaism neither preaches nor offers proof for life after death, the concept is totally valid.

But, of course, this is just Albert's story. He has had *his* proof, while many of us are still searching for ours. Stephen, it must be said, has no problem with people putting him to the test and he tells the following tale of a message he gave to a lady in Grimsby some three years ago.

'Her son came through, and I remember it was a very emotional message because he'd died tragically as a result of a stupid and unnecessary accident that took place virtually on the steps of the Grimsby town hall where I was demonstrating. He told her that it was his own fault and that he'd been clumsy and careless. That he was always a hyperactive little boy and that he'd been seven years old when he'd died, although there was something wrong about his age. Anyway the lady confirmed all this was true, even down to his age. He was actually *nine* years old when he'd died, but someone had put the wrong age on his birth certificate.

'The little boy's mum was very upset about it all, and she'd mulled over what I'd told her, especially the bits where I said she had to work hard at getting on with her own life and put the past behind her. It was easy enough for me to say, but not that easy for her to do and, anyway, she decided she was going to come and see me again in Grimsby in the hope of getting another message, and this time she wanted absolute proof that her little boy was okay. So, when she heard I was going to be back in Grimsby, and this was only a couple of months ago, what she did was this. She's never done much with his bedroom even though he'd been gone for quite a few years by then, so she went into the bedroom and tore a piece of wallpaper off the wall, just one long thin strip, and put it in her hand bag. Apparently, she told herself that if her son were alive in the spirit world he would come through and tell her what she had in her bag.

'Anyway, against all the odds, he came through to her again! I think maybe it might have had something to do with the fact that he was killed only a few yards from where I was standing doing the demonstration, and he told her pretty well the same things as he'd told her the first time. Only he finished off the message by saying that just before she'd come out that evening he'd seen her in the bedroom ripping something off the wall.

'At this point the lady in question stood up and shouted "He's right! He's right!" then she opened her handbag and pulled out the piece of wallpaper. At the end of the evening she came over and gave it to me, and I've still got it in my top drawer as a very important memento of a very important piece of evidence.'

Another example of "hard proof" comes from David and Christine Harley of Hull who lost their eight year old son to meningitis on May 26th 1999. In the morning Josh had been his bright and breezy self, but by lunchtime he was feeling poorly, and by the evening he had passed over. The family was totally devastated, especially as it had all happened so quickly, without any warning or without any rhyme or reason, and it took the better part of a whole year before they were even able to begin to come to terms with their loss. For twelve months they went through the motions of life in a daze, and then someone told them about Stephen Holbrook and his work and they went along to the Young Peoples' Institute in Hull to see what it was all about.

This was the first of seventeen visits over a two year period. Stephen says he was getting embarrassed seeing this same couple sitting in the audience at every demonstration, but that he couldn't just magick up a message to order. Nonetheless, their patience and persistence paid off, and finally they did get their message in the spring of this year (2002).

When I spoke to Christine Harley on the phone yesterday and asked her what Stephen had told her that convinced her that Josh was still alive and well, albeit in another dimension, she was quite candid in her reply.

'Everything, every single thing that Stephen said, was absolutely correct and accurate. He said he wanted to talk to a couple who had lost their son when he was still only seven or eight years old, and when we put up our hands and said yes, he told us about the photographs that we kept all over the house, the photograph we had *just* put on the fridge that very day. He told us about the pictures we both wore in lockets around our necks and he told us that it was the same photo in both lockets and that Josh was wearing a blue tea shirt. He also told us about Josh's photograph that we kept permanently on our key rings. He told us that we'd been watching a video with Josh playing with two other children, that he was getting distress in his head and that there was still some mystery about the nature of the strain of meningitis virus and that the hospital was dragging its heals in making any announcements or giving out any information. He told us about the star that Josh had made at school and that we always used it on top of the Christmas tree. He told us about the photographs of the family we had put in Josh's coffin and the letter with "the little writing" that Gemma, his sister, had written for him. He told me that I'd kissed Josh full on the lips, and he also named Gemma and Jacob as being his sister and brother. He spoke about the garden that we had especially for him, and that was so true because we never spoke of the cemetery, but always of Josh's garden...'

201

'And there is no way that Stephen could have known about any of this?' I asked.

'Absolutely no way at all. As far as I'm concerned Steve Holbrook has proved beyond all shadow of a doubt that Josh is alive and well in the spirit world and David feels exactly the same way too.'

I suppose another aspect of proof must come in the form of the countless emails Steve gets, care of his website. In fact, just a few weeks ago, Roger Prior who runs the website for Steve sent up a whole batch of emails for us to have a look through. There were hundreds of them, and when Steve phoned Roger to say that it was going to take forever to read through them all, Roger quietly pointed out that he'd only sent us up a handful and that there were another few thousand on file back in his office. By and large, the emails fall into a solid category of praise, although there are a few which are the exception to the norm.

Dear Mr Holbrook I am writing to you to suggest that you give up your life of sin and join us in the worship of the one true God, Jesus Christ... Rev. Andrew Causeway.

Saw you last night in Selby and you looked wrecked. Are you overdoing it! Anyway you were still excellent.... Get some R'n'R because bags and blue eyes don't mix. I know!!! From S.Poulton.

Dear Stephen I saw you last night in Gateshead and I thought you were pretty good, but not quite at the level that I'm at myself. Therefore I'd be grateful if you could send me the name of your agent so he can get me some work. Clive.

However, on a much more typical note, here are a handful from people who have had their own proof from Stephen.

I went to one of Stephen's demonstrations at a social club in Oldham. I was pregnant at the time and very nervous about the whole labour situation that I knew I had to face a few months from then. My great aunt had died about six weeks before the demonstration and Stephen got a message from her for me. He was so accurate that there was no way he could have just

202

guessed all the details. He told me things that my nan had said to my great aunt when she went to see her in the chapel of rest that I hadn't even heard at the time and it was only later that my nan confirmed that everything that she'd said in the chapel was word for word what Stephen had said... Another message I got from my great aunt was that 14 was going to be very significant with regard to my baby, which puzzled me because the baby wasn't due on the 14th... But it then turned out that I had to have an emergency c. section and I ended up in room number 14. After that I knew that my aunt had been with us all along, watching over me and my baby, and it really gave me a sense of security knowing that... Debbie Bowley.

Dear Steve I came to see one of your demonstrations and was contacted by my brother. He'd died about six months previously. My friend did not believe in any of this and was shocked not only when you got my brother's name, but also went on to say how he'd died. I used to go to the cemetery and feel distraught and couldn't come away, but now I know he is all around me I can go and sit and talk to him and not feel afraid.... Samantha X

Hi Stephen, I saw your remarkable performance at The Marmaville last night and I am still trying to get over it! It was amazing to see you bring so much hope and happiness to so many. Yours, David.

Dear Steve, I just want to thank you so much! I went to see you for the first time this evening, 17th October, at Swinton. Not only did I feel so lucky in getting a message from you, incredibly it was the message I had asked the spirits for, and something that was so deeply personal and important to me. When my questions that had tormented me were answered through yourself, I did feel so very very lucky. I talk to my Dad every single day as though he was still here, even though he passed away fourteen years ago. He was my best friend and the most amazing Dad anyone could ever have. So thank you for giving me so much comfort and allowing me to have contact with him through you. You have a wonderful gift and it's so wonderful to see you use it for the care and concern of others... Jane.

Many thanks for two excellent demonstrations on Saturday and Sunday. We have been searching for the truth with the help of spiritualism since the tragic death of our son three years ago. You gave us a short but very touching message on Sunday that moved us greatly. You are without doubt the best medium we have seen demonstrate and have helped us believe that one day we will see our son again. The really moving thing was when you said he had got the letter which we placed between his fingers on the day of the funeral. Once again thank you and God bless... Janet Alan & Paul Hubball.

I would just like to say a huge thank you to Steve for passing on a message to me from my cousin Dan. I've seen Steve twice at Retford Little Theatre, but the last time (September 4th) I actually got a message. I sat and watched the show from the front as I'm in a wheel chair, and I was really shocked when Steve had the message for me. He told me about my blue hair (the last time I'd seen Dan I'd had blue hair) and many other things that only Dan could have known about. I'm so grateful because it has always been so hard to imagine a life after death and it was so hard when Dan was tragically killed so young. He was only twenty six, not much older than myself... I can't find the words to say how grateful I am. Thank you so much! From Nicola Smith.

Just wanted to say that in the last twenty four hours I have seen three mediums demonstrating their gift and Stephen Holbrook was far and away the most astounding and the most moving. I am new to the idea of a spirit world but am finding the evidence very comforting. Grateful thanks, Kerri Wing.

There are literally baskets full of such emails, and I've plucked the first dozen at random from the top of the pile. In this day and age it is all too common for us to write in criticism and complaint and all too rare for us to write letters of praise and commendation, and therefore this plethora of positive comment and corroborative testimony has got to represent something both very tangible and powerful. You may not have had your hard proof, and maybe you won't get it until Steve Holbrook comes directly to you with a message from someone you have loved who has passed from this life to the next, but you need to be aware that there are thousands of people out there who *have* had their proof and their testimony cannot be ignored.

CHAPTER TWENTY THREE
London At The End

On July 15th of 2001 I found myself in London, at a loose end and with some time to kill. The day before I'd been with my old buddy Adrian Spendlow doing a poetry and music festival in Henley-on-Thames, and as Adrian had an appointment with his literary agent in London on the 15th I drove him down to our capital city and while Ade was with the big wigs that make money and emotion move with the power of the printed verse word, I decided to put my time to good use and make some preliminary enquiries into finding a London venue for Stephen. Our night at The Cochrane had been a full nine months before, and we had never really capitalised on our London exposure. I think we would have done if Steve had gone for the TV offers, but he hadn't, and that was that, but I had a hunch that another London venue would be useful in the next dozen months or so.

I dropped Adrian off in Covent Garden, and began my quest by visiting The Cochrane. I had no appointment and the person I needed to see wasn't available, but at least I did come away with a ball park figure of what it might cost to hire the theatre. It was enough to know that it was way out of my modest reach. My name is James Christie not Henrik Brixen and I knew I would have to look elsewhere.

From Holborn I tubed over to Shepherd's Bush to check out a small arts theatre that I remembered from the 1970's but that had been turned into a restaurant complex – undaunted, I caught a taxi to Chiswick to have a look at another little theatre that I *thought* I remembered, but after trawling both lengths of Chiswick High Street, I couldn't find the damn place anywhere and in the end I gave up in disgust and hopped on a bus heading back towards central London.

It is amazing how both time and memory play strange tricks. During the 60's and the 70's London had been my stamping ground. I'd lived there rich and I'd lived there poor and either way it represented an important chunk of my history. Once, London had been my exciting young mistress and at a later time it had become a seedy old whore; I'd left when it was time to leave and on the few times since when I'd visited for a day or was just passing through, I had felt like a parochial interloper, the country boy out of his depth in the great metropolis. Even so, taken on its own terms, London was a seminal influence in my life and, over all, with thirty years of hindsight and nostalgia, the memories are warm and precious.

There are some days when you know you are going to get things done and there are other days when you know that no matter how hard you try, nothing is going to fall into place. That London Monday fell into the second category, so I aborted my mission to find the "right" venue for Stephen and went and had an early lunch. There are some truly fabulous restaurants in the West End but the nostalgia virus was wiggling its way into my consciousness, and I ended up strolling across Trafalgar Square and up the Charing Cross Road for a few yards before turning into Villiers Street which runs down by the side of Charing Cross Station. It was one of those hot sultry summer days filled with flat white skies and oppressive heat contaminated by the fumes of a million cars, and by the time I reached Joe's Café, I was hot and sticky and sweaty...

Except, of course, Joe's Café wasn't called Joe's Café any more. I mean, it *had* been Joe's Café between 1965 and 1974, but it had changed hands (and names) a dozen times since then. Even so, it was still recognisable as the rendezvous and watering hole that most of the out of work actors and musicians had used back in my London youth – the view from the window was just the same, the floor was just as dirty and the chairs were just as plasticky. Not the most salubrious venue for a nice lunch but it was one of "my" places, and I felt comfortable and comforted to be in surroundings that were marginally familiar.

I ordered a couple of bagels and a cappuccino (once it had been bacon butties and frothy espresso) and found myself staring moodily into space wondering what the hell I was going to do to fill the rest of the day.

I know some writers who can only write to a disciplined regime in front of their typewriters or word processors, but for me it's never been like that and most of the good stuff I've ever churned out has come from doodling on serviettes or scribbling in scratty note books over cold cups of tea. Sitting in Joe's I was all too well aware that the publishing deadline for this book was rapidly approaching and I was still minus the last chapter. More with a sigh of resignation than the thrill of expectation, I pulled out the aforementioned scratty notebook, and started scribbling... not so much in an attempt to be creative, but more as an exercise in getting my thoughts in order.

London. It had been nine months since we'd done the event at The Cochrane and, incredibly, it had been thirty eight months since I'd first met Stephen at The Queens Hotel in Leeds. They had been thirty eight of the most unusual and eventful months in my life, and it was very true to say that those thirty eight months had changed my life beyond all recognition. Gone were the days of turning over Tarot cards and compiling horoscopes, and instead my days and nights were filled with long car journeys, the frenzy of book sales, and the contemplative study of the evidence that Stephen had brought through in this period. Reading palms had been replaced by reading maps in search of routes and venues, and placing a couple of adverts every month or so to keep my little psychic practice going had been replaced by placing adverts every week for venues as far apart as Southend and Glasgow. Thirty eight months previously my cash flow had been worryingly low, but thirty eight months on, it was more stable. Having said that, back in 1999 I'd had an overdraft of several hundred pounds, whilst now, in 2002, that overdraft was tipping the scales at several thousands of pounds!

At the beginning of my journey with Steve I had resolved to peel away the layers of the onion, and although I have, I think, been marginally successful in doing this, it has not happened easily or quickly. Stephen is a man of many contradictions, and he will only let you into his confidence very slowly, degree by degree. At first your vision of the man is obfuscated by his extraordinary clairaudient gifts and you tend to look for more than is there: you assume that because his gift is special, so must he also be special...

Now while we are *all* special in our own ways, the secret to knowing Steve is to recognise that away from the public platform, he is a very ordinary man, totally devoted to his family and totally devoted to his work. He's quirky about his personal privacy, is vehemently protective of his family and, by his own admission, he is something of a control freak when it comes to organising the professional side of his life. He does not go around communing with spirits all day long or meditating on pathways of celestial guidance; he does not have expensive or outlandish tastes (in fact he's got "charitable constipation syndrome" insofar as he simply cannot pass a charity shop without going in and coming out with an armful of bargains).

His greatest weakness is for designer label shirts, normally costing sixty or seventy quid, but available through Oxfam for £3.50! Caroline, his long suffering wife has told him that if he buys one more second hand designer shirt, then all the shirts (and husband as well) are going out of the window, so to scratch the itch he has now started buying charity shop designer shirts for *me!*

He believes in spending his money where it is most needed and most useful, and the work that he himself does for charity is something that he takes very seriously – so much so that in one short eighteen month period he raised over £15,000 for The Wakefield Hospice.

He takes his pleasures from some of the truly simple things in life. Ask him what his favourite music is and he's likely to answer "the sound of my kids having a real good laugh about something".

He has a wicked sense of humour, but paradoxically can be very straight laced about some things. "James, you are simply *not* going to put that in the book! It's much too rude!" We are not talking here about anything salacious or scandalous, but, for example, when I've quoted him as saying "oh bollocks" he's insisted that I change it to "oh bother"!

And yet, Stephen has one of the most truly infectious senses of humour I have ever come across and no matter how grim or grotty you might be feeling, a few minutes in this man's company will have your spirits soaring. I don't think that he is aware of this gift: it is part of his mandate for healing, and it is certainly true that he does heal troubled souls. His humour comes out in other less subtle ways and he will frequently send a letter to his mother addressed to "Margaret Hot Lips Holbrook" or to "Pat Rottweiler Barking Mad Johnson" – and it does make you wonder what the postman might think, doesn't it?

Sense of humour apart, Stephen is a funny man to be with... Not in the sense of telling jokes, because oddly this is something he seldom does (and even when he does try he gets it all wrong) but, for example, it was hilarious watching him the other night after a very long drive back to Yorkshire from East Anglia. He was curled up in the back of the car, came awake as we turned into his drive and started to struggle into his denim jacket. Well, he struggled and struggled and struggled, all to no avail, for the said denim jacket was in the boot of the car and Stephen was trying to get his arms into the legs of his spare pair of jeans!

In three years I've driven something like forty odd thousand miles with Steve and we have talked about everything under the sun, cabbages and kings, ceiling wax and strings et al, but he has always drawn the distinction between what he calls "car talk" and "book talk". Even so, as we've rumbled along the motorways of England in the trusty old Volvo (289,000 on the clock, bless her) he has recalled many an anecdote that has put a grin on my face from Liverpool to Leicester or Bournemouth to Brighouse.

One priceless tale that he tells is of an occasion when he was doing a demonstration with Sue Cunningham in a rather large venue over in West Yorkshire. The acoustics in the building were appalling, thick carpets and low ceilings, and like it or not Stephen was told he was going to have to use a microphone. Thus, with a button mike on his lapel and a radio transceiver clipped on his belt, he loitered with intent as Sue went on to do the first half. Thinking he'd better go to the loo before it was his turn to demonstrate, Steve found his way to the little boy's room at the back of the hall but somewhere on route he must have knocked the transceiver switch on his belt, and while he was whistling away in the gents and doing all the things that guys do when they're in the gents, he was broadcasting live to the capacity audience over the top of Sue's demonstration. Sue, poor love, had no choice other than to stop what she was doing while the whole audience rocked with laughter. When Stephen finally emerged from the loo at the back of the room Sue asked very casually, "Could you hear us in there, Steve?" to which, of course, Mr Holbrook replied "No" – which gave Sue the magnificent counter line of "Well love, we could certainly hear you!"

Some of the most amusing stories revolve around what Steve actually says on stage and on a couple of occasions I've watched an audience fall about laughing while Steve has looked on in bewilderment, wondering what he's said to solicit such a reaction. Once in Darlington, he was delivering a very poignant message to a gentleman on the front row, but the flow was erratic, caused by the gentleman's nervousness.

'Is this your first time at anything like this?' Stephen asked gently.

'Oh no I've been lots of times,' the gentleman replied.

'Oh it is so nice to meet a man who comes more than once,' Stephen reposted... and then stood gobsmacked while the audience collapsed.

On another occasion he was giving a message to a lady from her departed husband and trying to link in with a health condition that caused major fluctuations to her body temperature.

'He's saying that you're very hot in bed,' Stephen reported, and again had to stop mid message while the audience picked themselves up off the floor. In this instance the inference of what he'd said suddenly dawned on him and he made matters worse by rambling on inanely – 'No, not that you're hot in bed in *that* sense, which isn't to say that you're *not*, of course, I mean I don't know, do I, but when you're in bed at night you *do* get, well, you know, sort of *very* hot...' Ah, poor Stephen! He has yet to learn that when you're in a big hole you should stop digging.

One aspect of Stephen's life that I have often been curious about is whether or not his clairvoyant gifts extend to other members of his family. When I asked him about this recently he had a good chuckle and told me the tale of Robbie, his eldest son...

'Robbie was in the loo and I was passing the door and I heard him muttering to himself "Get back up there! Go on, get back *up* there 'cos I don't want you down here! Get – back – up – there!" I was absolutely convinced he was talking to a spirit but when I peaked around the door to make sure he was all right, he was sat there trying to push a dribble of mucous back up into his nose, saying "Get back *UP* there..." But then, oh yes, I've got to tell you this, Caroline was watching the world cup match the other day and right out of the blue she said "Andy Cole is going to lose one of his boots" – and would you believe it, it came through on the commentary five minutes later that Andy Cole had, in fact, just lost one of his boots. Cheeky witch, she actually turned around to me and said "You know, all these years I thought you were a fraud, but now I *know* there's something in this clairvoyance lark!"'

As I've said, Steve does not spend his waking life communing with the past souls of the dearly departed. He has long since learned how to control his gift, and away from the platform he's an ordinary guy with an extraordinary amount of energy and enthusiasm for life. Having said that, there is, I suppose, quite a spooky side to his nature that comes out in some extremely odd ways.

One of his party tricks (and I call it that because he himself has got no idea of how he does it) is to be able to identify virtually any perfume with just a couple of whiffs. "That," he will say "is Dune..." then he will turn to somebody else and exclaim "Number 5 by Channel" or "someone over there is wearing Joop!". I won't say that he never gets it wrong, but he's right twenty nine times out of thirty, much to his own delight and everybody else's amazement.

Another uncanny thing is his ability to know in advance just how many people will be in an audience regardless of how many tickets have been sold or how many reservations we might have taken. Jo and I frequently have a lottery going with him... Jo will say 156, I will say 167, and Steve will say 161... and again, nine times out of ten he will be spot on to the last digit. We were in the delightful town of Bury St. Edmunds a few weeks ago and I think I'd put my audience number in as being 139, Jo had committed herself to 117 and Stephen had told us that we were both miles out and that there would be 151 people present. By half past seven we had exactly 150 people in the room and I was all for closing the doors and getting on with the evening, but Steve was quite insistent that there was going to be a late comer, and sure enough at 7.31 a lady came rushing around the corner doing battle with her brolly in the rain, paid for her ticket and took the numbers up to the exact count of 151.

Ask him how he does this and he hasn't a clue. Ask him to give you the winning lottery numbers or the winning horse in the third race, and he'll politely tell you to take a hike...

211

Stephen is not a fortuneteller but he does have premonitions and he will briefly but succinctly put them into words when the occasion demands. I have noticed some significant enhancement of this ability since he gave up the hairdressing salon – it's almost as though having forsaken that very tiring and time consuming business he has opened up another sphere of sensitivity within his psyche. One is mindful of the Royal funeral prophecies and, on a more personal note, I remember him turning around to Jo one evening, very shortly after she'd finished a three year course in horticulture as a mature student, and telling her that she would really do very little in this field of work, and that increasingly she would be doing more and more to help me. True to say, that is exactly the way that it has worked out, and jolly darn glad I am of it as well!

A few months ago Jo and I met him at our usual rendezvous point before heading down the A1 for some southerly destination, and as we were pulling out of the car park he casually remarked "you've been talking about selling the car, haven't you?" Jo and I looked at each other in amazement because that's exactly what we *had* been discussing all day long, although Steve had absolutely no knowledge of this! Only a couple of weeks ago, while we were driving from Kettering to Corby, I remarked that I thought I could hear a wheel bearing beginning to squeak... and Steve smugly passed Jo a piece of note paper upon which he had written "James will mention a problem with the car within the next one and a half hours – Steve, 10am." Immediately we all looked at the car clock and registered the time as being 11.25!

These "flashes" are spontaneous and are not called to order, but nonetheless they do serve Stephen very well, and give some indication of how the spirit world is able to help with some of his earthly needs.

A couple of years back when he was still going through his "Austin Montegos are the best cars in the world" phase, he was looking for a new car of this marque. In his own mind he knew it had to be a low mileage, late registration model, automatic, and with all of the goodies. He'd been looking for weeks without any success, but then one night while he was driving back home along the M62 he felt impelled to turn off two junctions early. Pat, who was travelling with him, asked what the heck he was playing at

212

and he said he didn't know, but he was just going where the spirit moved him.

Winding their way back towards Wakefield through some of the back roads, Steve knew that they were going to find the right car and that the mileage would be around 59,000. They happened to pass a pub car park, and there sitting beneath one of the street lamps was an Austin Montego with a 'for sale' sign in the window. Steve screeched to a halt and ran across to check it out; it appeared to be exactly what he was looking for. He peered through the window trying to see what the mileage might be, but of course it was much too dark... but when he went back to buy the car at eight o'clock the following morning the odometer read 58,995! There are other stories about clairvoyants and their cars but they'll have to wait until the next book.

Stephen is often asked if he can see into his own future and his answer is a qualified "no". He feels that the year 2006 is going to be a major turning point year in his life, but has no precognition with regard to the details. He senses that a long time in the future he might have something to do with a healing centre, but this is not a visualisation that lifts from within his own spirit but rather a recurring prophecy that he has received over the years from other clairvoyants.

None of us, no matter how strong our powers of precognition may be, have a totally clear vision of our future – at best we are occasionally permitted a brief glimpse. But in any case, this is not where Stephen is coming from. He makes links with our *past* and in so doing guarantees that we do have a future both in and out of this world.

By mid afternoon the skies in London were darkening and the storm that had been brooding all day was beginning to make its presence felt. My waiter brought me over another cup of coffee, and staring moodily out of the window I rammed another plug of tobacco into my smelly old pipe. Samuel Barber's 'Adagio For Strings' was playing quietly in the background but rather than bringing me the usual inspiration that I take from this gorgeous piece of music, on this day it just made me feel incredibly sad.

On the other side of the road the bare brick wall of Charing Cross station acted as a backdrop to the window glass and I found myself staring at my own ghostly reflection. Not a pretty sight, James, not a pretty sight – too much grey in my hair, too much grey in my beard, too many dark rings around tired eyes. I was getting old; not dealing with so called "middle age" very well at all. Perhaps I had to accept that my challenge for the future might revolve around learning how to grow old gracefully while every fibre of my being cried treason at the passing years.

As the first raindrops began to fall, I wondered what Stephen's challenges might be. Certainly he was going to have to get to grips with the television thing, and certainly he was going to have to embrace the idea of working in America. It might not happen immediately or all at once, but it was there for him in his future, drawing his present towards that time like iron filings to a magnet.

So often I have heard him say 'James, I'm quite happy, in fact I'm very happy with what I've got right now. I don't want anything else. I don't need anything more!' But the truth is that we do not always dictate the direction of our own pathways and nor are we always able to have what we want to have – and certainly not if spirit (some people may call it fate or destiny) has other plans for us.

My grandmother used to say that there are three kinds of people in the world, that ninety percent of them are sheep, that five percent are wolves, and that the other five percent are the shepherds. It seems glaringly obvious to me that Stephen is one of the shepherds, and that as such he carries a weight of responsibility for the flock. He might not like this concept, but I believe it to be valid.

As for myself, if anything I suppose I'm one of the wolves – or at least, I have been for a goodly portion of my life. There certainly seems to be some interlinking between Stephen's pathway and my own, for if one word he utters and one word I write does something to remove the fear from someone's heart and mind, helping that one person live a brighter and richer life without being constantly haunted by the spectre of death, then I suspect we are both serving the One Spirit in our different ways.

Choose your own words, but if Stephen is to fulfil his "destiny" or is to follow his "ministry" he will be challenged to rise above his own image of himself.

My own ghostly image mocked me from the plate glass window and I found myself wondering, just who exactly are we?

Stephen says that we are spirits first who use these earthly bodies as a vehicle. On one level I have no argument with this philosophy, but I suspect that it cannot be quite that simple, for within the framework of our humanity while there is certainly spirit, there is also emotion, ego and self identity, and at the end of the day different people are, well, different.

I have met a few truly spiritual people over the years who seem to move on a different plane than the rest of us. Some people have described *me* as being a spiritual man and yet although I would regard myself as being knowledgeable about spirit, when I look honestly within myself I detect very little true spirituality. On the other hand I *am* aware of an extremely powerful sense of self-identity.

Is this, I wonder, the same thing? I don't have the objectivity to know for sure one way or the other, but I do see a very close similarity between my own personality and Stephen's. He does have an incredibly powerful spiritual gift but in essence he is not what you would call *spiritual*... As I said before, he's a very down to earth man who avoids the clichés and celestial beckonings of other worldliness.

Perhaps it comes down to one basic question. Are we what we see ourselves as being or are we, in essence, what other people perceive us to be? This is a difficult and a *dangerous* question and the cop out clause would be to claim that we are, perhaps, a bit of both... But in Steve Holbrook's case the ramifications are profound, for either way, he cannot remain where he is on his present level of spiritual evolution. There must be an element of spiritual expansion and the acquisition of a higher international profile, and if he can hold on to his Wakefield roots and privacy, so well and good, and that might be a bonus, but if he can't, let him at least take solace in the following thought.

He has brought so much hope and so much healing to so many thousands of people over these last few years. In the time ahead he will, I believe, respond to the challenge of recognising that there are so many *millions* more people out there in the world who have yet to be touched and lifted by his most beautiful gift.

And on that note I shoved my pen back into the camera bag and ordered another cup of coffee.

I walked through the late London afternoon in the pouring rain and by the time I met Adrian on the end of St. Martin's Lane I was thoroughly soaked to the skin. Adrian also was dripping like The Big Lebowski, but at least he had his enormous black and red umbrella and he generously made some space beneath the spokes to give me some shelter from the deluge.

'How'd you get on?' I asked him.

'Oh great,' he said in his lovely Yorkshire drawl. 'They loved the stuff I'm doing for the schools project and they're dead keen to do something with the new collection on the internet... Anyway, how about you?'

'Didn't have much luck finding a theatre,' I admitted, 'but on the other hand, I think I might just have finished the new book.'

'Oh James, that's marvellous!' Adrian wrapped an arm around my shoulders and gave me a big hug. 'I was wondering why you looked a bit phased out... You've had that "I'm on a different planet" look about you all weekend.'

'Yeah,' I managed a weak smile. 'I've got to admit, I do feel a bit out of this world.'